Corporations and Partnerships in Slovenia

Corporations and Partnerships in Slovenia

Second Edition

Rado Bohinc

This book was originally published as a monograph in the International Encyclopaedia of Laws/Corporations and Partnerships.

Founding Editor: Roger Blanpain
General Editor: Frank Hendrickx
Volume Editors: Koen Geens & Sofie Cools

Wolters Kluwer

Published by:
Kluwer Law International B.V.
PO Box 316
2400 AH Alphen aan den Rijn
The Netherlands
E-mail: international-sales@wolterskluwer.com
Website: lrus.wolterskluwer.com

Sold and distributed by:
Wolters Kluwer Legal & Regulatory U.S.
7201 McKinney Circle
Frederick, MD 21704
United States of America
Email: customer.service@wolterskluwer.com

ISBN 978-94-035-3013-0

e-Book: ISBN 978-94-035-2935-6
web-PDF: ISBN 978-94-035-2940-0

The Author

Dr Rado Bohinc (b. 1949) graduated from the University of Ljubljana, Faculty of Law, Slovenia (1971). He received a Master of Laws (Ljubljana, 1985) and Doctor of Law (Ljubljana, 1987). His doctoral thesis was on the relationship between property rights and corporate governance. He was appointed as an assistant professor at the University of Ljubljana, Faculty of Social Sciences in 1986 and has been teaching Company, Securities, Labour and European Union (EU) Law since then. He served as a Minister of Science and Technology (1992–1996) and as Minister of Internal Affairs (2000–2004) in the Slovenian government. In 1999, he was a Fulbright scholar at the University of California School of Law, Berkeley. In 2003, he was appointed a full-time professor at the University of Ljubljana and the University of Maribor, Slovenia. In November 2007, he was elected rector of the University of Primorska, Slovenia. Since November 2011, he is again Full-Time Professor of Corporate, Securities and EU Law at the University of Ljubljana, Faculty of Social Sciences. In 2015, he was elected the dean of the Faculty of Social Sciences, University of Ljubljana.

He researches comparative corporate law and governance, corporations, partnerships and public law entities, public and corporate governance and social responsibility. His early books are: *Property and Governance*, 1988 (GV); *Joint Stock Company* 1990, (GV); *Corporate Governance in Europe and the United States*, 2001 (FDV); *Public Law Entities* (in co-authorship), 2003 (GV). His most important scientific monographs are: *Corporations*, 2009 (Nebra), *Comparative Corporate Law*, 2010 (VerlagDM, Saarbrücken), *Corporations and Partnerships*, 2006, 2009, 2012, 2018 (Kluwer), *Media Law*, 2014 (Kluwer), *Insurance Law* (co-author), 2018 (Kluwer), *EU Law and Institutions*, 2007, 2012 (FDV), *Social Responsibility* 2017 (FDV). He is the editor and co-author of several joint publications, for example: *For Social Responsibility*, 2018 (FDV); *Corporate Social Responsibility*, 2016 (FDV), *Corporate Governance as a Tool for Economic Growth*, 2016 (FDV). He lectured at many universities abroad (USA – Fullbright, Germany, Spain, Italy, Austria, Czech, Sweden, Norway, Russia, India, Nepal, South Korea, New Zealand, etc.) and acted as an introductory speaker or as a speaker at numerous national and international scientific conferences and symposia.

See more on: https://radobohinc.si/en/home/.

The Author

Table of Contents

Table of Contents

List of Abbreviations (English and Slovene)

I. Institutions

ARLRS	Agency of the Republic of Slovenia for Public Legal Records and Related Services (APLRS, Slovene: AJPES)
BL	Banking Law
DL	Dematerialization Law
ESMA	European Securities and Markets Authority
EU	European Union
GDP	Gross Domestic Product
IFRS	International Financial Reporting Standards
IL	Insurance Law
LEPP	Law on Employee Participation in Profit
LSE	Ljubljana Stock Exchange (Slovene: LB)
MFIL	Market in Financial Instruments Law
OSS	One Stop Shop
PIE	Public-Interest Entities
PPP	Purchasing Power Parity
SEA	Security Exchange Agency (Slovene: ATVP)
SIA	Slovenian Institute of Auditors (Slovene: SIR)
SML	Securities Market Law
SORS	Statistical Office of the Republic of Slovenia (Slovene: SURS)
SSH	Slovene Sovereign Holding (Slovene: SDH)
UK	United Kingdom
US	United States

II. Companies and Partnerships

DP	Dual Company (Slovene: DvD)
EIG	Economic Interest Grouping (Slovene: GIZ)

List of Abbreviations (English and Slovene)

EPLC	European Public Limited Company (Slovene: EDD)
LLC	Limited Liability Company (Slovene: DOO)
LP	Limited Partnership (Slovene: KD)
PLC	Public Limited Company (Slovene: DD)
SE	European Company (Societé Européene)
UC	Unlimited Company (Slovene: DNO)
III. Laws	
BA	The Banking Act – 1 of the Banking Act (Official Gazette of RS, No. 131/06 of 14. 12. 2006), BA
	Law on amending and supplementing the Law on Banking – 1A Banking Act (Official Gazette of RS, No. 1/08 of 4. 1. 2008), BA-1A
	Act Amending the Banking Act – 1B Banking Act (Official Gazette of RS, No. 109/08 of 19. 11. 2008), BA-1B
	Act Amending the Banking Act – 1C Banking Act (Official Gazette of RS, No. 19/09 of 13. 3. 2009), BA-1C
	Act Amending the Banking Act – 1D Banking Act (Official Gazette of RS, No. 98/09 of 4. 12. 2009), BA-1D
	Act Amending the Banking Act – 1E Banking Act (Official Gazette of RS, No. 79/10 of 8. 10. 2010), BA-1E
	The Banking Act – official consolidated text – ZBan-1-UPB5 (Official Gazette of RS, No. 99/10 of 12. 7. 2010), BA-OCT5
	Act Amending the Banking Act – 1F Banking Act (Official Gazette of RS, No. 35/11 of 13. 5. 2011), BA-1F
	Act Amending the Banking Act – 1G Banking Act (Official Gazette of RS, No. 59/11 of 25. 7. 2011), BA-1G
	Act Amending the Banking Act – 1H Banking Act (Official Gazette of RS, No. 85/11 of 25. 10. 2011), BA-1H
	Act Amending the Banking Act – 1I Banking Act (Official Gazette of RS, No. 48/12 of 26. 6. 2012), BA-1I

Act Amending the Banking Act – 1J Banking Act (Official Gazette of RS, No. 105/12 of 27. 12. 2012), BA-1J

Law Amending the Law on Banking – Banking Act 1K (Official Gazette of RS, No. 56/13 of 2. 7th 2013), BA-1K

Act Amending the Banking Act – 1L Banking Act (Official Gazette of RS, No. 96/13 of 22. 11. 2013), BA-1L

The Banking Act – 2 of the Banking Act (Official Gazette of RS, No. 25/15 of 13. 4. 2015), BA-2

Act Amending the Banking Act – ZBan-2A (Official Gazette of the Republic of Slovenia, No. 41/17 of 28 July 2017)

Market in Financial Instruments Act – ZTFI-1 (Official Gazette of the Republic of Slovenia, No. 77/18 of 30 November 2018)

Act Implementing the Regulation (EU) establishing a general framework for securitization and establishing a specific framework for simple, transparent and standardized securitisations – ZIUDSOL (Official Gazette of the Republic of Slovenia, No. 22/19 of 5 April 2019)

Decision on annulment of the fourth paragraph of Article 33 of the Banking Act (Official Gazette of the Republic of Slovenia, No. 44/19 of 5 July 2019)

IA — Insurance Act – the Insurance Act (Official Gazette of RS, No. 13/00 of 17. 2. 2000), IA

Correction of the Law on Insurance – Insurance Act (Official Gazette of RS, No. 91/00 of 6. 10. 2000)

Law Amending the Law on Insurance – Insurance Act (Official Gazette of RS, No. 21/02 of 11. 3. 2002), IA-A

The annulment of the fifth paragraph of Article 22 and the second and third paragraphs of Article 29 of the Insurance Act (Official Gazette of RS, No. 29/03 of 21. 3. 2003)

Law Amending the Law on Insurance – IA-B (Official Gazette of RS, No. 50/04 of 6. 5. 2004)

Insurance Act – official consolidated text – IA-UPB1 (Official Gazette of RS, No. 102/04 of 21. 9. 2004)

Law Amending the Law on Insurance – IA-C (Official Gazette of RS, No. 79/06 of 27. 7. 2006)

	Insurance Act – official consolidated text – IA-UPB2 (Official Gazette of RS, No. 109/06 of 23. 10. 2006)
	Law Amending the Law on Insurance – IA-D (Official Gazette of RS, No. 102/07 of 9. 11. 2007)
	Law Amending the Law on Insurance – IA-E (Official Gazette of RS, No. 69/08 of 8. 7. 2008)
	Law Amending the Law on Insurance – IA-F (Official Gazette of RS, No. 19/09 of 13. 3. 2009)
	Law Amending the Law on Insurance – IA-G (Official Gazette of RS, No. 49/09 of 29. 6. 2009)
	Law Amending the Law on Insurance – Insurance Act-H (Official Gazette of RS, No. 79/10 of 8. 10. 2010)
	Insurance Act – official consolidated text – IA-UPB7 (Official Gazette of RS, No. 99/10 of 12. 7. 2010)
	Law Amending the Law on Insurance – IA-I (Official Gazette of RS, No. 90/12 of 30. 11. 2012)
	Law Amending the Law on Insurance – IA-J (Official Gazette of RS, No. 56/13 of 2. 7. 2013)
BSA	Bank of Slovenia Act – BAS-1 (Official Gazette of RS, No. 58/02 of 4. 7. 2002), BSA
	Correction of the Law on the Bank of Slovenia – ZBS-1 (Official Gazette of RS, No. 85/02 of 4. 10. 2002)
	Law Amending the Law on the Bank of Slovenia – ZBS-1A (Official Gazette of RS, No. 39/06 of 13. 4. 2006), BSA-1A
	Bank of Slovenia Act – official consolidated text – BAS-1-UPB1 (Official Gazette of RS, No. 72/06 of 11. 7. 2006), BSA-OCT1
BSAct	Law Amending the Law on the Bank of Slovenia – ZBS-1B (Official Gazette of RS, No. 59/11 of 25. 7. 2011). BSA-1B
	The Business Secrets Act – BSAct (Official Gazette of the Republic of Slovenia, No. 22/19 of 5 April 2019)
LC	Law on Cooperatives (Official Gazette of RS, No. 13/92 of 20. 3. 1992), LC
	Law Amending the Law on Cooperatives (Official Gazette of RS, No. 7/93 of 4. 2. 1993), LC-A
	Law Amending the Law on Cooperatives – ZAD-B (Official Gazette of RS, No. 41/07 of 11. 5. 2007), LC-B

	Cooperatives Act – official consolidated text – ZAD-UPB1 (Official Gazette of RS, No. 62/07 of 12. 7. 2007), LC-OCT1
	Law Amending the Law on Cooperatives – ZAD-C (Official Gazette of RS, No. 87/09 of 2. 11. 2009), LC-C
	Cooperatives Act – official consolidated text – ZAD-UPB2 (Official Gazette of RS, No. 97/09 of 30. 11. 2009), LC-OCT2
LCC	Correction of the Companies Act – ZGD-1 (Official Gazette of RS, No. 60/06 of 9. 6. 2006)
	Act Amending the Companies Act – ZGD-1A (Official Gazette of RS, No. 10/08 of 30. 1. 2008), LCC-1A
	Act Amending the Companies Act – ZGD-1B (Official Gazette of RS, No. 68/08 of 8. 7. 2008), LCC-1B
	Act Amending the Companies Act – ZGD-1C (Official Gazette of RS, No. 42/09 of 5. 6. 2009), LCC-1C
	Companies Act – official consolidated text – CA-1-UPB3 (Official Gazette of RS, No. 65/09 dated 14. 8. 2009), OCT-UPB3
	Law on Amendments to the Companies Act – ZGD-1D (Official Gazette of RS, No. 33/11 of 3. 5. 2011), LCC-1D
	The annulment of the first to the fourth paragraph of Article 10a and the fourth paragraph of Article 10b, and partly repealing the seventh paragraph of Article 10a of the LCC, and the finding that the fifth and sixth paragraphs of Article 10a, part of the Seventh paragraph of Article 10a and the first to the third paragraph of Article 10b and twelfth indent of Article 50 of the companies Act insofar as it relates to the first and second paragraphs of Article 10b of the companies Act are not inconsistent with the Constitution (Official Gazette of RS, No. 44/13 of 24. 5. 2013)
LCC-1E	Law on Amendments to the Companies Act – ZGD-1E (Official Gazette of RS, No. 91/11 of 14. 11. 2011), LCC-1E
LCC-1F	Act Amending the Companies Act – ZGD-1F (Official Gazette of RS, No. 32/12 of 4. 5. 2012) LCC-1F
LCC-1G	Act Amending the Companies Act – ZGD-1G (Official Gazette of RS, No. 57/12 of 27. 7. 2012) LCC-1G

List of Abbreviations (English and Slovene)

LCC-1H	Act Amending the Companies Act – ZGD-1H (Official Gazette of the Republic of Slovenia, No. 82/13 of 8 October 2013)
LCC 1-I	Act Amending the Companies Act – ZGD-1I (Official Gazette of the Republic of Slovenia, No. 55/15 of 24 July 2015)
LCC1-J	Act Amending the Companies Act – ZGD-1J (Official Gazette RS, No. 15/17 of 31 March 2017)
LCPS	The Law on commercial public services, Official Gazette of the RS, Nos 32/93, 30/98 – ZZLPP, 127/06 – ZJZP (Slovene: ZGJS)
LCP	The Law on the completion of privatization and privatization of legal persons owned by the Slovenian Development Corporation – LCP, Slovene ZZLPPO (Official Gazette of RS, No. 30/98 of 16. 4. 1998)
LEPM	The Law on workers' participation in management (Official Gazette of RS, No. 42/93 of 22. 7. 1993), LEPM
	Law Amending the Law on workers' participation in management – ZSDU-A (Official Gazette of RS, No. 56/01 of 6. 7. 2001), LEPM-A
	Law Amending the Law on workers' participation in management of governance – ZSDU B (Official Gazette of RS, No. 26/07 of 23. 3. 2007), LEPM-B
	The Law on workers' participation in management of governance – official consolidated text
	ZSDU UPB1 (Official Gazette of RS, No. 42/07 of 15. 5. 2007), LEPM-OCT1
LEPMEC	The Law on employee's participation in management of European Company
	(SE) Official Gazette of the RS, No. 28/2006 of 17 March 2006 (Slovene: ZSDUED)
LEWC	The Law on European Worker's Councils, Official Gazette of the RS, Nos 59/2002, 103/2007 (Slovene: ZEDS)
LF	Law on Foundations (Official Gazette of RS, No. 60/95 of 20. 10. 1995)
	Law Amending the Law on Foundations – ZU-A (Official Gazette of RS, No. 53/05 of 31. 5. 2005), LF
	The Law on Foundations – official consolidated text – ZU-UPB1 (Official Gazette of RS, No. 70/05 of 26. 7. 2005), LF-OCT1

Correction Official consolidated text of the Law on Foundations – ZU-UPB1 (Official Gazette of RS, No. 91/05 of 14. 10. 2005)

LFOIPCD — The Financial Operations, Insolvency Proceedings and Compulsory Dissolution – ZFPPIPP (Official Gazette of RS, No. 126/07 of 31. 12. 2007) LFOIPCD

Law Amending the Law on Financial Operations, Insolvency Proceedings and Compulsory Dissolution – ZFPPIPP-A (Official Gazette of RS, No. 40/09 of 29. 5. 2009), LFOIPCD-A

Law Amending the Law on Financial Operations, Insolvency Proceedings and Compulsory Dissolution – ZFPPIPP-B (Official Gazette of RS, No. 59/09 of 30. 7. 2009), LFOIPCD-B

Law Amending the Law on Financial Operations, Insolvency Proceedings and Compulsory Dissolution – ZFPPIPP-C (Official Gazette of RS, No. 52/10 of 30. 6. 2010), LFOIPCD-C

Law Amending the Law on Financial Operations, Insolvency Proceedings and Compulsory Dissolution – ZFPPIPP-D (Official Gazette of RS, No. 26/11 of 8. 4. 2011), LFOIPCD-D

The decision on repealing Article 34 of the Law on Amendments and Supplements to the Law on Financial Operations, Insolvency Proceedings and Compulsory Dissolution Act, insofar as it relates to the provision of point 2 of the first paragraph of Article 114 of the Financial Operations, Insolvency Proceedings and Compulsory Dissolution and task manager in the bankruptcy proceedings to which this Act binds awards manager, made before the entry into force of the law amending the law on financial operations, insolvency proceedings and compulsory Dissolution Act. The decision revoking the decision of the Higher Court of Koper and the decision of the District Court of Nova Gorica and the decision of the District Court in Nova Gorica (Official Gazette of RS, No. 23/12 of 26. 3. 2012)

Law Amending the Law on Financial Operations, Insolvency Proceedings and Compulsory Dissolution – ZFPPIPP-E (Official Gazette of RS, No. 47/13 of 31. 5. 2013) LFOIPCD-E

	The Financial Operations, Insolvency Proceedings and Compulsory Dissolution Act – official consolidated text – UPB7-ZFPPIPP (Official Gazette of RS, No. 63/13 of 26. 7. 2013) LFOIPCD-OCT13
	Law Amending the Law on Financial Operations, Insolvency Proceedings and Compulsory Dissolution – ZFPPIPP-F (Official Gazette of RS, No. 100/13 of 6. 12. 2013) LFOIPCD-F
	Correction of the Law on Amendments and Supplements to the Law on Financial Operations, Insolvency Proceedings and Compulsory Dissolution – ZFPPIPP-F (Official Gazette of RS, No. 10/15 of 16. 2. 2015)
	The Financial Operations, Insolvency Proceedings and Compulsory Dissolution Act – official consolidated text – UPB8-ZFPPIPP (Official Gazette of RS, No. 13/14 of 17. 2. 2014), LFOIPCD-OCT14
	Adjustment of the Financial Operations, Insolvency Proceedings and Compulsory Dissolution Act – official consolidated text – UPB8-ZFPPIPP (Official Gazette of RS, No. 10/15 of 16. 2. 2015) LFOIPCD-OCT15
	Law Amending the Law on Financial Operations, Insolvency Proceedings and Compulsory Dissolution – ZFPPIPP-G (Official Gazette of RS, No. 27/16 of 11. 4. 2016), LFOIPCD-G
	Decision finding that the Law on Financial Operations, Insolvency Proceedings and Compulsory Dissolution in conflict with the Constitution (Official Gazette of RS, No. 31/16 of 29. 4. 2016)
	Decision finding that the Law on Financial Operations, Insolvency Proceedings and Compulsory Dissolution in conflict with the Constitution and the repeal of the decision of the Higher Court in Ljubljana (Official Gazette of RS, No. 38/16 of 27. 5. 2016)
LI	The Law on Institutions, Official Gazette of the RS, Nos 12/91, 17/91, 55/92, 13/93, 8/96, 31/2000, 66/2003 127/2006-ZJZP (Slovene: ZZav), LI
	Law amending the Law on Institutions – ZZ-A (Official Gazette of RS, No. 8/96 of 12. 2. 1996), LI-A
ITMCL	Law on Investment Funds and Management Companies – ZISDU-1 (Official Gazette of RS, No. 110/02 of 18. 12. 2002), ITMCL

	Authentic interpretation of the first paragraph of Article 137 of the Law on Investment Funds and Management Companies – ORZISDU137 (Official Gazette of RS, No. 32/04 of 2. 4. 2004), ITMCL-AE1
	Law Amending the Law on Investment Funds and Management Companies – ZISDU-1A (Official Gazette of RS, No. 42/04 of 23 4 2004), ITMCL-1A
	Decision of the Constitutional Court of the Republic of Slovenia on repealing the eleventh paragraph of Article 237 of the Act, the Investment Funds and Management Companies, No. U-I-127/03-44 (Official Gazette of RS, No. 68/05 of 18. 7. 2005)
	Law Amending the Law on Investment Funds and Management Companies – ZISDU-1B (Official Gazette of RS, No. 92/07 of 10. 10. 2007), ITMCL-1B
	Correction of the Law on Amendments and Supplements to the Law on Investment Funds and Management Companies – ZISDU-1B (Official Gazette of RS, No. 109/07 of 30. 11. 2007)
	The Law amending the Law on Amendments and Supplements to the Law on Investment Funds and Management Companies – ZISDU-1C (Official Gazette of RS, No. 65/08 of 30. 6. 2008), ITMCL-1C
LPPP	The Law on public private partnership Official Gazette of the RS, No. 127/06 (Slovene: ZJZP)
LS	Law on Societes – SA-1 (Official Gazette of RS, No. 61/06 of 13. 6. 2006)
	Law Amending the Law on Societes – SA-1A (Official Gazette of RS, No. 58/09 of 27. 7. 2009)
	Law Amending the Law on Societes – SA-1B (Official Gazette of RS, No. 39/11 of 25. 5. 2011)
	Societies Act – official consolidated text – SA-1 UPB2 (Official Gazette of RS, No. 64/11 of 12. 8. 2011)
MFIL	Law on Markets in Financial Instruments – ZTFI (Official Gazette of RS, No. 67/07 of 27. 7. 2007), MFIL
	Correction of the Market in Financial Instruments – ZTFI (Official Gazette of RS, No. 100/07 dated 2. 11. 2007)
	Law Amending the Law on Markets in Financial Instruments – ZTFI-A (Official Gazette of RS, No. 69/08 of 8. 7. 2008), MFIL-1A

	Law Amending the Law on Markets in Financial Instruments – ZTFI-B (Official Gazette of RS, No. 40/09 of 29. 5. 2009), MFIL-1B
	Law Amending the Law on Markets in Financial Instruments – ZTFI-C (Official Gazette of RS, No. 88/10 of 11. 5. 2010), MFIL-1C
	Law on Markets in Financial Instruments – official consolidated text – ZTFI -UPB3 (Official Gazette of RS, No. 108/10 dated 30. 12. 2010), MFIL-OCT-3
	Law Amending the Law on Markets in Financial Instruments – ZTFI-D (Official Gazette of RS, No. 78/11 of 10. 5. 2011), MFIL-1D
	Law Amending the Law on Markets in Financial Instruments – ZTFI-E (Official Gazette of RS, No. 55/12 of 20. 7. 2012), MFIL-1E
	Law Amending the Law on Markets in Financial Instruments – ZTFI-F (Official Gazette of RS, No. 30/16 of 25. 4. 2016), MFIL-1F
	Law Amending the Law on Market in Financial Instruments – ZTFI-G (Official Gazette of the Republic of Slovenia, No. 9/17 of 24 February 2017)
	Law on Market in Financial Instruments – ZTFI-1 (Official Gazette of the Republic of Slovenia, No. 77/18 of 30 November 2018)
OL	Code of Obligations – OZ (Official Gazette of RS, No. 83/01 of 25 October 2001) OL
	Decision on the partial annulment of Article 1060 of the Code of Obligations (Official Gazette of RS, No. 28/06 of 17. 3. 2006)
	Law on amending and supplementing the Code of Obligations – OZ-A (Official Gazette of RS, No. 40/07 of 7. 5. 2007), OL-A
PILPA	Code of Obligations – official consolidated text – OZ-UPB1 (Official Gazette of RS, No. 97/07 of 24. 10. 2007), OL-OCT1
	Private International Law and Procedure Act (PILPA, Slovene: ZMZPP) Official Gazette RS, No. 56/99 in 45/08 – ZArbit)
TAL	Takeovers Law – 1 (Official Gazette of RS, No. 79/06 of 27. 7. 2006), TL

	Law on the Amendment of the Takeovers Law1A Takeover Act (Official Gazette of RS, No. 1/08 of 4. 1. 2008), TL 1-A
	Law Amending the Law on Takeovers – TL 1-B (Official Gazette of RS, No. 68/08 of 8. 7. 2008), TL -1B
	The annulment of the second sentence of the second paragraph of Article 75 and Article 63 in conjunction with the second sentence of the second paragraph of Article 75 of the Takeover Act in respect of the content that they made it authentic interpretation of the second paragraph of Article 75 and Article 63 in conjunction with the second paragraph of Article 75 of the Takeover Law (Official Gazette of RS, No. 105/11 of 23. 12. 2011)
	Law Amending the Law on Takeovers – Takeover Law 1C (Official Gazette of RS, No. 10/12 of 10. 2. 2012), TL-1C
	Law Amending the Law on Takeovers – 1D Takeover Law (Official Gazette of RS, No. 38/12 of 25. 5. 2012), TL-1D
	Law on Amendments to the Law on Takeovers – 1E Takeover Law (Official Gazette of RS, No. 56/13 of 2. 7th 2013), TL-1E
	Law Amending the Law on Takeover – Takeover Law 1F (Official Gazette of RS, No. 25/14 of 11. 4. 2014), TL-1F
	Law Amending the Law on Takeovers – 1G Takeover Law (Official Gazette of RS, No. 75/15 of 8. 10. 2015), TL-1G
CRL	Court Register Act (Official Gazette of RS, No. 13/94 of 10. 3. 1994), CRL
	Court Register Act – official consolidated ZSReg text – UPB1 (Official Gazette of RS, No. 114/05 of 19. 12. 2005), CRL-OCT1
	Court Register Act – official consolidated ZSReg text – -UPB2 (Official Gazette of RS, No. 54/07 of 18. 6. 2007), CRL-OCT2
	The Law amending the Law on Amendments and Supplements to the Law on the Court Register – ZSReg-C (Official Gazette of RS, No. 93/07 of 12. 10. 2007), CRL-C

	Law Amending the Law on the Court Register – ZSReg-F (Official Gazette of RS, No. 17/15 of 13. 3. 2015), CRL-F
CRL-A	Law Amending the Law on the Court Register – ZSReg-A (Official Gazette of RS, No. 91/05 of 14. 10. 2005), CRL-A
CRL-B	Law Amending the Law on the Court Register – ZSReg-B (Official Gazette of RS, No. 33/07 of 13. 4. 2007), CRL-B
CRL-D	Law Amending the Law on the Court Register – ZSReg-D (Official Gazette of RS, No. 65/08 of 30. 6. 2008), CRL-D
CRL-E	Law Amending the Law on the Court Register – ZSReg-E (Official Gazette of RS, No. 49/09 of 29. 6. 2009), CRL-E
CRL-F	The Law Amending the Court Register Law – ZSReg-F (Official Gazette of the Republic of Slovenia, No. 17/15 of 13 March 2015)
CRL-G	Law Amending the Court Register Law – ZSReg-G (Official Gazette of the Republic of Slovenia, No. 54/17 of 29 September 2017)
DSL-1	-Dematerialized Securities Law – DLL-1, – DZNVP-1 (Official Gazette of the Republic of Slovenia, No. 75/15 of 8 October 2015)
BRL-1	Act Amending the Dematerialized Securities Law – DLL-1A, – ZNVP-1A (Official Gazette of the Republic of Slovenia, No. 5/17 of 3 February 2017)
	Decision to annul the first and second sentences of the fourth paragraph of Article 48 of the Dematerialized Securities Act (Official Gazette of the Republic of Slovenia, No. 15/18 of 7 March 2018)
	Act Amending the Dematerialized Securities Act Law – DLL-1B, – ZNVP-1B (Official Gazette of the Republic of Slovenia, No. 43/19 of 28 June 2019
	Business Register Law of Slovenia – ZPRS-1 (Official Gazette of the Republic of Slovenia, No. 49/06 of 12. 5. 2006)

Law Amending the Business Register of Slovenia Law – BRL-1A, Slovene: ZPRS-1A (Official Gazette of the Republic of Slovenia, No. 19/15 of 20 March 2015)

Law Amending the Business Register of Slovenia Law – BRL-1B, Slovene: ZPRS-1B (Official Gazette RS, No. 54/17 of 29 September 2017)

List of Abbreviations (English and Slovene)

General Introduction

§1. General Background of the Country

I. Geography

1. The Republic of Slovenia (Republika Slovenija) lies in southern Central Europe bordering Italy on the west, the Adriatic Sea on the southwest, Croatia on the south and east, Hungary on the northeast and Austria on the north.[1] The capital of Slovenia is Ljubljana. Four major European geographic regions meet in Slovenia: the Alps, the Dinarides, the Pannonian Plain and the Mediterranean. Slovenia's highest peak is Triglav (2,864 m); the country's average height above sea level is 557 m.

II. Cultural Composition

2. The official language is Slovenian, which is a member of the South Slavic language group. Hungarian and Italian enjoy the status of official languages in the ethnically mixed regions along the Hungarian and Italian borders. By religion, Slovenians have traditionally been largely Roman Catholic.

3. Slovenia's first book was printed by the Protestant reformer Primož Trubar (1508–1586). Mainly two books, Catechismus (a catechism) and Abecedarium, were published in 1550 in Tübingen, Germany. Slovenia's two greatest writers were the poet France Prešeren (1800–1849) and the writer Ivan Cankar (1876–1918). The most important Slovenian painters are Ivana Kobilca and impressionist Rihard Jakopič. The most famed Slovenian architect is Joee Plečnik, who worked in Vienna as well as in Prague.

4. The Slovenian educational system consists of pre-school education, basic education – there is one structure for primary and lower secondary education – and (upper) secondary education, which includes vocational and technical education, secondary general education, higher vocational education and higher education. Specific parts of the system are adult education, music and dance education, special

1. Most of the data in this monograph are taken from Wikipedia, the free encyclopaedia, en.wikipedia.org/ wiki/Slovenia, and the Statistical Office of the Republic of Slovenia, www.stat.si /eng/.

needs education and programmes in ethnically and linguistically mixed areas. Currently, there are four universities in Slovenia: University of Ljubljana, University of Maribor, University of Primorska and University of Nova Gorica.

III. Political System

5. According to its Constitution,[2] Slovenia is a democratic republic, a State governed by the rule of law and a social State. At various points in Slovenia's history, the country has been part of the Roman Empire; the Duchy of Carantania; Austria-Hungary; the State of Slovenes, Croats and Serbs; the Kingdom of Serbs, Croats and Slovenes (renamed the Kingdom of Yugoslavia in 1929) between the World Wars; and the Socialist Federal Republic (SFR) of Yugoslavia from 1945 until gaining independence in 1991.

6. The Slovenian head of State is the president, who is elected by popular vote every five years. The executive branch is headed by the prime minister and the council of ministers or cabinet, which are elected by the Parliament. The bicameral Parliament of Slovenia consists of the National Assembly (Državni zbor) and the National Council (Državni svet). The National Assembly has ninety seats, which are partially filled with directly elected representatives and partially with proportionally elected representatives (two seats reserved for autochthonous Hungarian and Italian minorities). The National Council has forty seats and is made up of representatives of social, economic, professional and local interest groups. Parliamentary elections are held every four years.

7. Slovenia's statistical regions exist solely for legal and statistical purposes. The government, however, is preparing a plan for new administrative regions. The number of these regions has not yet been decided but is said to be between twelve and fourteen. Constitutional changes allowing the creation of regions have already been approved by the National Assembly. Slovenia is divided into 210 municipalities, of which eleven have urban status.

8. Slovenia is a member of the European Union (EU), the Council of Europe and North Atlantic Treaty Organization (NATO). Slovenia is also a founding member of the World Trade Organization, joined Central European Free Trade Agreement (CEFTA) in 1996, and joined the EU on 1 May 2004. Slovenia was the first of new Member States (accession 2004) to hold the Presidency of the Council of the EU in the first half of 2008.

2. The Constitution of the Republic of Slovenia (CRS) was adopted on 23 Dec. 1991, and amended on 14 Jul. 1997, 25 Jul. 2000 and 7 Mar. 2003, URS.

IV. Population and Employment Statistics

9. On 1 January 2019, Slovenia had a population of 2,080,908. The number of Slovene citizens decreased while the number of foreign citizens increased. According to the Statistical Office of Slovenia, the population of Slovenia increased by 14,028 in 2018. The number of citizens of Slovenia decreased by almost 2,300, while the number of foreign citizens increased by more than 16,300 (13.4%). On 1 January 2019, the 138,193 foreign citizens represented 6.6% of Slovenia's population (Table 1).

On 1 January 2019, the population of Slovenia consisted of 1,038,656 men and 1,042,252 women. The share of women among citizens of Slovenia was 51.2% (this share has been slowly decreasing for a number of years); among foreign citizens there were 34.3% women (after several years of increase, their share decreased by one percentage point in 2018).

Table 1 Population by Groups and Sex, Slovenia

	1. 1. 2018	1. 4. 2018	1. 7. 2018	1. 10. 2018	1. 1. 2019
Population	*2.066.880*	*2.067.284*	*2.070.050*	*2.076.595*	*2.080.908*
men	1.027.041	1.028.014	1.030.234	1.034.966	1.038.656
women	1.039.839	1.039.270	1.039.816	1.041.629	1.042.252
Citizens of the RS	1.945.005	1.943.441	1.943.127	1.943.075	1.942.715
men	948.185	947.657	947.569	947.657	947.826
women	996.820	995.784	995.558	995.418	994.889
Foreign citizens	121.875	123.843	126.923	133.520	138.193
men	78.856	80.357	82.665	87.309	90.830
women	43.019	43.486	44.258	46.211	47.363

Source: SURS.

10. Total Slovenian population is composed of the working-age population and persons aged 15 or less. The working-age population is then divided into inactive and active population. Active population is divided into unemployed and employed persons. Furthermore, employed persons are employees, self-employed or unpaid family members.[3]

11. The unemployment rate at 4.8% in the first quarter of 2019 was 1.1 percentage point lower than a year ago. In the first quarter of 2019, there were 14,000 more employed persons and 11,000 fewer unemployed persons than in the previous year.

3. http://www.stat.si/StatWeb/en/show-news?id=5951&idp=3&headerbar=12.

The number of unemployed men decreased by 20.9% and the number of unemployed women by 15.9%. There were 23,000 long-term unemployed persons (unemployed twelve months or more), 18.2% fewer than in the previous year. In the past few years, the ILO unemployment rate was higher than the EU-28 average in Italy and Croatia and lower in Hungary and Austria. The rate in Slovenia was slightly below the EU-28 average.[4] In June 2016, the number of persons in employment increased to around 820,000 at a monthly level. In June 2016, the number of persons in employment increased by 0.3%; it increased the most in manufacturing (by 0.3%). On the monthly level, the registered unemployment rate decreased by 0.3 of a percentage point, to 10.8%.[5]

The number of employed persons (978,000) in the first quarter of 2019 increased by 1.5% compared to the previous year. Among employed persons there were 2.5% more employees, 4.6% more self-employed persons and 38% fewer unpaid family workers. The number of unpaid family workers (19,000) was the lowest in the past ten years. In the first quarter of 2019 the number of student workers decreased by 8.7% compared to the previous year. Around 720,000 employees were permanently employed and 117,000 were temporarily employed. The share of permanently employed compared to the previous year increased by 6%. The share of temporarily employed decreased by 14.6% (Table 2).[6]

Table 2 Population by Activity, Slovenia (Number in 1,000)

	I–III 2018			*I–III 2019*		
	Total	*Men*	*Women*	*Total*	*Men*	*Women*
Population – total	2,067	1,027	1,040	2,081	1,039	1,042
Labour force	1,025	547	478	1,028	556	472
Employed	964	517	446	978	533	446
Employees	816	422	394	837	435	402
Self-employed	117	81	36	122	87	35
Unpaid family workers	31	14	17	19	11	8M
Unemployed	61	30	31	50	23	26
Inactive	731	320	411	739	321	418

Source: SURS.[7]

12. Among the working population, in Slovenia, 14.6% of people were born abroad. Of these, half were born in Bosnia and Herzegovina, while the majority of the people were born in Croatia (slightly less than 18% of the economically active

4. https://www.stat.si/StatWeb/en/News/Index/8140.
5. http://www.stat.si/StatWeb/en/show-news?id=6126&idp=3&headerbar=12.
6. https://www.stat.si/StatWeb/en/News/Index/8140.
7. https://www.stat.si/StatWeb/en/News/Index/8140.

foreign born). Among the working population, born in Slovenia, most have secondary education (almost 60% of people), as well as the workforce born abroad, is dominated by persons with secondary education, but their proportion is lower (almost 48%). Of the people born in Slovenia, majority are tertiary educated (almost 26%), whereas those born abroad, are primary educated or less (41%).[8] In Slovenia, the main ethnic group comprises Slovenians (84%). Nationalities from the former Yugoslavia (Serbs, Croats, Bosniaks and Muslims by nationality) form 6.3%, and the Hungarian, Italian and Roma minorities form 0.6% of the population. The ethnic affiliation of 9.1% is either undeclared or unknown. With 101 inhabitants per square kilometre (256/sq. mi.) in 2009, Slovenia ranks low among the European countries in population density (compared with 320/km^2 for the Netherlands or 195/km^2 for Italy). Approximately 51% of the population lives in urban areas and 49% in rural areas.

V. Economy

13. From 1996 until 2010, Slovenia's average quarterly Gross Domestic Product (GDP) growth was 0.80% reaching a historical high of 4.19% in June of 1999 and a record low of –6.04% in March 2009.[9] According to the Statistical Office of the Republic of Slovenia (Slovene: SURS) (SORS), GDP decreased by 4.8% in the first quarter of 2013 compared with the first quarter of 2012. GDP has been decreasing since 2010. According to SORS, in the first quarter of 2016, Slovenia's GDP was 2.5% higher than in the first quarter of 2015. In the first quarter of 2016, exports had a positive impact on the economic activity.[10] In the first quarter of 2019, GDP increased by 3.2% over the first quarter of 2018. Seasonally adjusted GDP increased by 0.8% over the previous quarter and by 3.7% over the first quarter of 2018. Domestic expenditure increased by 1.8% in the first quarter of 2019, which was the lowest increase in the past three years. Important impact on the domestic expenditure growth had gross capital formation, which decreased by 1.3% compared to the first quarter of 2018. The final consumption expenditure grew by 2.9%, which is somewhat higher growth than in the previous three quarters. Compared to growth rates in the previous quarters, the increase in the first quarter of 2019 was more significant in household final consumption expenditure (2.6%) and in government final consumption expenditure (3.6%).

After two-quarters of slightly lower growth of exports (5.4% and 6.8%), in the first quarter of 2019, we observed higher growth of exports (7.6%). Imports increased less (by 6.4%), which resulted in high external trade surplus. This time it contributed 1.6 percentage points to GDP growth.

14. In 2009, GDP per capita in Purchasing Power Standards in Slovenia amounted to 88% of that in the EU-27. Actual individual consumption per capita in

8. Socio-Economic characteristics of the population (1 Jan. 2009) and international migrants (2009), detailed data, Slovenia – final data.
9. www.businessmonitor.com/bmo/europe/?gclid=CNKY6dba4qYCFcULfAod2FIm6w.
10. http://www.stat.si/StatWeb/en/show-news?id=5973&idp=1&headerbar=10.

purchasing power standards in Slovenia in 2015 lagged behind the EU-28 average by 26%. Slovenian GDP per capita (EUR 18,093 in 2014) in purchasing power standards in 2015 was 17% lower than the EU-28 average; same as in 2014. The GDP per capita in Slovenia was last recorded at USD 32,742.51 in 2018, when adjusted by purchasing power parity (PPP). The GDP per Capita, in Slovenia, when adjusted by PPP is equivalent to 184% of the world's average. GDP per capita PPP in Slovenia averaged USD 24,759.30 from 1990 until 2018, reaching an all-time high of USD 32,742.51 in 2018 and a record low of USD 16,289.49 USD in 1992.[11]

15. Macroeconomic and financial stability[12] has allowed Slovenia to complete the process of European integration by joining the euro area on 1 January 2007. Slovenia was the first new member to adopt the euro as the country's only currency on 1 January 2007. In June 2004, it joined the European Exchange Rate Mechanism.

16. Slovenia's trade is oriented towards Western (EU) countries, mainly Germany, Austria, Italy and France. This is the result of a wholesale reorientation of trade towards the West and the growing markets of Central and Eastern Europe in the wake of the collapse of its Yugoslav markets. Slovenia's economy is highly dependent on foreign trade. Trade equals about 120% of GDP (exports and imports combined). About two-thirds of Slovenia's trade is with EU members, a primary motivation for seeking EU membership.

17. Industry and construction comprise over one-third of the GDP. As in most industrial economies, services make up an increasing share of output (57.1%), notably in financial services.

In 2015, EUR 548 million dividends were paid. In comparison with 2014, this is 2.2% less. Most dividends were paid to the government sector, EUR 181 million.[13] A comparable series of data on performance of enterprises in the 2005–2014 period showed that as in 2005 also in 2014 turnover was the highest in wholesale and retail trade, while the biggest increase was recorded in electricity, gas, steam and air conditioning supply.[14]

Average gross earnings for April 2019 amounted to EUR 1,730.70 and net earnings to EUR 1,114.98. Compared to earnings for April 2018, average earnings for April 2019 increased, gross earnings in nominal terms by 4.0% and in real terms by 2.3%, and net earnings in nominal terms by 3.3% and in real terms by 1.6%.[15]

To increase GDP in Slovenia, it is crucial to ensure a stable macroeconomic environment and raise productivity and thus the long-term competitiveness of the economy. It is essential to strengthen long-term factors of productivity, such as innovative capacity of the economy and human capital. Slovenia should also enhance

11. https://tradingeconomics.com/slovenia/gdp-per-capita-ppp.
12. Bank of Slovenia, *Financial Stability Review*, Expert Papers on Financial Stability 2006, www.bsi.si/ en/default.asp.
13. http://www.stat.si/StatWeb/en/show-news?id=6101&idp=23&headerbar=20.
14. http://www.stat.si/StatWeb/en/show-news?id=6018&idp=16&headerbar=7.
15. http://www.stat.si/StatWeb/en/show-news?id=6018&idp=16&headerbar=7.

the efficiency of the government and its institutions and create an environment that is conducive to the establishment and growth of businesses.[16]

VI. Enterprises, Statistics

18. In comparison to previous years, there are more enterprises, greater turnover and more persons employed in Slovenia.[17] In 2018 there were 146,196 active enterprises which generated EUR 102.4 billion of turnover, 7.5% more than in 2017, and EUR 24.1 billion of value added, 7.0% more than in 2017. In 2018 there were also more employed persons in enterprises, namely 654,831 employees and self-employed persons, which is 4.2% more than in 2017. As regards sections of activity, the highest increase was recorded in construction (by 8.3%) and in real estate sectors (by 8.5%). Water supply, sewerage, waste management and remediation activities sectors generated 9.0% more turnover in 2018; their turnover represented 3.6% of total turnover in the industry. In manufacturing activities enterprises generated 6.6% more turnover; their turnover represented 78% of total turnover in industry. Electricity, gas, steam and air conditioning supply sectors generated less turnover than in 2017.

Manufacturing sector generated the most turnover and value added in industry. The largest share of turnover was generated by enterprises in manufacture of fabricated metal products, except machinery and equipment, in manufacture of electrical equipment and in manufacture of motor vehicles. The largest value added was generated by enterprises in manufacture of basic pharmaceutical products and pharmaceutical preparations, in manufacture of fabricated metal products, except machinery and equipment, and in manufacture of electrical equipment. In 2018 there were 19,220 active enterprises in construction, 552 more than a year before. Enterprises involved in construction generated EUR 6 billion of turnover in 2018 and had among all sections in structural business statistics the highest (22.9%) increase.

Value added in construction sector increased by 17.8% to EUR 1.7 billion. The highest increase was recorded in enterprises engaged in construction of buildings.

Most enterprises in construction were registered in specialized construction activities. In 2018 they generated 49.5% of total turnover, 59.4% of total value added, 50.5% of total production value, and employed 65.2% of all persons in construction. In wholesale and retail trade activity and repair of motor vehicles and motorcycles, there were 126 fewer enterprises in 2018 than in the previous year. In 26,265 enterprises there were 120,160 persons employed, who in 2018 generated EUR 36.7 billion of turnover or 8.5% more than a year before. Enterprises in trade generated EUR 4.5 billion of value added, which is 6.4% more than in the previous year.

Most enterprises are microenterprises with fewer than 9 persons employed. Their share in the total number is 94.4%. In 2018 these enterprises generated 5.2% more

16. http://www.umar.gov.si/en/topics/competitiveness/.
17. https://www.stat.si/StatWeb/en/News/Index/8156.

turnover and 6.8% more value added. Turnover of 79,104 active enterprises registered in other service activities was 7.9% higher than in 2017. The highest increase in turnover was recorded in professional, scientific and technical activities (by 9.6%), followed by transportation and storage (by 9.3%), real estate activities (by 8.9%), and accommodation and food service activities (by 7.9%). The lowest increase in turnover was recorded in information and communication activity (by 3.7%). Value added in 2018 amounted to EUR 7.8 billion, which is 8.1% more than in 2017.

Enterprises in other service activities employed almost the same number of persons as industry. In 2018, the number of persons employed increased in these activities as in the industry sector. It was higher by 4.4%. In 2018 there were 232,639 persons employed in these activities or 9,702 more than a year earlier.

19. There were 186,433 active enterprises in Slovenia in 2014, 2.4% more than in the previous year. They generated 3.3% more turnover.

20. As regards the size of enterprise by the number of persons employed, in Slovenia microenterprises dominate (93.8%), although the maximum turnover is created by medium-sized (25.2%) and large enterprises (34.7%). More than half (56.3%) of the persons employed worked in enterprises with more than fifty employees (Source: SORS).

21. Number of enterprises, by legal form in 2009 (statistical data):

- Limited liability companies (LLC): 33,530.
- Public limited companies (PLC) and limited partnership (LP) public companies: 999.
- General partnerships: 2,088.
- LP: 829.

VII. Social and Cultural Values

22. According to its Constitution, Slovenia, in its own territory, protects human rights and fundamental freedoms. It is a Constitutional obligation to provide for the preservation of the natural wealth and cultural heritage and create opportunities for the harmonious development of society and culture in Slovenia.

23. The right to social security is a Constitutional right. Citizens have the right to social security under conditions provided by law. The State regulates compulsory health, pensions, disability and other social insurance, and ensures its proper functioning. The right to health care is also a Constitutional right, as follows: Everyone has the right to health care under conditions provided by law. By law, cost of health care must be provided from public funds.

24. Freedom of Education is Constitutionally guaranteed. Primary education is compulsory and is financed from public funds. Secondary and tertiary education is also financed from public funds, and it is for students free of charge. The State creates opportunities for citizens to obtain a proper education. State universities and institutions of higher education are autonomous. The freedom of scientific and artistic endeavour is Constitutionally guaranteed.

25. The Constitutional framework of economic and social relations consists of the following provisions:

- The State creates opportunities for employment and work, and ensures the protection of both by law (Labor Act).
- The manner in which property is acquired and enjoyed is established by law, so as to ensure its economic, social and environmental function. Ownership rights to real estate may be revoked or limited in the public interest with the provision of compensation in a kind or monetary compensation under conditions established by law.
- Special rights to use national assets may be acquired, subject to conditions established by law. The conditions under which natural resources may be exploited are established by law. The law may provide that natural resources may also be exploited by foreign persons and establishes the conditions for such exploitation.
- The law establishes special conditions for land utilization in order to ensure its proper use. Special protection of agricultural land is provided by law. The State promotes the economic, cultural and social advancement of the population living in mountainous and hilly areas.
- Everyone has the right, in accordance with the law, to a healthy living environment. The State promotes a healthy living environment. To this end, the conditions and manner in which economic and other activities are pursued are established by law.
- The law establishes under which conditions and to what extent a person who has damaged the living environment is obliged to provide compensation. The protection of animals from cruelty is regulated by law.
- Everyone is obliged to protect natural sites of special interest, rarities and cultural monuments in accordance with the law. The State and local communities promote the preservation of the natural and cultural heritage.
- Free economic initiative is guaranteed. The conditions for establishing commercial organizations are established by law (Law on Commercial Companies, LCC). Commercial activities may not be pursued in a manner contrary to the public interest. Unfair competition practices and practices, which restrict competition in a manner contrary to the law, are prohibited.
- Employees participate in the management of commercial organizations and institutions in a manner and under conditions provided by law. The freedom to establish, operate and join trade unions is guaranteed.
- Employees have the right to strike. Where required by the public interest, the right to strike may be restricted by law, with due consideration given to the type and nature of activity involved.

VIII. Privatization Efforts in the Economy

A. *Privatization: General*

26. In the search for a new equilibrium between the private, public and social sectors, Slovenia faces the challenge of the post-privatized ownership structure of the economy, significant for the strong public, weak social and emerging, newly formed and consolidating private sectors. Furthermore, there is an important historical and ideological burden of cultural patterns (and real experiences) that derives from certain similar concepts of the former socialist State.

27. However, when talking about the cultural environment in countries in transition, it is necessary to say that the enthusiasm of the early 1990s for private property and a market economy still prevails over the concepts of public and social principles of the economy. But, paradoxically, the privatization of the economy (more correctly: the transformation from social to private forms of enterprises) caused the strengthening of the public sector. The State as an owner thereby took over total public services and, in addition, became the owner of substantial parts of other businesses. State and parastatal institutions (funds, investment companies, public banks) today own more than 50% of the economy in Slovenia.

B. *Politically Inspired Ownership and Market Economy Reforms*

28. Property rights-based corporate governance is a rather new theoretical and legal concept in Slovenia, emerging only after the beginning of politically inspired ownership and market economy reforms and privatization at the beginning of the 1990s. Previous systems of corporate governance were not at all comparable, being under self-management, labour based, or public administration controlled. Thus, there is little tradition, property rights culture and little experience on the part of shareholders, managers, creditors and other participants in corporate dialogue. There is still not enough theoretical and empirical knowledge about it.

29. The predominant institutional ownership structure strongly influences decision-making in Slovenian companies. It is very typical of Slovenian companies that only institutional investors are able to acquire enough expertise to be involved in active corporate participation. On the other hand, it must not be forgotten that, besides banks, there are a number of other institutional investors in Slovenia that have emerged as a result of the privatization process, involving the so-called privatization certificates and later on privatization shares; therefore, it is difficult to say that Slovenia matches one model (market) or the other (bank).

30. To make things even more complicated, Slovenia's securities market legislation (takeover bid regulation, insider trading restrictions, institutions such as the Stock Exchange, Security Exchange Agency (SEA), centralized Clearing Depository Service, the concept of brokerage companies, closed and open investment trusts and funds, investment corporations) are to some degree patterned on the United

States (US) model; while on the other hand, it is obvious that other items of corporate legislation (company law, banking law (BL), law on the participation of employees, etc.) are copied from the German or at least EU systems.

C. Ownership Structure of the Slovenian Economy

31. From the analysis of privatization issues (*see* below, Chapter 2) in Slovenia, we can derive some conclusions regarding the structure of ownership in the Slovenian economy. The predominant institutional ownership structure in terms of size and, even more, influence on decision-making, is very typical for Slovenia's post-privatization economy. Institutional owners, be they pension or indemnity companies, banks, insurance and investment companies, be they State or municipal administration directly, are usually under the political control of the existing political hierarchy.

32. The substantial extent of internal ownership with organized labour's influence on managerial decisions is another specific factor of a relevant part of the economy that makes business decisions subordinated to the interests and pressures of organized employed shareholders.

33. An important part of the national economy is still owned by the State, and thus it is not privatized. This part includes, mainly, wholly or majority controlled stock at the level of the corporation, which in itself carries the danger of subordinating the interests of the State as an owner to the interests of the State as the public regulator, or the agent of political parties.

D. The Culture of the New Shareholders

34. As far as the culture (behaviour) of shareholders, business (investment) motives and goals, and the tradition of different types of ownership are concerned, their characteristics are as follows:

- Institutional shareholders are ever more active and professional with regard to the current business performance of corporations, at least those where they own a substantial part. They regularly participate in shareholders' meetings, lobby and de facto choose and influence the candidates for supervisory board members, giving them informal but very significant instructions (e.g., as regards the nomination of management board members). They also permanently lobby for controlling and decision-making packages of shares, arranging informal (and sometimes formal) shareholders' agreements, putting informal pressure on management board business conduct and even personnel decisions, and so on.; in short they are organized to exercise sufficient power to control the corporations in which they are interested.
- The State as an owner behaves in much the same way as other institutional owners, that is, as an active professional owner, particularly in the industrial branches

of public interest where it combines and mostly mixes its position as owner with that of authority and regulator. This frequently makes corporate decisions dependent on political goals, including the goals of political parties that control a particular field.

- Employees as an 'internal' shareholder group are normally well organized; they act in the interests of employees unless they are a minority, when they either enter into a shareholders' agreement with the institutional owners (which is unfortunately very rare) or they behave like an opposition, which is more usual. It is very typical and significant that the internal shareholders' group representative on the supervisory board makes coalitions with labour representatives on supervisory boards, making the employee alliance stronger than the number of their shares would otherwise permit.
- Diffused shareholders acquiring their shares through public (privatization) sale or on the securities market are not organized by banks or brokerage firms, or at least by the management as proxies, nor by themselves. They are thus without influence as regards decision-making within the company; nevertheless, their ownership stake is not to be underestimated. According to their position, they actually do not attend the shareholders' meeting nor participate as individuals or groups in a shareholders' dialogue, having in addition no relation developed with the supervisory and even less with the management boards.

E. Ownership Structures and Securities Market Regulation System

35. Let us briefly comment on ownership structures from the point of view of the following question: Which type of securities market regulation system is more appropriate to Slovenia, with its high concentration of ownership and voting power? Concentrated ownership and concentrated voting power weaken the position of managers and empower direct influence on the part of block shareholders. The risk of acquiring managers' private benefit is less expressed, but the danger of squeezing out outstanding shareholders is more substantial. The European type of shareholders' activism can thus potentially increase (in Europe, 'shareholder activism' refers to small shareholders defending their interests against controlling block holders), rather than that of the US (in the US and in the United Kingdom (UK), 'shareholder activism' refers to increased monitoring of managers by weak shareholders).

36. Rather than to protect shareholders against the management, the main policy objective of legislation (*ratio legis*) should be the protection of outstanding shareholders against squeezing them out by block holders. Monitoring of managerial performance from the point of view of block shareholders is presumably not a legal problem, considering that blocks are composed of active (institutional) shareholders. But the problem of manipulative behaviour of influential block holding over the management of the corporation remains, as well as the problem of independent management. These problems cannot be solved simply by leaving management and the shareholders' block to make an agreement and leave other shareholders to solve their problems by court actions.

37. Legal regulation of the securities market can affect much dispersion of ownership and deconcentration of monopolistic powers and prevent the forming of huge block holdings and voting pools, all of which have negative implications on corporate governance efficiency and fair competition in the securities market. Legal regulation of the securities market, especially concerning the issues of full disclosure requirements, mandatory takeover bids, fair dealings rules and regulation, insider trading prohibitions, together with tax regulation of the transfer of shares within a short period of time, can contribute to securities market fair competitiveness as a prerequisite for efficient corporate governance and protection of minority shareholder's rights. The problem of Slovene securities market legislation is to find out how it copes, and whether at all it copes, with the issue of concentrated ownership and influential institutional owners emerging as a result of the privatization process.

§2. The Historical Background of Companies (Corporations) and Partnerships

I. The Development of Slovene Company Law

38. The Parliament of Slovenia adopted the new Company Law (Law on Commercial Companies) in May 1993.[18] The Law on Commercial Companies 1993 is the most comprehensive and one of the most important laws enacted since the country's independence in 1991. The Law on Commercial Companies 1993 was in August 2006 replaced by the new Law on Commercial Companies 2006 (ZGD-1), LCC-1 (hereinafter: 'LCC').[19]

39. The new Law on Commercial Companies 2006 (ZGD-1), LCC-1 was since then several times amended or corrected, by the following laws and Constitutional Court's decisions:

- Correction of the Companies Act – ZGD-1 (Official Gazette of RS, No. 60/06 of 9 June 2006).
- Act Amending the Companies Act – ZGD-1A (Official Gazette of RS, No. 10/08 of 30 January 2008), LCC-1A.
- Act Amending the Companies Act – ZGD-1B (Official Gazette of RS, No. 68/08 of 8 July 2008), LCC-1B.
- Act Amending the Companies Act – ZGD-1C (Official Gazette of RS, No. 42/09 of 5 June 2009), LCC-1C.
- Companies Act – official consolidated text – CA-1-UPB3 (Official Gazette of RS, No. 65/09 of 14 August 2009), OCT-UPB3.
- Law on Amendments to the Companies Act – ZGD-1D (Official Gazette of RS, No. 33/11 of 3 May 2011), LCC-1D.

18. The Law on Commercial Companies (LCC), Official Gazette of the RS, Nos 30/93, 29/94, 82/94, 20/98, 84/98, 6/99, 45/2001 (ZGD).
19. The Law on Commercial Companies (LCC), Official Gazette of the RS, No. 46/2006 (ZGD-1).

- Law on Amendments to the Companies Act – ZGD-1E (Official Gazette of RS, No. 91/11 of 14 November 2011), LCC-1E.
- Act Amending the Companies Act – ZGD-1F (Official Gazette of RS, No. 32/12 of 4 May 2012) LCC-1F.
- Act Amending the Companies Act – ZGD-1G (Official Gazette of RS, No. 57/12 of 27 July 2012) LCC-1G.
- The annulment of the first to the fourth paragraph of Article 10a and the fourth paragraph of Article 10b, and partly repealing the seventh paragraph of Article 10a of the LCC, and the finding that the fifth and sixth paragraphs of Article 10a, part of the Seventh paragraph of Article 10a and the first to the third paragraph of Article 10b and twelfth indent of Article 50 of the companies Act insofar as it relates to the first and second paragraphs of Article 10b of the companies Act are not inconsistent with the Constitution (Official Gazette of RS, No. 44/13 of 24 May 2013).
- Act Amending the Companies Act – ZGD-1 H (Official Gazette of RS, No. 82/13 of 8 October 2013), LCC-1H.
- Act Amending the Companies Act – ZGD-1I (Official Gazette of RS, No. 55/15 of 24 July 2015), LCC-1I.
- Act Amending the Companies Act – ZGD-1J (Official Gazette RS, No. 15/17 of 31 March 2017).

40. The Law on Commercial Companies of 1993 replaced the Enterprise Law enacted in the last period of the former Yugoslavia (1988), and attempted to introduce, for the first time after five decades of social and State ownership, as well as traditional property-rights-based legal forms of companies. Legal forms of the former system, based on the Law on Associated Labor (1976) and contract, rather than a market economy (associations of labour and later social enterprises), were labour managed or self-managed and were not at all comparable with the traditional US corporation.

41. Slovenia's Law on Commercial Companies is based on the European tradition in this field. To be more specific, it follows the German Aktiengesetz, so that many institutions including management on its own responsibility; the two-tier governance system and employee participation in Management and Supervisory Boards are similar to and comparable with those of Germany and Austria.

II. The Previous Self-Management System

42. We can easily say that there is a long and rich tradition of employee participation in Slovenia. As a matter of fact, the previous self-management system that ultimately proved to be economically inefficient, and as such politically unsustainable, was based on a contractual economy as opposed to a market economy, and labour rights as opposed to the concept of property rights.

43. The non-ownership concept of business enterprises imposed labour-based corporate governance, with a workers' council in the role of a board of directors, with the power to appoint and remove managers, to monitor them and to make strategic and long-term business decisions. The legal form of business was a so-called organization of associated labour, which was not capital but labour governed.

44. Reforms in the early 1990s abolished this concept. The self-management and non-ownership concepts were abandoned, and the privatization process brought about the transformation of organizations of associated labour, first into so-called enterprises with social capital and later, after the adoption of the modern European-patterned company law, to traditional corporate forms. However, some of the tradition, whether the self-management culture or related feelings and understanding, has remained among employees and, of course, in certain political and especially trade union circles.[20] That tradition, together with the German (Austrian) tradition that for historical reasons prevails as a legislative pattern in the corporate law, caused the Slovenian legislators to follow and even exceed not merely the German two-tier system, but also its employee participation model.

III. Security Market Legislation at the First Stage of Transition

45. Slovenia's Ljubljana Stock Exchange (LSE) was the first official bourse in any former socialist country in the world, despite the fact that the Slovenian process of privatization was one of the slowest privatization processes of all the former socialist countries. The LSE first listed fully privatized shares (and dematerialized them at the same time) on 8 January 1996.

46. The present legal basis for the capital market in Slovenia was established in March 1994, when the Securities Market Law (SML) replaced the two former federal (Yugoslav) laws on securities and capital markets, regulating the issuance and trading of securities and defining the roles of the stock exchange, the SEA, the Central Clearing Depository Service and securities market participants. The legislation was based on the Anglo-American legislature and also followed the European Directives of that time. Within the framework of the SML, the LSE and the SEC have developed their own regulations (the official LSE rules, approved by the SEA and the Articles of Association of the LSE).

20. Nowadays, the following laws regulate structural participation (participation of employees in management):

- The Law on workers' participation in management (Official Gazette of RS, No. 42/93 of 22. 7. 1993), LEPM.
- Law Amending the Law on workers' participation in management – ZSDU-A (Official Gazette of RS, No. 56/01 of 6. 7. 2001), LEPM-A.
- Law Amending the Law on workers' participation in management of governance – ZSDU B (Official Gazette of RS, No. 26/07 of 23. 3. 2007), LEPM-B.
- The Law on workers' participation in management of governance – official consolidated text – ZSDU UPB1 (Official Gazette of RS, No. 42/07 of 15. 5. 2007), LEPM-OCT1.

47. Conversely to company law that followed German tradition, legislation in the field of the securities market, such as the SML (1999),[21] Securities Dematerialization Law (DL) (1999),[22] Takeover Law (1997),[23] Investment Funds and Management Companies Law (IFMCL) (1994)[24] and BL,[25] which all formed the security market legislation at the first stage of transition, were more patterned on the US model.

48. The first takeover legislation dealt with public companies and private companies emerging from the privatization process. A legal entity or physical person who intended to acquire more than 25% of the voting rights of a particular company was obliged to make a public bid for the purchase of the rest of the shares. Unless his purchase succeeded, he was obliged to repeat such a bid for every consecutive 5% of voting rights from 25% up. In addition, the SEA supervises the execution of the public offer and the operations of brokerage companies and banks, which obtained permission for securities activities from the Bank of Slovenia. It also supervises the business operations of the Stock Exchange (including insider trading).

IV. Privatization of Slovenia's Social-Owned Enterprises

49. Privatization of Slovenia's social-owned enterprises in the early 1990s was effected by a mandatory allocation of shares to a combination of public funds, employees, former employees, plus a public sale of shares. As a result, Slovene corporate share ownership is now bifurcated between large, potentially influential institutional shareholders and diffuse, relatively powerless, smallholders.[26] Privatization law has predominantly influenced the ownership structure, where three main models of privatization were brought about.

Model 1

50. Privatization by public sale (offer), where a substantial part (40%) of privatized company shares were sold to the general public in the market, after mandatory free distribution of up to 20% of shares to the employees, ex-employees and their relatives and after allocating a mandatory 40% to the three funds (Development – 20%, Indemnity – 10% and Pension Funds – 10%), which caused most of the widely diffused ownership structure.

21. Former Securities Market Law, SML, Official Gazette of the RS, No. 56–2654/1999.
22. Former Dematerialization Law, Official Gazette of the RS, No. 23–1034/1999.
23. Former Takeover Law, Official Gazette of the RS, No. 47–2504/1997, RS 56–2654/1999.
24. Former Law on Management Companies and Investment Funds, Official Gazette of the RS, Nos 6-268/1994, RS 68–3745/1996, RS 25–1487/1997, 10–436/1998, 26–1213/1999, RS 56–2654/1999.
25. Former Banking Law, Official Gazette of the RS, No. 7-286/1999.
26. *See*: Act on the completion of privatization and privatization of legal persons owned by the Slovenian Development Corporation – ZZLPPO (Official Gazette of RS, No. 30/98 of 16. 4. 1998).

Model 2

51. Privatization by internal buy out where a substantial part (40%) of privatized shares were sold to the employees, with five-year deferred payment terms, possibly out of the corporation's profits, after the mandatory free distribution of up to 20% of shares to the employees, ex-employees and their relatives and allocating a compulsory 40% to the three funds (Development – 20%, Indemnity – 10% and Pension Funds – 10%) which created the majority (up to 60%) of the internal diffused ownership structure.

Model 3

52. Privatization by management or other buy outs, where a substantial part (40%) of privatized shares were sold to a group of managers, or a corporation formed for that specific purpose (usually called a by-pass corporation because it normally continued the business after the privatized corporation went bankrupt), again after the mandatory free distribution of up to 20% of shares to the employees, ex-employees and their relatives and allocating a compulsory 40% to the three funds (Development – 20%, Indemnity – 10% and Pension Funds – 10%) which normally led to a closed corporation in the sense of firm control of the privatized corporation by the acquiring corporation or group.

53. It is difficult to say which of the models described dominated the privatization process, but we estimate that, in practice, the three models were applied, in many different combinations, in equal proportions, to the total number of privatized companies. However, taking into account the value and size of the privatized companies, model 1 (public sale) prevailed over model 2 (internal buyout) and both of them were outnumbered by the third (management buyout).

54. In Slovenia, the institutional ownership structure has, due to the specifics of the privatization models, always prevailed. Institutional owners, be they State or municipal administrations directly, or Pension or Indemnification Companies, Slovenian Development Companies, banks, insurance and investment companies and funds and other companies still own more than 80% of shares in an average company. The average individual institutional share would be between 10% and 20%, but institutional owners normally act in concert or conclude shareholders' agreements.

55. The Slovenian Development Company, transformed from the Slovenian Development Fund, was established under privatization legislation as an institution, entitled to up to 20% of the shares of each privatized company. The Slovenian Development Fund had held the majority of shares in approximately 400 mainly poorly performing corporations. According to privatization rules, it sold a certain portion of these shares to so-called authorized investment companies, that is, investment corporations especially established for the purpose of holding and trading in privatized shares, and acting as institutional owners.

56. Pension and indemnification funds were later reorganized as Pension and Indemnification Companies and still act as institutional, mainly portfolio, owners. The share of diffused ownership has been getting smaller and smaller. In 95% of companies, the share of diffused shareholders has decreased, in more than half of those by more than 5%. Substantial internal ownership as a result of the privatization method (internal free distribution up to 20% and employee buy outs up to 40% under half price) is still applicable to a relevant part of the economy (mainly middle-sized and small companies). In companies with more than 50% internal ownership (which does not prevail), business decisions are subordinated to the interests and pressures of employed shareholders. Approximately half of the remaining 20% of the diffused ownership is internal.

57. Another important factor, not to be neglected when talking about ownership structure, is the forming of new companies *ab initio*: new entries not affected by existing corporation structures and privatization. Newly formed corporations after the reforms at the end of the 1980s emerged in enormous numbers (close to 100,000, compared to several thousands of the existing ones), but their value or size in terms of turnover, profit or number of employees (average 1.4% employees per corporation) was and still is unimportant in relation to the GDP. However, typical of these companies is that nearly all of them are private limited companies, with almost no public companies and literally none listed on the Stock Exchange.

V. Corporate Governance Developments

58. Under the LCC-1993, a Supervisory Board was compulsory for companies fulfilling certain conditions imposed by law, relating to the size of a company, the number of its employees and shareholders, the way it was founded and whether it is listed on the Stock Exchange.

59. In smaller Slovenian public companies (less than a certain amount of share capital, less than an average of 500 employees, less than 100 named shareholders; if a company is not listed on the Stock Exchange, if the company was founded simultaneously) and in private companies, it was left to the founders to decide whether or not to prescribe a Supervisory Board in the Articles of Incorporation. In the year 2006, the system of compulsory two-tier corporate governance was abandoned. However, in fact, the two-tier system still prevails in Slovenia nowadays due to the fact that the great majority of public companies transformed themselves from former social companies through the process of privatization and legal transformation.

60. Bearing in mind the methods of privatization that included the free distribution of shares to employees, former employees and their relatives and, in addition, public sale, it is obvious that former social enterprises became public companies with widespread diffused ownership. In Slovenia, almost all former social enterprises privatized by the internal distribution of shares, buyout or public sale, have taken the legal form of PLC.

§3. DEFINITIONS, NOTIONS AND STRUCTURE OF COMPANIES AND PARTNERSHIPS

I. Different Forms of Companies and Partnerships

A. *The Concept of a Commercial Company*

61. To clarify what types of corporate structure have to be compared and to help the reader understand what type of corporate structure will be treated as a company and what type as a partnership, some comparative and linguistic clarifications must be recorded.

62. The LCC derives its rules from the concept of a commercial company. Within the meaning of the LCC, a commercial company is a legal person which independently pursues an activity with a view to profit (any activity for the purposes of deriving a profit) in the market. Commercial companies are, according to the LCC, legal entities, operating for profit and governed by private (company) law. Commercial companies are organized either as so-called personal companies, which correspond to partnerships, or as companies with share capital, which correspond to US corporations.

B. *PLC in Some EU Countries*

63. To make it perfectly clear, the PLC under the Slovene LCC corresponds to the following types of companies in the hereunder-listed EU countries: die Aktiengesellschaft (Germany and Austria), la société anonyme (France, società per azioni (Italy) la sociedad anónima (Spain) and the public company limited by shares, public company limited by guarantee having a share capital (UK).

C. *LLC in Some EU Countries*

64. A LLC under the Slovene LCC corresponds to the following types of companies in the hereunder-listed EU countries: die Gesellschaft mit beschränkter Haftung (Germany and (Austria), la sociedad de responsabilidad limitada (Spain), la société à responsabilité limitée (France), società a responsabilità limitata (Italy) and the private company limited by shares, private company limited by guarantee having a share capital (UK). (Greece);

D. *Company or Corporation*

65. In translating LCC, UK English does not, in contradistinction to US English, employ the word ‘corporation’ at all for a PLC. Nor does it use ‘closed corporation’ or ‘closely held corporation’. Rather, ‘company’ is used in every case.

66. In Slovenia, the distinction between companies and partnerships is not a distinction between entities with and without legal personality. In Slovenia, all partnerships have a separate legal personality. In Slovenia, one can usually distinguish partnerships from companies by the following rule: the members of a company enjoy limited liability, while the partners of a partnership do not. It is necessary to mention that ambiguous forms of LPs by shares (commandite par actions), or Dual Company (DP) also exist under LCC. The main difference between a corporation and a partnership lies in the fact that no contractual relationship between the members remains after the formation of a company, whereas the members of a partnership remain each other's partners.

II. Distinction Between Structures and Consequences

67. As far as Slovene corporate law is concerned, there is no difficulty in distinguishing between a PLC (US corporation or UK public company limited by shares) and an LLC (US closely held corporation or UK private company limited by shares).

68. The differences and similarities are very clearly stipulated in the law (*see* below). It is not like some countries where the designation as a closely held corporation follows solely from the reading of the Articles of Incorporation, and generally no specific statutory consequences are attached to such qualifications (as in the US). In Slovene company law, as in some other countries, characterization or classification as a private company also follows from the reading of the articles, but specific legal consequences are attached to it (as in the UK).

69. According to Slovene company law, members can freely choose the legal form of a business entity, be it from a group of personal companies (partnerships), or from companies limited by shares (private or public companies). Of course, different legal consequences must follow, according to the type of company that has been chosen. Conversion from one to another type of company is free and is subject to the decision reached at a general meeting.

III. Commercial Companies and Civil Associations: Sole Proprietorship

70. Slovenia belongs to a group of countries where a clear and legally distinctive difference between civil associations and commercial partnerships is made. The basic impact of such a difference is in the legal status between the two. All forms of commercial companies and all forms of partnerships are, according to the LCC, legal entities. On the other hand, civil associations are not legal entities but contractual associations of partners, aiming towards common goals.

71. An individual (independent) entrepreneur (sole proprietorship) is, according to the LCC, a natural person who independently pursues an activity with a view to profit (a natural person independently performing a profit-making activity in the market as his sole activity).

IV. Non-profit Associations

A. Economic Interest Grouping

72. According to the LCC, business activities can be performed in the form of an Economic Interest Grouping (EIG). An EIG can be founded by at least two companies or entrepreneurs with the aim of facilitating and accelerating the activities carried out by its members with a view to profit and to improve and increase the results of such activities, but not to create a profit of its own.

73. The activity of the grouping must be connected to the commercial activities of its members but may only be of an auxiliary nature with respect to such activities. A grouping may be formed without subscribed capital. The rights of the members of a grouping may not be expressed in securities. A grouping acquires legal personality upon its entry in the Court Register, henceforth 'the register'. Members are responsible for the liabilities of the grouping with all their assets.

B. Companies as Non-profit Associations

74. Companies may perform activities not for profit. However, under the LCC, companies are also deemed to be companies if, pursuant to the law, they pursue an activity wholly or partly without a view to profit.

C. Cooperatives, Private Institutions, Foundations and Societies

75. We can briefly mention here other private, non-profit legal persons, cooperatives, private institutions, foundations and societies, which are not regulated by the LCC, but by separate laws.

76. Cooperatives[27] are private non-profit legal entities, performing common activities that are for the benefit of its members, mainly in the field of agriculture,

27. The following laws regulate cooperatives in the Republic of Slovenia, since its independence:

- Law on Cooperatives (Official Gazette of RS, No. 13/92 of 20. 3. 1992), LC.
- Law Amending the Law on Cooperatives (Official Gazette of RS, No. 7/93 of 4 2 1993), LC-A.
- Law Amending the Law on Cooperatives – ZAD-B (Official Gazette of RS, No. 41/07 of 11. 5. 2007), LC-B.

construction, commerce, and so on. They are governed under the principle of 'one man one vote', rather than 'one share one vote'.

77. Institutions[28] are legal entities, founded to perform activities in the fields of education, science, culture, sport, health, social work, care of children, care of the disabled, and so on. The aim of the activity must not be making profit. Institutions are either public (established by the State or by local communities to perform public services) or private legal entities (formed by private entities). Private institutions normally carry on their activities as public services under concession.

78. Foundations[29] are private legal entities, founded by natural persons or private legal entities for the purpose of financing or performing charitable, religious or other non-profit aims in different fields such as education, research, social care, and so on. Foundations may also carry on public services, subject to concession.

79. Societies[30] are private legal entities founded mainly by natural persons to carry on different activities of common interest, not for profit, for instance in the

---

- Cooperatives Act – official consolidated text – ZAD-UPB1 (Official Gazette of RS, No. 62/07 of 12. 7. 2007), LC-OCT1.
- Law Amending the Law on Cooperatives – ZAD-C (Official Gazette of RS, No. 87/09 dated 2. 11. 2009), LC-C.
- Cooperatives Act – official consolidated text – ZAD-UPB2 (Official Gazette of RS, No. 97/09 dated 30. 11. 2009), LC-OCT2.

28. The following laws regulate institutions in the Republic of Slovenia, since its independence:

- Law on Institutions, LI, Official Gazette of the RS, Nos 12/91, 17/91, 55/92, 13/93, 8/96, 31/2000, 66/2003 (Slovene: ZZav).
- Law amending the Law on Institutions – ZZ-A (Official Gazette of RS, No. 8/96 of 12. 2. 1996).

29. The following laws regulate foundations in the Republic of Slovenia, since its independence:

- Law on Foundations (Official Gazette of RS, No. 60/95 dated 20. 10. 1995).
- Law Amending the Law on Foundations – ZU-A (Official Gazette of RS, No. 53/05 of 31. 5. 2005), LF.
- The Law on Foundations – official consolidated text – ZU-UPB1 (Official Gazette of RS, No. 70/05 of 26. 7. 2005), LF-OCT1.
- Correction Official consolidated text of the Law on Foundations – ZU-UPB1 (Official Gazette of RS, No. 91/05 dated 14. 10. 2005).

30. The following laws regulate associations in the Republic of Slovenia, since its independence:

Societies Act – SA-1 (Official Gazette of RS, No. 61/06 of 13. 6. 2006),
- Law Amending the Law on Associations – SA-1A (Official Gazette of RS, No. 58/09 of 27. 7. 2009),
- Law Amending the Law on Associations – SA-1B (Official Gazette of RS, No. 39/11 of 25. 5. 2011),
- Societies Act – official consolidated text – SA-1 UPB2 (Official Gazette of RS, No. 64/11 dated 12. 8. 2011),

fields of sport, culture, entertainment, education, social services, and so on. Societies can gain the status of societies in the public interest and become subsidized by a State or local community budget. To a limited extent, societies may perform business activities.

V. Different Forms of Partnerships and Companies under the LCC

A. *Partnerships (Personal Companies) and Companies with Share Capital*

80. Partnerships are, under the LCC, organized in one of the following legal forms:

- An Unlimited Company (UC)[31] is a company formed by two or more persons who are personally liable for the obligations of the company with all their assets. It is formed by means of a contract concluded by the members.
- An LP[32] is a company formed by two or more persons in which at least one of the partners is personally liable for the liabilities of the company with all his assets (a general partner) and at least one partner is not personally liable for the liabilities of the company (a limited partner).
- A DP[33] is an LP of which the sole general partner is a company in which there are no partners who are personally liable or where all general partners are such companies, or a UC in which all the partners are companies which are not personally liable.

Silent Partnership does not exist in Slovenian LCC any more since the amendment of LCC-1 G (Official Gazette RS. 57/2012 as of 27 July 2012).

81. Companies with share capital (US corporations) are, under the LCC, organized in one of the following legal forms:

- A PLC[34] is a company which has a subscribed capital divided into shares. It is liable to creditors for its obligations with all its assets. Shareholders are not personally liable to creditors for the obligations of the company.
- An LP with Share Capital[35] is a company in which at least one partner (general partner) is personally liable for the liabilities of the company with all his assets (general partner) while the limited shareholders who have a share in the subscribed capital are not personally liable for liabilities of the company to creditors.

- Law on Non-Governmental Organizations – ZNOrg (Official Gazette of the Republic of Slovenia, No. 21/18 of 30 March 2018).

31. Slovene: *Družba z neomejeno odgovornostjo, DNO.*
32. Slovene: *Komanditna družba*, KD.
33. Slovene: *Dvojna družba*, DvD.
34. Slovene: *Delniška družba*, DD.
35. Slovene: *Komanditna delniška družba*, KDD.

- An LLC[36] is a company whose subscribed capital consists of contributions by members, who obtain shares in the subscribed capital in proportion to their contributions, and are not personally liable for the liabilities of the company to creditors. It is not possible to issue securities for their investments in the company.
- A European Public Limited Company (EPLC)[37] (Societas Europea) is a PLC, regulated in the LCC for the purpose of implementation of Regulation 2157/2001/EC. The LCC defines the method of foundation, management, transfer of registered office and dissolution of EPLC.

82. All companies are legal entities. Companies in their capacities as legal persons may own movable and immovable property, acquire rights and assume obligations, and may sue or be sued. Companies acquire the status of a legal person upon being entered in the court register.

83. Prior to the entry of the company in the register, the relations between partners are governed by the rules governing civil law contracts. Anyone who, prior to company's entry into the register, acts on behalf of a company is personally liable for such acts, to the full extent of his assets; if there are several such persons, they are jointly and severally liable. If partners in so acting acquire certain rights, they are bound to transfer those rights to the company after the company has been entered in the register, unless the company opposes that transfer.

B. Similarities and Distinctions Between Companies and Partnerships

84. As an entity, a company with share capital has several similarities and distinctions in comparison to a partnership. Both companies (public and private) and partnerships (unlimited and limited) are, according to the LCC, separate legal entities. On registration under law, a company or a partnership becomes a separate legal entity as distinct from its members. There are several defining characteristics of companies, similar to or distinctive from the characteristics of partnerships.

85. Both a company and a partnership are different and distinct from their members in law. Both of them have their own name and their own assets and liabilities, which are separate and distinct from those of its members. Both companies and partnerships are capable of owning property, incurring debt and borrowing money, having a bank account, employing people, entering into contracts and suing and being sued separately.

86. The basic distinction between companies and partnerships has to do with liability of the members to the creditors of the company or partnership. The liability of a member (shareholder) of a company is limited to payment of any uncalled money due on shares held by him, when called upon to pay, and nothing more, even if the liabilities of the company far exceed its assets.

36. Slovene: *Družba z omejeno odgovornostjo*, DOO.
37. Slovene: *Evropska delniška družba*, EDD.

87. On the other hand, partners of a partnership company have unlimited liability to pay the debts of a partnership. That applies to all partners in an unlimited partnership and to general partners in an LP. However, they are only liable if the company fails to fulfil a liability to a creditor (subsidiary liability of partners).

88. Companies may have perpetual succession. A company does not cease to exist unless it is wound up, or the purpose for which it was formed has been completed. Membership of a company may keep on changing, but that does not affect the existence of the company. The death or insolvency of a member does not affect the existence of the company. But, like a partnership, a company may also be dissolved upon the expiry of the period for which it was formed, or by resolution of a general meeting, which must be adopted by a majority of at least three-quarters of the subscribed capital represented. On the other hand, a partnership is dissolved upon the expiry of the period for which it was formed. It must be dissolved upon the death or dissolution of a member, unless otherwise provided in the members' contract. A partnership can be founded for the lifetime of a member.

89. A company and a partnership is a distinct legal entity and its property is its own. A member or a partner cannot claim to be the owner of the company's property during the existence of the company or partnership. A company and a partnership is an artificial person and accordingly, it acts through its representatives: in the case of a company, through the members of the board of directors or management board and in the case of partnership through one or more partners. The members (in the case of a public company, shareholders) are simply the holders of shares in the company and need not necessarily be the managers of the company.

90. Partners in the partnership would, as a rule, be managers and representatives of the partnership as a legal entity, unless otherwise stipulated in the partnership contract. A limited partner may not conduct the business of a partnership; otherwise, he or she becomes personally liable for the partnership's debts. In carrying out its activities, representatives enter into various legal activities, binding a company or a partnership directly as a separate legal entity.

91. Companies and partnerships both have the capacity to sue or be sued. A company or a partnership can sue or be sued in its own name as distinct from the names of its members or partners.

92. A partner cannot transfer his shares in the partnership company without the consent of all other partners. In the case of a public company, shares may be transferred without the permission of the other members, in the absence of provisions to the contrary in the Articles of Association of the company. In the case of a private company, shares may not be transferred without first being offered to the other members, unless permission of the other members is provided for in the contract.

93. A public company may have as many members as it desires. The minimum number of members necessary for a PLC or for a private limited company is one.

A private company cannot have more than fifty members. But there must be at least two members in order to form a partnership.

C. *Commercial and Civil Partnerships (Association Contract under the Obligation's Law) The Obligation's Law (OL), Official Consolidated Text, Official Gazette of the RS, No. 97/2007 (Slovene: OZ, UPB-1).*

94. According to the Obligation's Law, two or more persons (natural or legal) can come together and oblige themselves to contribute towards a common goal. Such a contractual association is not a legal entity and thus does not need to be registered as a commercial partnership under the LCC. Any contractual association which does not comply with the LCC norms is treated as a civil association (association contract), regulated by the Obligation's Law. Therefore, a partnership of two or more members is a civil association under the Obligation's Law, if not registered as a commercial partnership under the LCC (civil partnership).

There are several distinctions between civil partnerships and commercial partnerships.

95. A civil partnership is a group of (two or more) persons who have come together to contribute towards a common goal and to share the profits of the business carried on by them. It does not have a separate legal entity. A commercial partnership is an association of persons who have come together for a specific business purpose. It has a separate legal entity as soon as it is registered under the LCC.

96. The liability of the partners of a civil partnership is unlimited because the property involved in its business belongs to the partners individually or they are collectively entitled to it. However, a commercial partnership is, as a legal entity, primarily liable to the creditors with all its assets. The members of a commercial partnership are jointly and severally liable to creditors for the liabilities of the company with all their assets. But their liability is subsidiary (they are only liable if the company fails to fulfil a liability to a creditor).

97. The liability of members of a commercial partnership depends on the kind of partnership, either a general (unlimited) partnership, or LP. Only in a general (unlimited) partnership are all partners personally liable for the liabilities of the company with all their assets. On the other hand, in the case of an LP, only a general partner is personally liable for the liabilities of the company; a limited partner, of which there must be at least one, is not liable for the liabilities of the company.

VI. Sole Entrepreneur

98. An entrepreneur under the LCC-1 is a natural person who independently carries out a gainful activity within the organized company. The following provisions of this LCC apply *mutatis mutandis* to an entrepreneur: activities (Article 6), name

(Articles 12–23), seat (paragraphs 29 and 30), branches (Article 31), procures (paragraphs 33 to 37) and business secrets (paragraphs 39 and 40).

However there are special provisions on the entrepreneur for the name; the name of the entrepreneur has to contain the name and surname of the entrepreneur, the abbreviation of a sole proprietor (s.p.), the activity and any additional ingredients. The name of the branch of an entrepreneur must also include his name, surname and indication that it is a branch. An entrepreneur may also use an abbreviated file containing at least his name, surname and surname.

99. The manner of keeping accounts and compiling the financial statements of an entrepreneur is governed by a special Slovenian accounting standard, regardless the size of an entrepreneur; LCC-1 J, 2017 erased the wording, 'whose company meets the criteria for small enterprises'. An entrepreneur may keep accounts under the system of simple bookkeeping in accordance with the above-mentioned special accounting standard, if he has not exceeded two of the following criteria in the last financial year: the average number of workers does not exceed three, the annual revenue is less than EUR 50 000, the average value of assets, calculated as half of the sum of the asset value on the first and last day of the financial year, does not exceed EUR 25 000. This also applies to an entrepreneur who starts an activity and does not employ on average more than three workers in the first fiscal year.

100. An entrepreneur can start an activity when he or she is registered with the APRRS in the Business Register of Slovenia. In the application for entry in the business register, the entrepreneur must indicate: the proposed date of entry, information about the entrepreneur: name and surname, EMŠO, residence, tax number, an indication of the activities that the entrepreneur will perform, the business address information, which includes the country, street and house number, settlement, municipality, postal code and place.

101. If the entrepreneur is not the owner of the facility at the business address or at the business address of the branch specified in the application, the application must enclose a certified statement from the owner of the facility to allow the business owner to operate at this address. The statement, however, according to the LCC-1 J, 2017, does not need to be authenticated if the owner of the facility makes a statement at the OSS (one stop shop) or if the entrepreneur obtains an authorization to engage in an activity from the Republic of Slovenia, a municipality, or a competent state or municipal fund, responsible for housing.

An entrepreneur may, during his lifetime, transfer the enterprise to another natural person (acquirer). The transfer contract must state the name and the seat of the entrepreneur and explicit consent for the use of the name and surname of the entrepreneur in the enterprise of the acquirer, the value of the enterprise (assets and rights and obligations) on the date of the transfer, with reference to the annual balance sheet, the interim balance sheet or the corresponding financial statement. APRRS enters the acquirer in the Business Register of Slovenia, if it has not yet been registered and, from its own motion, erases the entrepreneur from it.

Special Forms of Companies

A. *Banks*

102. A bank may be organized either as a PLC or as a European company (SE). The provisions of the LCC apply to banks unless otherwise stipulated by the BL.[38]

103. A bank may not perform activities other than banking activities, as stipulated by the BL. The minimum amount of share capital of a bank is EUR 5 million.

Shares in a bank may only be registered shares. Shares in a bank may only be paid in cash and must be fully paid up prior to the entry of either establishment or a capital increase in the Companies' Register. Shares of a bank must be issued in dematerialized form.

---

38. The Banking Act – 1 of the Banking Act (Official Gazette of RS, No. 131/06 dated 14. 12. 2006), BA:

- Law on amending and supplementing the Law on Banking – 1A Banking Act (Official Gazette of RS, No. 1/08 of 4 1 2008), BA-1A.
- Act Amending the Banking Act – 1B Banking Act (Official Gazette of RS, No. 109/08 dated 19. 11. 2008), BA-1B.
- Act Amending the Banking Act – 1C Banking Act (Official Gazette of RS, No. 19/09 of 13. 3. 2009), BA-1C.
- Act Amending the Banking Act – 1D Banking Act (Official Gazette of RS, No. 98/09 of 4. 12. 2009), BA-1D.
- Act Amending the Banking Act – 1E Banking Act (Official Gazette of RS, No. 79/10 dated 8. 10. 2010), BA-1E.
- The Banking Act – official consolidated text – ZBan-1-UPB5 (Official Gazette of RS, No. 99/10 of 12. 7. 2010), BA-OCT5.
- Act Amending the Banking Act – 1F Banking Act (Official Gazette of RS, No. 35/11 of 13. 5. 2011), BA-1F.
- Act Amending the Banking Act – 1G Banking Act (Official Gazette of RS, No. 59/11 of 25. 7. 2011), BA-1G.
- Act Amending the Banking Act – 1H Banking Act (Official Gazette of RS, No. 85/11 dated 25. 10. 2011), BA-1H.
- Act Amending the Banking Act – 1I Banking Act (Official Gazette of RS, No. 48/12 of 26 6 2012), BA-1I.
- Act Amending the Banking Act – 1J Banking Act (Official Gazette of RS, No. 105/12 dated 27. 12. 2012), BA-1J.
- Law Amending the Law on Banking – Banking Act 1K (Official Gazette of RS, No. 56/13 of 2 7th 2013), BA-1K.
- Act Amending the Banking Act – 1L Banking Act (Official Gazette of RS, No. 96/13 dated 22. 11. 2013), BA-1L.
- The Banking Act – 2 of the Banking Act (Official Gazette of RS, No. 25/15 of 13 4 2015), BA-2.
- Act Amending the Banking Act – ZBan-2A (Official Gazette of the Republic of Slovenia, No. 41/17 of 28 Jul. 2017).
- Market in Financial Instruments Act – ZTFI-1 (Official Gazette of the Republic of Slovenia, No. 77/18 of 30 Nov. 2018).
- Act Implementing the Regulation (EU) establishing a general framework for securitization and establishing a specific framework for simple, transparent and standardized securitisations – ZIUDSOL (Official Gazette of the Republic of Slovenia, No. 22/19 of 5 Apr. 2019).
- Decision on annulment of the fourth paragraph of Article 33 of the Banking Act (Official Gazette of the Republic of Slovenia, No. 44/19 of 5 Jul. 2019).

104. There is a prohibition of cross-shareholdings of banks with a share higher than 20%.[39]

B. Insurance Companies

105. An insurance company may be organized either as a PLC or as a mutual company. The provisions of the LCC apply to insurance companies unless otherwise stipulated by the Insurance Law (IL).[40] An insurance company may not perform activities other than insurance activities, stipulated by the IL. The minimum amount of share capital of an insurance company is EUR 3 million.

---

39. With BA-2, the following directives are transferred to, the legal system of the Republic of Slovenia:- Directive 2013/36 / EU of the European Parliament and of the Council of 26 Jun. 2013 on access to the activity of credit institutions and the prudential supervision of credit institutions and investment firms and amending Directive 2002/87 / EC and repealing Directives 2006/48 / EC and 2006 / 49 / EC (OJ L No. 176 of 27 Jun. 2013, p. 338; hereinafter: 'Directive 2013/36 / EU'):

    (1) Directive 2014/59 / EU of the European Parliament and of the Council of 15 May 2014 establishing a framework for the recovery and resolution of credit institutions and investment firms and amending the Sixth Council Directive 82/891 / EEC and Directives 2001/24 / EC, 2002 / 47 / EC, 2004/25 / EC, 2005/56 / EC, 2007/36 / EC, 2011/35 / EU 2012/30 / EU and 2013/ 36 / EU and regulation (EU) No. 1093/2010 and (EU) No. 648/2012 of the European Parliament and of the Council (OJ L No. 173, dated 12 Jun. 2014, p. 190; hereinafter: Directive 2014/59 / EU).
    (2) Council Directive 86/635 / EEC of 8 Dec. 1986 on the annual accounts and consolidated accounts of banks and other financial institutions (OJ L No. 372 of 31 Dec. 1986, p. 1), as last amended by Directive 2006/46 / EC of the European Parliament and of the Council of 14 Jun. 2006 amending Council Directives 78/660 / EEC on the annual accounts of certain types of companies, 83/349 / EEC on consolidated accounts, 86/635 / EEC on the annual accounts and consolidated accounts of banks and other financial institutions and 91/674 / EEC on the annual accounts and consolidated accounts of insurance undertakings (OJ L No. 224 of 16 Aug. 2006, p. 1);
    (3) Council Directive 89/117 / EEC of 13 Feb. 1989 on the obligations of branches established in a Member State of credit institutions and financial institutions established outside that Member State regarding the publication of annual accounts (OJ L No. 44 on 16 Feb. 1989, p. 40).

40. Insurance Act – the Insurance Act (Official Gazette of RS, No. 13/00 of 17. 2. 2000), IA:

    - Correction of the Law on Insurance – Insurance Act (Official Gazette of RS, No. 91/00 dated 6. 10. 2000).
    - Law Amending the Law on Insurance – Insurance Act (Official Gazette of RS, No. 21/02 of 11. 3. 2002), IA-A.
    - The annulment of the fifth paragraph of Article 22 and the second and third paragraphs of Article 29 of the Insurance Act (Official Gazette of RS, No. 29/03 of 21. 3. 2003).
    - Law Amending the Law on Insurance – IA-B (Official Gazette of RS, No. 50/04 of 6 5. 2004).
    - Insurance Act – official consolidated text – IA-UPB1 (Official Gazette of RS, No. 102/04 dated 21. 9. 2004).
    - Law Amending the Law on Insurance – IA-C (Official Gazette of RS, No. 79/06 of 27. 7. 2006).
    - Insurance Act – official consolidated text – IA-UPB2 (Official Gazette of RS, No. 109/06 dated 23. 10. 2006).

106. Shares in an insurance company may only be registered shares. Shares in an insurance company may only be paid in cash and must be fully paid up prior to the entry of either establishment or capital increase in the Companies' Register. Shares of an insurance company must be issued in dematerialized form.

C. Brokerage Companies

107. A brokerage company may be organized as either a PLC, an SE or a private limited company. The provisions of the LCC apply to brokerage companies unless otherwise stipulated by the Market in Financial Instruments Law (MIFL).[41]

- Law Amending the Law on Insurance – IA-D (Official Gazette of RS, No. 102/07 dated 9. 11. 2007).
- Law Amending the Law on Insurance – IA-E (Official Gazette of RS, No. 69/08 of 8. 7. 2008).
- Law Amending the Law on Insurance – IA-F (Official Gazette of RS, No. 19/09 of 13. 3. 2009).
- Law Amending the Law on Insurance – IA-G (Official Gazette of RS, No. 49/09 of 29. 6. 2009).
- Law Amending the Law on Insurance – Insurance Act-H (Official Gazette of RS, No. 79/10 dated 8. 10. 2010).
- Insurance Act – official consolidated text – IA-UPB7 (Official Gazette of RS, No. 99/10 of 12. 7. 2010).
- Law Amending the Law on Insurance – IA-I (Official Gazette of RS, No. 90/12 dated 30. 11. 2012).
- Law Amending the Law on Insurance – IA-J (Official Gazette of RS, No. 56/13 of 2 7th 2013).
- Insurance Law – ZZavar-1 (Official Gazette RS, No. 93/15 of 7 Dec. 2015).
- Law Amending the Insurance Act – ZZavar-1A (Official Gazette of the Republic of Slovenia, No. 9/19 of 11 Feb. 2019).

41. Law on Markets in Financial Instruments – ZTFI (Official Gazette of RS, No. 67/07 dated 27. 7. 2007), MFIL:

- Correction of the Market in Financial Instruments – ZTFI (Official Gazette of RS, No. 100/07 dated 2. 11. 2007), MFIL.
- Law Amending the Law on Markets in Financial Instruments – ZTFI-A (Official Gazette of RS, No. 69/08 of 8. 7. 2008), MFIL-1A.
- Law Amending the Law on Markets in Financial Instruments – ZTFI-B (Official Gazette of RS, No. 40/09 of 29. 5. 2009), MFIL-1B.
- Law Amending the Law on Markets in Financial Instruments – ZTFI-C (Official Gazette of RS, No. 88/10 of 11. 5. 2010), MFIL-1C.
- Law on Markets in Financial Instruments – official consolidated text – ZTFI -UPB3 (Official Gazette of RS, No. 108/10 dated 30. 12. 2010), MFIL-OCT-3.
- Law Amending the Law on Markets in Financial Instruments – ZTFI-D (Official Gazette of RS, No. 78/11 of 10. 5. 2011), MFIL-1D.
- Law Amending the Law on Markets in Financial Instruments – ZTFI-E (Official Gazette of RS, No. 55/12 of 20. 7. 2012), MFIL-1E.
- Law Amending the Law on Markets in Financial Instruments – ZTFI-F (Official Gazette of RS, No. 30/16 dated 25. 4. 2016), MFIL-1F.

  Law Amending the Market in Financial Instruments Law – ZTFI-G (Official Gazette of the Republic of Slovenia, No. 9/17 of 24 Feb. 2017).

108. The provisions of the MFIL regarding shares and shareholders of a brokerage company organized as a PLC, also apply as appropriate to holdings and members of a brokerage company organized as a limited company. A brokerage company may not perform activities other than those related to securities.

109. The minimum amount of share capital in a brokerage company is EUR 125,000. However, the minimum amount of share capital in a brokerage company is EUR 50,000 in cases where the brokerage company in question does not provide services with regard to public offerings with mandatory buyout or services with regard to trade in securities.

110. Shares in a brokerage company may only be registered shares. Shares in a brokerage company may only be paid in cash and must be fully paid up prior to the entry of either establishment or capital increase in the Companies' Register. Shares of a brokerage company must be issued in dematerialized form. The acquisition of shares in a brokerage company, whereby a person directly or indirectly reaches or exceeds the qualifying holding in the brokerage company (25% of its votes), is subject to the authorization of the SEA.

D. *Investment Funds*

111. According to the Investment Funds and Management Companies Act,[42] an investment fund is an undertaking with the sole purpose of public gathering of assets of natural and legal persons and investment of these assets in marketable securities and other liquid financial assets in accordance with the principles of risk diversification. An investment fund may be founded as a mutual fund or established

---

- Law on Market in Financial Instruments – ZTFI-1 (Official Gazette of the Republic of Slovenia, No. 77/18 of 30 Nov. 2018).

42. Law on Investment Funds and Management Companies – ZISDU-1 (Official Gazette of RS, No. 110/02 dated 18. 12. 2002), ITMCL:

- Authentic interpretation of the first paragraph of Article 137 of the Law on Investment Funds and Management Companies – ORZISDU137 (Official Gazette of RS, No. 32/04 of 2. 4. 2004), ITMCL-AE1.
- Law Amending the Law on Investment Funds and Management Companies – ZISDU-1A (Official Gazette of RS, No. 42/04 of 23. 4. 2004), ITMCL-1A.
- Decision of the Constitutional Court of the Republic of Slovenia on repealing the eleventh paragraph of Article 237 of the Act, the Investment Funds and Management Companies, No. U-I-127 / 03-44 (Official Gazette of RS, No. 68/05 of 18. 7. 2005).
- Law Amending the Law on Investment Funds and Management Companies – ZISDU-1B (Official Gazette of RS, No. 92/07 dated 10. 10. 2007), ITMCL-1B.
- Correction of the Law on Amendments and Supplements to the Law on Investment Funds and Management Companies – ZISDU-1B (Official Gazette of RS, No. 109/07 dated 30. 11. 2007).
- The Law amending the Law on Amendments and Supplements to the Law on Investment Funds and Management Companies – ZISDU-1C (Official Gazette of RS, No. 65/08 of 30. 6. 2008). 2007), ITMCL-1C.

as an investment company. A mutual fund is an investment fund established as a separate fund, which is divided into units. Upon a unit holder's request, the value of his units is payable out of the fund's assets, and the assets of this fund are managed by a management company.

E. Management Companies

112. A management company is organized either as a PLC or as a private limited company. Unless otherwise stipulated in ITMCL, provisions of the LCC apply to management companies. A management company may not perform any activity besides services related to managing investment funds. The minimum amount of the subscribed capital in a management company is EUR 200,000. A management company's shares may only be paid in cash, and full payment must be effected prior to the management company's entry into the Companies' Register, or, prior to the entry of the increased share capital into the Companies' Register.

113. The management board of a management company must comprise at least two members acting jointly as agents and representatives of the management company in legal transactions. Members of the management board of a management company must be in full-time employment of that company, either on the basis of an employment contract with the company, or on the basis of some other legal relationship. At least one of the management board members must have a good command of the Slovenian language. At least one of the management board members must regard the Republic of Slovenia as a focus for realizing his/her life objectives.

F. Investment Companies

114. The provisions of the LCC on PLC are applicable to investment companies, unless otherwise stipulated by the ITMCL. An investment company may not perform any activity other than of investing assets in securities and other liquid financial investments in accordance with the principles of risk diversification. An investment company may only be established pursuant to the procedure of a successful establishment of a PLC.

115. An investment company may be established by a management company as a sole founder, by adopting the statute and by making a public invitation for subscription and payment of the investment company shares.

116. The minimum amount of the share capital of an investment company must amount to a euro equivalent of EUR 800,000. An investment company may increase its share capital, if the prescribed conditions are fulfilled. The pre-emptive rights of the existing shareholders to the subscription and payment of new shares cannot be excluded. The investment company may not increase its share capital out of the company's assets, if this increase causes the occurrence of partial rights. An investment company may only issue registered shares of the same class (in a dematerialized form). Investment company shares must be freely transferable. Prior to initiating the procedure for the subscription and payment of shares in an investment company, the management company must make a public invitation for subscription and payment of shares.

117. The invitation for subscription and payment of investment company shares must include the important data in respect of the investment company and the management company, as well as on the investment policy of the investment company and other data that, pursuant to the MIFL, must be included in the invitation for subscription and payment of securities applicable to a public offering.

118. The investment company has no management board. Obligations and authorizations, which would normally be assumed by the management board pursuant to the LCC, must be assumed by the management board of the management company which is to manage the investment company.

119. The management company conducts the transactions of the investment company and represents it in all matters except those where the supervisory board of the investment company is authorized to represent the investment company.

120. The investment company must have a supervisory board. Supervisory board members must have appropriate professional skills and experience in the field of managing financial assets.

G. Foreign Undertakings

121. Foreign undertakings within the meaning of the LCC -1 are natural or legal persons pursuing an activity with a view to profit and having their residence or registered office outside the Republic of Slovenia; it can be an undertaking from the EU or from a non-Member State (i.e., a third country). The status of a foreign undertaking is assessed in accordance with the law of the country to which that undertaking belongs, unless otherwise provided in law. Regarding business conduct in the Republic of Slovenia, the rights, obligations and responsibilities of a foreign undertaking are equated with domestic undertakings or entrepreneurs.

H. Branches

122. A foreign undertaking may pursue an activity for profit in the Republic of Slovenia through branches. The LCC rules on activity, on registered names, on registered offices, on procurator and on business secrets apply *mutatis mutandis* to branches. A branch must be entered in the register. An application to enter a branch in the register must contain the name and registered office of the branch, the activity and the business carried out by the branch, the name of the person who represents the branch and the foreign undertaking, identification data about founder or shareholder, the nature and scope of responsibilities of the founder or shareholder, the date of the entry and exit of the founder or shareholder, the amount of the contribution of the founder or shareholder (LCC-1I, 2015, Article 677/1), and other data required by law.

123. A branch must operate in the name and for the account of the foreign undertaking, and in so doing, it must use the registered name of the parent undertaking, its registered office and its own name. All communications, official correspondence, order forms and other documents of the branch must indicate apart from its registered name, the register containing the documents in respect of the branch, including the number of the branch in the register. Where the legislation of the home country of a foreign undertaking requires the entry of the undertaking in a register, the register in which the undertaking from a third country is entered must be indicated, as well as its registration number in the Slovenian register. A foreign undertaking may not take up and pursue activities in the Republic of Slovenia before the branch is entered in the register. The provisions laid down in the LCC on books of account and annual reports apply *mutatis mutandis* to branches.[43]

124. A branch of a foreign undertaking from a third country must submit the annual report of the undertaking if it has been drawn up, revised and disclosed on the basis of the legislation of the home country[44] of the undertaking.

125. For each branch, one or more representatives must be appointed to represent the foreign undertaking. The foreign undertaking may appoint the same representatives for more than one branch, but the representatives of the principal branch may by law also be representatives in other branches, even when other representatives are appointed to them.

126. The foreign undertaking is liable with all its assets for the liabilities arising from the business conduct of its branches.

VII. Micro, Small, Medium-Sized and Large Companies

127. With the amendment to the LCC-1-I, 2015, the threshold for the classification of companies is adapted; the EU provisions on the content, form and obligations of preparing the consolidated annual report and the general rules for the

43. A branch of a foreign undertaking from ES must submit the annual report of this undertaking if it has been drawn up, revised and disclosed on the basis of the legislation of a European Community Member State applying to an undertaking in accordance with Directive 78/660/EEC, Directive 83/349/EEC and Directive 84/253/EEC.
44. Where an annual report of a foreign undertaking from a third country has not been drawn up pursuant to Directive 78/660/EEC and Directive 83/349/EEC, or in a corresponding manner, an annual report must be drawn up and disclosed for the activities of the branch.

valuation of items in the financial statements are brought in the legal order of Slovenia; and there are also simplifications for micro-companies. For the purposes of applying the provisions of general accounting rules (how to keep the books of account and render year-end accounts), companies are classified, according to the LCC, into micro-, small-, medium-sized and large on the basis of the following criteria:

- average number of employees in a financial year;
- net sales income; and
- value of assets.

128. A micro company is a company meeting two of the following criteria:

- the average number of employees in a financial year does not exceed ten;
- the net sales income does not exceed EUR 700,000; and
- the value of assets does not exceed EUR 350,000.

129. A small company is a company meeting two of the following criteria:

- the average number of employees in a financial year does not exceed fifty;
- the net sales income does not exceed EUR 8 million; and
- the value of assets does not exceed EUR 4 million.

130. A medium-sized company is a company which is neither a micro company nor a small company, meeting the following criteria:

- the average number of employees in a financial year does not exceed 250;
- the net sales income does not exceed EUR 40 million; and
- the value of assets does not exceed EUR 20 million.

All other companies are large companies. In any event, the large companies are Public-Interest Entities (PIEs), Stock Exchange, the companies which must according to Article 56 of LCC-1 prepare a consolidated annual report (Article 54, LCC-1I 2015).

PIE is a company whose securities are traded on a regulated securities market, or a credit institution as defined by the law governing banking, or insurance company as defined by the law governing insurance (Article 53, LCC-1I 2015).

Large companies can also check the items using recognized mathematical and statistical methods based on sampling techniques, and reflect an assessment that is a good approximation of the physical inventory of reality (Article 54, LCC-1I 2015).

§4. Sources and Hierarchy of the Law on Company and Partnerships

I. Sources and Hierarchy of the Law in Slovenia: General

131. As far as the relationship between statutory law and the articles of a company is concerned, one should understand the nature of a particular rule: either the rule is mandatory (*ius cogens*), or just optional or recommended (*ius dispositivum*). The Articles of Association must be strictly in accordance with those rules, which are of a strict nature, including mandatory legal provisions (*ius cogens*).

132. Concerning the extent of shareholders' freedom in setting up the rules on companies, internal legal relations in the Articles of Association, the following LCC rules must be strictly applied:

– the matters regulated by law may only be stipulated differently by the Articles of Association where the law explicitly allows this; and
– additional matters may only be stipulated by the Articles of Association where such matters are not comprehensively regulated by law.

133. Other issues of importance for the company which are not regulated in the Articles of Association may be regulated in the company's other acts (bylaws), in accordance with the Articles of Association and the LCC.

134. In addition to statutory rules, autonomous rules in the Articles of Association and membership contracts, the Corporate Governance Code and bylaws of other professional organizations (the Stock Exchange, the Association of Supervisory Board Members of Slovenia and the Managers' Association of Slovenia, Chamber of Industry and Commerce) are of great importance, containing, in accordance with law, mainly the best practice recommendations relating to corporate governance, compensation, remuneration and nomination of the companies' bodies.

135. Slovenia is not a federal State, so no problems regarding the relationship between federal law and State law exist.

II. EU Sources of Company and Partnership Law

A. *Main EU Sources of Company Law*

136. Except for the Lisbon Treaty,[45] there are a number of directives and regulations, mainly from the field of company and SML. The LCC regulates the transposition of directives and implementation of regulations of the European

45. Treaty of Lisbon amending the Treaty on the European Union and the Treaty establishing the European Community (OJ C306 of 17 Dec. 2007), entry into force on 1 Dec. 2009.

Community. The LCC transposes the following directives of the European Community in the field of company law into the company law legislation of the Republic of Slovenia:

- First Council Directive 68/151/EEC of 9 March 1968 on the coordination of safeguards which, for the protection of the interests of members and others, are required by Member States in respect of companies within the meaning of the second paragraph of Article 58 of the Treaty, with a view to making such safeguards equivalent throughout the Community (OJ L No. 65, 14. 3. 1968, p. 8) with amendments (hereinafter: 'Directive 68/151/EEC').
- Second Council Directive 77/91/EEC of December 1976 on the coordination of safeguards which, for the protection of the interests of members and others, are required by Member States in respect of companies within the meaning of the second paragraph of Article 58 of the Treaty, in respect of the formation of public LLC and the maintenance and alteration of their capital, with a view to making such safeguards equivalent (OJ L No. 26, 31. 1. 1977, p, 1) with amendments (hereinafter: 'Directive 77/91/EEC'); Directive 2012/30/EU of the European Parliament and of the Council of 25 October 2012 on the coordination of safeguards to protect the interests of members and others, are required by Member States of companies within the meaning of the second paragraph of Article 54 of the Treaty on the Functioning of the European Union, on the establishment public LLC and the maintenance and alteration of their capital, with a view to making such safeguards equivalent throughout the Community (OJ No. 315, 14. 11. 2012, p. 74; hereinafter: 'Directive 2012/30/EU').
- Third Council Directive 78/855/EEC of 9 October 1978 based on Article 54(3)(g) of the Treaty concerning mergers of public LLC (OJ L No. 295, 20. 10. 1978, p. 36) with amendments (hereinafter: 'Directive 78/855/EEC'). Directive 2011/35/EU of the European Parliament and of the Council of 5 April 2011 concerning mergers of public LLC (OJ L No. 110, 29. 4. 2011, p. 1), as last amended by Directive 2014/59/EU of the European Parliament and the Council of 15 May 2014 establishing a framework for the recovery and resolution of credit institutions and investment firms and amending the Sixth Council Directive 82/891/EEC and Directives 2001/24/EC, 2002/47/EC, 2004/25/EC, 2005/56/EC, 2007/36/EC, 2011/35/EU 2012/30/EU and 2013/36/EU and regulation (EU) No. 1093/2010 and (EU) No. 648/2012 of the European Parliament and of the Council (OJ L No. 173, 12. 6. 2014, p. 190) (hereinafter: 'Directive 2011/35/EU').
- Fourth Council Directive 78/660/EEC of 25 July 1978 based on Article 54(3)(g) of the Treaty on the annual accounts of certain types of companies (OJ L No. 222, 14. 8. 1978, p. 11) with amendments (hereinafter: 'Directive 78/660/EEC'); Last amended by Directive 2006/46/EC was published in the Official Journal on 16 August with an implementation date of 5 September 2008. Directive 2006/43/EC of the European Parliament and of the Council of 17 May 2006 on statutory audits of annual accounts and consolidated accounts, amending Council Directives 78/660/EEC and 83/349/EEC and repealing Council Directive 84/253/EEC (OJ L No. 157, 9. 6. 2006, p. 87), as last amended by Directive 2014/56/EU of

the European Parliament and of the Council of 16 April 2014 amending Directive 2006/43/EC on statutory audits of annual accounts and consolidated accounts (OJ L No. 158, 27. 5. 2014, p. 196) (hereinafter: 'Directive 2006/43/EC').
- Directive 2013/34/EU of the European Parliament and of the Council of 26 June 2013 on the annual financial statements and related reports of certain types of undertakings, amending Directive 2006/43ES the European Parliament and of the Council and repealing Council Directives 78/660/EEC and 83/349/EEC (OJ L No. 182, 29. 6. 2013, p. 19; hereinafter: 'Directive 2013/34/EU').
- Sixth Council Directive of 17 December 1982 concerning the division of public LLC, based on Article 54(3)(g) of the Treaty (OJ L No. 378, 31. 12. 1982, p. 47), as last amended by Directive 2014/59/EU of the European Parliament and of the Council of 15 May 2014 establishing a framework for the recovery and resolution of credit institutions and investment firms and amending the Sixth Council Directive 82/891/EEC and Directives 2001/24/EC, 2002/47/EC, 2004/25/EC, 2005/56/EC, 2007/36/EC, 2011/35/EU 2012/30/EU and 2013/36/EU and regulation (EU) No. 1093/2010 and (EU) No. 648/2012 of the European Parliament and of the Council (OJ L No. 173, 12. 6. 2014, p. 190) (hereinafter: 'Directive 82/891/EU').
- Seventh Council Directive 83/349/EEC of 13 June 1983 based on Article 54(3)(g) of the Treaty on consolidated accounts (OJ L No. 193, 18. 7. 1983, p. 1) with amendments (hereinafter: 'Directive 83/349/EEC').
- Eighth Council Directive 84/253/EEC of 10 April 1984 based on Article 54(3)(g) of the Treaty on the approval of persons responsible for carrying out the statutory audits of accounting documents (OJ L No. 126, 12. 5. 1984, p. 20) with amendments (hereinafter: 'Directive 84/253/EEC'); Last amended by Directive 2006/43/EC on Statutory Audits of Annual and Consolidated Accounts.
- Eleventh Council Directive of 21 December 1989 on the disclosure of branches in a Member State by certain types of company governed by the law of another State (OJ L No. 395, 30. 12. 1989, p. 36), as last amended by Directive 2012/17/EU of the European Parliament and of the Council of 13 June 2012 amending Council Directive 89/666/EEC and Directives 2005/56/EC and 2009/101/EC of the European Parliament and of the Council as regards the interconnection of central, commercial registers as companies (OJ L No. 156, 16. 6. 2012, p. 1) (hereinafter: 'Directive 89/666/EU').
- Twelfth Council Company Law Directive 89/667/EEC of 21 December 1989 on single member private LLC (OJ L No. 395, 30. 12. 1989, p. 40) with amendments (hereinafter: 'Directive 89/667/EEC').
- Directive 2009/109/EC of the European Parliament and of the Council of 16 September 2009 amending Council Directives 77/91/EEC, 78/855/EEC and 82/ 891/EEC, and Directive 2005/56/EC as regards reporting and documentation requirements in the case of mergers and divisions.
- Directive 2007/63/EC of the European Parliament and of the Council of 13 November 2007 amending Council Directives 78/855/EEC and 82/891/EEC as regards the requirement of an independent expert's report on the occasion of merger or division of public LLC.
- Directive 2007/36/EC of the European Parliament and of the Council of 11 July 2007 on the exercise of certain rights of shareholders in listed companies (OJ L

No. 184, 14. 7. 2007, p. 17), as last amended by Directive 2014/59/EU of the European Parliament and of the Council of 15 May 2014 establishing a framework for the recovery and resolution of credit institutions and investment firms and amending the Sixth Council Directive 82/891/EEC and Directives 2001/24/EC, 2002/47/EC, 2004/25/EC, 2005/56/EC, 2007/36/EC, 2011/35/EU 2012/30/EU and 2013/36/EU and regulation (EU) No. 1093/2010 and (EU) No. 648/2012 of the European Parliament and of the Council (OJ L No. 173, 12. 6. 2014, p. 190) (hereinafter: 'Directive 2007/36/EU').

- Directive 2006/68/EC of the European Parliament and of the Council of 6 September 2006 amending Council Directive 77/91/EEC as regards the formation of public LLC and the maintenance and alteration of their capital.
- Directive of the European Parliament and Council Directive 2005/56/EC of 26 October 2005 on cross-border mergers of LLC (OJ No. 310, 25. 11. 2005, p. 1), as last amended by Directive 2014/59/EU of the European Parliament and of the Council of 15 May 2014 establishing a framework for the recovery and resolution of credit institutions and investment firms and amending the Sixth Council Directive 82/891/EEC and Directives 2001/24/EC, 2002/47/EC, 2004/25/EC, 2005/56/EC, 2007/36/EC, 2011/35/EU 2012/30/EU and 2013/36/EU and regulation (EU) No. 1093/2010 and (EU) No. 648/2012 of the European Parliament and of the Council (OJ L No. 173, 12. 6. 2014, p. 190) (hereinafter: 'Directive: 2005/56/EC').
- Directive 2009/102/EC of the European Parliament and of the Council of 16 September 2009 in the area of company law on single member private LLC.
- Directive 2009/101/EC of the European Parliament and of the Council of 16 September 2009 on coordination of safeguards which, for the protection of the interests of members and third parties, are required by Member States of companies within the meaning of the second paragraph of Article 48 of the Treaty, with a view to making such safeguards equivalent.
- Directive 2013/34/EU concerning the disclosure of non-financial information and information on the diversity of certain large enterprises and groups (OJ L No. 330 of 15.11. 2014, page 1).
- Directive 2014/95/EU of the European Parliament and of the Council of 22 October 2014 amending Directive 2013/34/EU concerning the disclosure of non-financial information and information on the diversity of certain large enterprises and groups (OJ L No. 330 of 15.11. 2014, page 1.
- Directive (EU) 2017/1132 of the European Parliament and of the Council of 14 June 2017 relating to certain aspects of company law.

Alignment with Directive (EU) 2017/828 of the European Parliament and of the Council of 17 May 2017 amending Directive 2007/36/EC as regards the promotion of long-term shareholder participation (EU) 2017/828) represents the main reason for the upcoming Law on Amendments to the Companies Act (LCC 1 K) which is under preparation; it will include a new regulation of the following issues regarding shareholders' rights and promotion of long-term participation of shareholders: (1) identification of shareholders, provision of information and facilitation of the exercise of rights shareholders; (2) directors' 'remuneration policy – shareholders' rights and information; (3) transparency and approval of the company's transactions with related parties and (4) transparency of institutional investors, asset managers and advisers to vote. However, the amendment to the law is not yet in the parliamentary procedure until September 2020.

137. The LCC in greater detail determines the implementation of the following European Community Regulations:

- Council Regulation (EEC) No. 2137/85 of 25 July 1985 on the European Economic Interest Grouping (EEIG) (OJ L No. 199, 31. 7. 1985, p. 1) (hereinafter: 'Regulation 2137/85/EEC').
- Regulation (EC) No. 1606/2002 of the European Parliament and of the Council of 19 July 2002 on the application of international accounting standards (OJ L No. 243, 11. 9. 2002, p. 1) (hereinafter: 'Regulation 1606/2002/EC').
- Commission Regulation (EC) No. 1725/2003 of 29 September 2003 adopting certain international accounting standards in accordance with Regulation (EC), No. 1606/2002 of the European Parliament and of the Council (OJ L No. 261, 13. 10. 2003, p. 1) with amendments (hereinafter: 'Regulation 1725/2003/EC').
- Council Regulation (EC), No. 2157/2001 of 8 October 2001 on the Articles of Association of an SE (OJ L No. 294, 10. 11. 2001, pp. 1–21) (hereinafter: 'Regulation 2157/2001/EC').
- Council Regulation EC 2157/2001 on the Statute for an SE, OJ L No. 294, 10. 11. 2001.
- Council Regulation 2157/2001/EC of 8 October 2001 on the Statute for an SE (OJ L No. 294, 10. 11. 2001, p. 1), as last amended by Council Regulation (EU) No. 517/2013 of 13 May 2013 adapting certain regulations and decisions in the areas of free movement of goods, free movement of persons, company law, competition policy, agriculture, food safety, veterinary and phytosanitary policy, transport policy, energy, taxation, statistics, trans-European networks, justice and fundamental rights, justice, freedom and security, environment, customs union, external relations, foreign, security and defence policy and institutions, by reason of the accession of the Republic of Croatia (OJ L No. 158, 10. 6. 2013, p. 1) (hereinafter: 'Regulation 2157/2001/EC').

B. Main EU Sources of SML

138. The Market on Financial Instruments Law (MFIL) transfers the following Directives into the legislation of the Republic of Slovenia:

- Council Directive 89/117/EEC of 13 February 1989 on the obligations of branches established in a Member State of credit institutions and financial institutions having their head offices outside that Member State regarding the publication of annual accounting documents (OJ L No. 44, 16. 2. 1989, p. 40; hereinafter: 'Directive 89/117/EEC').
- Directive 97/9/EC of the European Parliament and of the Council of 3 March 1997 on investor compensation schemes (OJ L No. 84, 26. 3. 1997, p. 22, hereinafter: 'Directive 97/9/EC').

- Directive 98/26/EC of the European Parliament and of the Council of 19 May 1998 on settlement finality in payment and securities settlement systems (OJ L No. 166, 11. 6. 1998, p. 45) as amended by Directive 2009/44/EC of the European Parliament and of the Council of 6 May 2009 amending Directive 98/26/EC on settlement finality in payment and securities settlement systems and Directive 2002/47/EC on financial collateral arrangements as regards linked systems and credit claims (OJ L No. 146, 10. 6. 2009, p. 37); last amended by Regulation (EU) No. 909/2014 of the European Parliament and of the Council of 23 July 2014 on improving securities settlement arrangements in the EU and on central securities depositories and amending Directives 98/26/EC and 2014/65/EU and Regulation (EU) No. 236/2012 (OJ No. 257, 28. 8. 2014, p. 1); hereinafter: 'Directive 98/26/EC').
- Directive 2001/34/EC of the European Parliament and of the Council of 28 May 2001 on the admission of securities to official stock exchange listing and on information to be published on those securities (OJ L No. 184, 6. 7. 2001, p. 1, last amended by Directive of the European Parliament and Council Directive 2005/1/EC of 9 March 2005 amending Council Directives 73/239/EEC, 85/611/EEC, 91/675/EEC, 92/49/EEC and 93/6/EEC and Directives 94/19/EC, 98/78/EC, 2000/12/EC, 2001/34/EC, 2002/83/EC and 2002/87/EC establishing a new organizational structure for financial services committees (OJ L No. 79, 24. 3. 2005, p. 9); hereinafter: 'Directive 2001/34/EC').
- Directive 2003/6/EC of the European Parliament and of the Council of 28 January 2003 on insider dealing and market manipulation (market abuse) (OJ L No. 96, 12. 4. 2003, p. 16;), as amended by Directive 2010/78/EU of the European Parliament and of the Council of 24 November 2010 amending Directives 98/26/EC, 2002/87/EC, 2003/6/EC, 2003/41/EC, 2003/71/EC, 2004/39/EC, 2004/109/EC, 2005/60/EC, 2006/48/EC, 2006/49/EC and 2009/65/EC as regards the powers of the European Supervisory Authority (European banking authority), the European Supervisory Authority (European insurance and occupational pensions authority) and the European Supervisory Authority (European securities and markets authority (ESMA)) (OJ L No. 331, 15. 12. 2010, p. 120); hereinafter: 'Directive 2003/6/EC').
- Directive 2003/71/EC of the European Parliament and of the Council of 4 November 2003 on the prospectus to be published when securities are offered to the public or admitted to trading and the amended Directive 2001/34/EC (OJ L No. 345, 31. 12. 2003, p. 64, and amending Directive 2001/34/EC (OJ L No. 345, 31. 12. 2003, p. 64), as last amended by Directive 2014/51/EU of the European Parliament and of the Council of 16 April 2014 amending Directives 2003/71/EC and 2009/138/EC and Regulation (EC) No. 1060/2009, (EU) No. 1094/2010 and (EU) No. 1095/2010 as regards the powers of the European Supervisory Authority (European Insurance and Occupational Pensions Authority) and the European Supervisory Authority (ESMA) (OJ L No. 153, 22. 5. 2014, p. 1); hereinafter: 'Directive 2003/71/EC').

- Commission Directive 2003/124/EC of 22 December 2003 implementing Directive 2003/6/EC of the European Parliament and of the Council as regards the definition and public disclosure of inside information and the definition of market manipulation (UL L 339, 24. 12. 2003, p. 70; hereinafter: 'Directive 2003/124/EC').
- Commission Directive 2003/125/EC of 22 December 2003 implementing Directive 2003/6/EC of the European Parliament and of the Council as regards the fair presentation of investment recommendations and the disclosure of conflicts of interest (UL L 339, 24. 12. 2003, p. 73; hereinafter: 'Directive 2003/125/EC').
- Directive 2004/39/EC of the European Parliament and of the Council of 21 April 2004 on markets in financial instruments amending Council Directives 85/611/EEC, 93/6/EEC and Directive 20 00/12/EC of the European Parliament and of the Council and repealing Council Directive 93/22/EEC (OJ L No. 145, 30. 4. 2004, p. 1), as last amended by Directive 2010/78/EU of the European Parliament and of the Council of 24 November 2010 amending Directives 98/26/EC, 2002/87/EC, 2003/6/EC, 2003/41/EC, 2003/71/EC, 2004/39/EC, 2004/109/EC, 2005/60/EC, 2006/48/EC, 2006/49/EC and 2009/65/EC as regards the powers of the European Supervisory Authority (European banking authority), the European Supervisory Authority (European insurance and occupational pensions authority) and the European Supervisory Authority (ESMA) (OJ L No. 331, 15. 12. 2010, p. 120); hereinafter: 'Directive 2004/39/EC'.
- Directive 93/22/EEC (OJ L No. 145, 30. 4. 2004, p. 1), amended by Directive 2007/44/EC of the European Parliament and of the Council of 5 September 2007 amending Council Directive 92/49/EC and Directives 2002/83/EC, 2004/39/EC, 2005/68/EC and 2006/48/EC as regards procedural rules and evaluation criteria for the prudential assessment of acquisitions and increase of holdings in the financial sector (OJ L No. 274, 21. 9. 2007, p. 1) – hereinafter: 'Directive 2004/39/EC'.
- Commission Directive 2004/72/EC of 29 April 2004 implementing Directive 2003/6/EC of the European Parliament and of the Council as regards accepted market practices, the definition of inside information in relation to derivatives on commodities, the drawing up of lists of insiders, the notification of managers' transactions and the notification of suspicious transactions (OJ L No. 162, 30. 4. 2004, p. 70; hereinafter: 'Directive 2004/72/EC').
- Directive 2004/109/EC of the European Parliament and of the Council of 15 December 2004 on the harmonization of transparency requirements in relation to information about issuers whose securities are admitted to trading on a regulated market and amending Directive 2001/34/EC (OJ L No. 390/38, 30. 12. 2004, p. 38; last amended by Directive 2013/50/EU of the European Parliament and of the Council of 22 October 2013 amending Directive 2004/109/EC of the European Parliament and of the Council on the harmonization of transparency requirements in relation to information about issuers whose securities are admitted to trading on a regulated market, Directive 2003/71/EC of the European Parliament and of the Council on the prospectus to be published when securities are offered or admitted to trading and the Commission Directive 2007/14/EC laying down detailed rules for implementing certain provisions of Directive 2004/109/EC (OJ L No. 294, 11. 6. 2013, p. 13), hereinafter: 'Directive 2004/109/EC').

- Directive 2006/48/EC of the European Parliament and of the Council of 14 June 2006 relating to the taking up and pursuit of the business of credit institutions (OJ L No. 177, 30. 6. 2006, p. 1) amended by Directive 2007/44/EC of 5 September 2007 amending Council Directive 92/49/EEC and Directives 2002/83/EC, 2004/39/EC, 2005/68/EC and 2006/48/EC as regards procedural rules and evaluation criteria for the prudential assessment of acquisitions and increase of holdings in the financial sector (OJ L No. 247, 21. 9. 2007, p. 1) amended by Directive 2009/111/EC of the European Parliament and of the Council of 16 September 2009 amending Directives 2006/48/EC, 2006/49/EC and 2007/64/EC as regards banks affiliated to central institutions, certain own funds items, large exposures, supervisory arrangements and crisis management (OJ L No. 302, 17. 11. 2009, p. 97); hereinafter: 'Directive 2006/48/EC', to the extent applied to brokerage companies.
- Directive 2006/49/EC of the European Parliament and of the Council of 14 June 2006 on the capital adequacy of investment firms and credit institutions (OJ L No. 177, 30. 6. 2006, p. 201) last amended by Directive 2009/111/EC of the European Parliament and of the Council of 16 September 2009 amending Directives 2006/48/EC, 2006/49/EC and 2007/64/EC as regards banks affiliated to central institutions, certain own funds items, large exposures, supervisory arrangements and crisis management (OJ L No. 302, 17. 11. 2009, p. 97); hereinafter: 'Directive 2006/49/EC'.
- Directive 2013/36/EU of the European Parliament and of the Council of 26 June 2013 on access to the activity of credit institutions and the prudential supervision of credit institutions and investment firms and amending Directive 2002/87/EC and repealing Directives 2006/48/EC and 2006/49/EC (OJ L No. 176, 27. 6. 2013, p. 338; hereinafter: 'Directive 2013/36/EU'), insofar as it relates to the brokerage company.
- Directive 2014/65/EU of the European Parliament and of the Council of 15 May 2014 on markets in financial instruments and amending Directive 2002/92/EC and Directive 2011/61/EU (OJ L No. 173 of 12. 6. 2014 p. 349), most recently amended by Commission Regulation (EU) 2017/1946 of 11 July 2017 supplementing Directives 2004/39/EC and 2014/65/EU of the European Parliament and of the Council as regards regulatory technical standards for a comprehensive list of information to be included in the notice of the proposed acquisition of a qualifying holding in an investment firm (OJ L No. 276 of 26. 10. 2017, p. 32), hereinafter referred to as Directive 2014/65/EU.
- Commission Implementing Directive (EU) 2015/2392 of 17 December 2015 on Regulation (EU) No. No. 596/2014 of the European Parliament and of the Council as regards reporting to the competent authorities of actual or potential infringements of that Regulation (OJ L No. 332 of 18. 12. 2015, p. 126), hereinafter referred to as Directive 2015/2392/EU.
- Directive (EU) 2016/1034 of the European Parliament and of the Council of 23 June 2016 amending Directive 2014/65/EU on markets in financial instruments (OJ L No. 175 of 30.6 2016, p. 8).
- Commission Directive (EU) 2017/593 of 7 April 2016 supplementing Directive 2014/65/EU of the European Parliament and of the Council with regard to the protection of financial instruments and assets belonging to customers, product

management obligations and rules are used to provide or receive fees, commissions or any monetary or non-monetary benefits (OJ L No. 87 of 31. 3. 2017, p. 500, hereinafter: Directive 2017/593/EU).

Further on The Market on Financial Instruments Law (MFIL) in greater detail regulate the implementation of the following European Community Regulations:

- Commission Regulation (EC) 2273/2003 of 22 December 2003 implementing Directive 2003/6/EC of the European Parliament and of the Council as regards exemptions for buy-back programmes and stabilization of financial instruments (UL L 336, 23 December 2003, 33; hereinafter: 'Regulation 2273/2003').
- Commission Regulation (EC) 809/2004 of 29 April 2004 implementing Directive 2003/71/EC of the European Parliament and of the Council as regards information contained in prospectuses as well as the format, incorporation by reference and publication of such prospectuses and dissemination of advertisements (OJ L No. 149, 30. 4. 2004, p. 1) as amended by Commission Regulation 1787/2006 of 4 December 2006 (OJ L No. 337, 5. 12. 2006, p. 17); hereinafter: 'Regulation 809/2004').
- Regulation (EU) No. 575/2013 of the European Parliament and of the Council of 26 June 2013 on prudential requirements for credit institutions and investment firms and amending Regulation (EU) No. 648/2012 (OJ No. 176, 27. 6. 2013, p. 1), as last amended by Commission Delegated Regulation (EU) 2015/62 of 10 October 2014 amending Regulation (EU) No. 575/2013 of the European Parliament and of the Council with regard to the coefficient of leverage (OJ No. 11, 17. 1. 2015, p. 37); hereinafter: 'Regulation 575/2013/EU'.
- Regulation (EU) No. 909/2014 of the European Parliament and of the Council of 23 July 2014 on improving securities settlement arrangements in the EU and on central securities depositories and amending Directives 98/26/EC and 2014/65/EU and Regulation (EU) No. 236/2012 (OJ No. 257, 28. 8. 2014, p. 1); hereinafter: 'Regulation 909/2014/EU'.
- Regulation (EU) 2016/1011 of the European Parliament and of the Council of 8 June 2016 on indices to be used as reference values in financial instruments and financial agreements or to measure the performance of investment funds and amending Directives 2008/48/EC and 2014/17/EU and Regulation (EU) No. 596/2014 (OJ L No. 171 of 29. 6. 2016, p. 1, hereinafter: Regulation 2016/1011/EU).
- Regulation (EU) 2017/1129 of the European Parliament and of the Council of 14 June 2017 on the prospectus to be published when securities are offered to the public or their listing for trading on a regulated market and repealing Directive 2003/71/EC (OJ L No. 168).

III. National Sources

A. *Law on Commercial Companies*

139. The LCC[46] (Slovene: Zakon o gospodarskih družbah, ZGD-1) defines the basic rules for the foundation and operation of companies, sole proprietors, related persons, subsidiaries of foreign companies and restructuring of their status. The LCC defines the concept and types of commercial companies (including partnerships), the legal personality of a company, its activities, liability, registered name, representation, business secrets and issues relating to the entry of a company into the court register.

140. The LCC elaborates each type of company and partnership separately and sole proprietor. The most extensive regulations refer to PLC, which include issues such as: the capital and shares, management and governing bodies of a PLC (management board, supervisory board and board of directors), shareholders' meetings, including minority rights, and different kinds of auditing (including special and extraordinary audits).

46. Companies Act – ZGD-1 (Official Gazette of RS, No. 42/06 dated 19. 4. 2006), LCC-1:

- Correction of the Companies Act – ZGD-1 (Official Gazette of RS, No. 60/06 of 9. 6. 2006).
- Act Amending the Companies Act – ZGD-1A (Official Gazette of RS, No. 10/08 of 30. 1. 2008), LCC-1A.
- Act Amending the Companies Act – ZGD-1B (Official Gazette of RS, No. 68/08 of 8. 7. 2008), LCC-1B.
- Act Amending the Companies Act – ZGD-1C (Official Gazette of RS, No. 42/09 dated 5. 6. 2009), LCC-1C.
- Companies Act – official consolidated text – CA-1-UPB3 (Official Gazette of RS, No. 65/09 dated 14. 8. 2009), OCT-UPB3.
- Law on Amendments to the Companies Act – ZGD-1D (Official Gazette of RS, No. 33/11 of 3. 5. 2011), LCC-1D.
- Law on Amendments to the Companies Act – ZGD-1E (Official Gazette of RS, No. 91/11 dated 14. 11. 2011), LCC-1E.
- Act Amending the Companies Act – ZGD-1F (Official Gazette of RS, No. 32/12 of 4. 5. 2012) LCC-1F.
- Act Amending the Companies Act – ZGD-1G (Official Gazette of RS, No. 57/12 of 27. 7. 2012) LCC-1G.
- The annulment of the first to the fourth paragraph of Article 10a and the fourth paragraph of Article 10b, and partly repealing the seventh paragraph of Article 10a of the LCC, and the finding that the fifth and sixth paragraphs of Article 10a, part of the Seventh paragraph of Article 10a and the first to the third paragraph of Article 10b and twelfth indent of Article 50 of the companies Act insofar as it relates to the first and second paragraphs of Article 10b of the companies Act are not inconsistent with the Constitution (Official Gazette of RS, No. 44/13 of 24. 5. 2013).
- Act Amending the Companies Act – ZGD-1 H (Official Gazette of RS, No. 82/13 dated 8. 10. 2013), LCC-1H.
- Act Amending the Companies Act – ZGD-1I (Official Gazette of RS, No. 55/15 of 24. 7. 2015), LCC-1I.
- Act Amending the Companies Act – ZGD-1J (Official Gazette RS, No. 15/17 of 31 Mar. 2017).

141. The provisions of the LCC on activities, registered names, registered office, branches, procuration and business secrets apply *mutatis mutandis* to sole entrepreneurs.

142. The LCC has extensive regulations regarding books of accounts and reports, such as general accounting and annual report rules, consolidated annual reports, publications, general rules on the categorization of financial statements, balance sheets, profit and loss accounts, business reports, and so on.

143. The LCC also regulates measures to increase and reduce the subscribed capital, exclusion of minority shareholders from the company, the right of minority shareholders to withdraw from the company, nullity and contestability of shareholders' resolutions and dissolution of a company.

144. The LCC also contains extensive provisions regarding affiliated companies (concerns and holdings) and on restructuring of companies, such as: mergers, division, transfer of assets and changing its organizational form (conversion).

B. Other Relevant Laws

145. Acquisitions and takeover procedures are regulated separately in the Takeover Act, TA (Slovene: Zpre).[47]

47. Takeovers Act – 1 of the Takeover Act (Official Gazette of RS, No. 79/06 of 27. 7. 2006), TA:

- Act on the Amendment of the Act on Takeovers – 1A Takeover Act (Official Gazette of RS, No. 1/08 of 4. 1. 2008), TA 1-A.
- Law Amending the Law on Takeovers – 1B Takeover Act (Official Gazette of RS, No. 68/08 of 8. 7. 2008), TA-1B.
- The annulment of the second sentence of the second paragraph of Article 75 and Article 63 in conjunction with the second sentence of the second paragraph of Article 75 of the Takeover Act in respect of the content that they made it authentic interpretation of the second paragraph of Article 75 and Article 63 in conjunction with the second paragraph of Article 75 of the Takeover Act (Official Gazette of RS, No. 105/11 dated 23. 12. 2011).
- Law Amending the Law on Takeover – Takeover Act 1C (Official Gazette of RS, No. 10/12 of 10. 2. 2012), TA-1C.
- Law Amending the Law on Takeovers – 1D Takeover Act (Official Gazette of RS, No. 38/12 of 25. 5. 2012), TA-1D.
- Law on Amendments to the Law on Takeovers – 1E Takeover Act (Official Gazette of RS, No. 56/13 of 2. 7th 2013), TA-1C.
- Law Amending the Law on Takeover – Takeover Act 1F (Official Gazette of RS, No. 25/14 dated 11. 4. 2014), TA-1F.
- Law Amending the Law on Takeovers – 1G Takeover Act (Official Gazette of RS, No. 75/15 dated 8. 10. 2015), TA-1G.

146. Bankruptcy procedures are not a part of the LCC, but are regulated by a separate law – Law on Company Finance, Insolvency and Winding up Procedures (LFIWP).[48]

---

48. The Financial Operations, Insolvency Proceedings and Compulsory Dissolution – ZFPPIPP (Official Gazette of RS, No. 126/07 dated 31. 12. 2007) LFOIPCD:

- Law Amending the Law on Financial Operations, Insolvency Proceedings and Compulsory Dissolution – ZFPPIPP-A (Official Gazette of RS, No. 40/09 of 29. 5. 2009), LFOIPCD-A.
- Law Amending the Law on Financial Operations, Insolvency Proceedings and Compulsory Dissolution – ZFPPIPP-B (Official Gazette of RS, No. 59/09 of 30. 7. 2009), LFOIPCD-B.
- Law Amending the Law on Financial Operations, Insolvency Proceedings and Compulsory Dissolution – ZFPPIPP-C (Official Gazette of RS, No. 52/10 of 30. 6. 2010), LFOIPCD-C.
- Law Amending the Law on Financial Operations, Insolvency Proceedings and Compulsory Dissolution – ZFPPIPP-D (Official Gazette of RS, No. 26/11 of 8. 4. 2011), LFOIPCD-D.
- The decision on repealing Article 34 of the Law on Amendments and Supplements to the Law on Financial Operations, Insolvency Proceedings and Compulsory Dissolution Act, insofar as it relates to the provision of point 2 of the first paragraph of Article 114 of the Financial Operations, Insolvency Proceedings and Compulsory Dissolution and task manager in the bankruptcy proceedings to which this Act binds awards manager, made before the entry into force of the law amending the law on financial operations, insolvency proceedings and compulsory Dissolution Act. The decision revoking the decision of the Higher Court of Koper and the decision of the District Court of Nova Gorica and the decision of the District Court in Nova Gorica (Official Gazette of RS, No. 23/12 of 26. 3. 2012).
- Law Amending the Law on Financial Operations, Insolvency Proceedings and Compulsory Dissolution – ZFPPIPP-E (Official Gazette of RS, No. 47/13 of 31. 5. 2013) LFOIPCD-E.
- The Financial Operations, Insolvency Proceedings and Compulsory Dissolution Act – official consolidated text – UPB7-ZFPPIPP (Official Gazette of RS, No. 63/13 of 26. 7. 2013) LFOIPCD-OCT13.
- Law Amending the Law on Financial Operations, Insolvency Proceedings and Compulsory Dissolution – ZFPPIPP-F (Official Gazette of RS, No. 100/13 dated 6. 12. 2013) LFOIPCD-F.
- Correction of the Law on Amendments and Supplements to the Law on Financial Operations, Insolvency Proceedings and Compulsory Dissolution – ZFPPIPP-F (Official Gazette of RS, No. 10/15 of 16. 2. 2015).
- The Financial Operations, Insolvency Proceedings and Compulsory Dissolution Act – official consolidated text – UPB8-ZFPPIPP (Official Gazette of RS, No. 13/14 of 17. 2. 2014), LFOIPCD-OCT14.
- Adjustment of the Financial Operations, Insolvency Proceedings and Compulsory Dissolution Act – official consolidated text – UPB8-ZFPPIPP (Official Gazette of RS, No. 10/15 of 16. 2. 2015) LFOIPCD-OCT15 – Law Amending the Law on Financial Operations, Insolvency Proceedings and Compulsory Dissolution – ZFPPIPP-G (Official Gazette of RS, No. 27/16 dated 11. 4. 2016), LFOIPCD-G.
- Decision finding that the Law on Financial Operations, Insolvency Proceedings and Compulsory Dissolution in conflict with the Constitution (Official Gazette of RS, No. 31/16 of 29. 4. 2016).
- Decision finding that the Law on Financial Operations, Insolvency Proceedings and Compulsory Dissolution in conflict with the Constitution and the repeal of the decision of the Higher Court in Ljubljana (Official Gazette of RS, No. 38/16 of 27. 5. 2016).
- Decision on the finding that the Financial Operations Act, insolvency proceedings and forcible termination are inconsistent with the Constitution and the annulment of the decision of the Higher Court in Ljubljana (Official Gazette of the Republic of Slovenia, No. 38/16 of 27 May 2016).
- Act Amending the Inheritance Act – ZD-C (Official Gazette of the Republic of Slovenia, No. 63/16 of 7 Oct. 2016).

147. In addition to the LCC provisions on shares, it is necessary to consult another law – the DL,[49] which regulates the method of issuing and transferring of dematerialized securities and the rules for keeping a central register of dematerialized securities.

148. Banks and insurance companies are special forms of companies which are regulated by the Law on Bank of Slovenia,[50] the BL and the Insurance, Law (IL).

The Bank of Slovenia is the central bank of the Republic of Slovenia. It is a public legal entity, sole State-owned, that independently manages its own assets. The Bank of Slovenia has financial and management autonomy; the members of its decision-making bodies are independent in the performance of their duties. They shall not be bound by the decisions, positions and instructions of government or any authority, nor may they seek instructions or guidelines

- Decision on the finding that the fourth paragraph of Article 192 of the Financial Operations Act, insolvency proceedings and compulsory winding up is partially inconsistent with the Constitution (Official Gazette of the Republic of Slovenia, No. 54/18 of 10 Aug. 2018).

49. Law on dematerialized securities – ZNVP (Official Gazette of RS, No. 23/99 of 8. 4. 1999), LDS:

- Law Amending the Law on dematerialized securities – ZNVP-A (Official Gazette of RS, No. 114/06 dated 9. 11. 2006), LDS-A.
- Act on the Book-Entry Securities – official consolidated text – ZNVP UPB1 (Official Gazette of RS, No. 2/07 of 9. 1. 2007), LDS -OCT1.
- Amending Act of dematerialized securities – ZNVP-B (Official Gazette of RS, No. 58/09 of 27. 7. 2009), LDS-B.
- Law Amending the Law on dematerialized securities – ZNVP-C (Official Gazette of RS, No. 78/11 of 10. 5. 2011), LDS-C.
- Dematerialized Securities Law – ZNVP-1 (Official Gazette of the Republic of Slovenia, No. 75/15 of 8 Oct. 2015), -Law Amending the Dematerialized Securities Law – ZNVP-1A (Official Gazette of the Republic of Slovenia, No. 5/17 of 3 Feb. 2017).
- Decision to annul the first and second sentences of the fourth paragraph of Article 48 of the Dematerialized Securities Law (Official Gazette of the Republic of Slovenia, No. 15/18 of 7 Mar. 2018).
- Law Amending and Supplementing the Dematerialized Securities Law – ZNVP-1B (Official Gazette of the Republic of Slovenia, No. 43/19 of.

50. Bank of Slovenia Law – BAS-1 (Official Gazette of RS, No. 58/02 dated 4. 7. 2002):

- Correction of the Law on the Bank of Slovenia – ZBS-1 (Official Gazette of RS, No. 85/02 of 4. 10. 2002).
- Law Amending the Law on the Bank of Slovenia – ZBS-1A (Official Gazette of RS, No. 39/06 dated 13. 4. 2006).
- Bank of Slovenia Law – official consolidated text – BAS-1-UPB1 (Official Gazette of RS, No. 72/06 of 11. 7. 2006).
- Law Amending the Law on the Bank of Slovenia – ZBS-1B (Official Gazette of RS, No. 59/11 of 25. 7. 2011).
- Law Amending the Bank of Slovenia Law – ZBS-1C (Official Gazette of the Republic of Slovenia, No. 55/17 of 6 Oct. 2017).

149. The securities market is regulated by the modern and very recent Market in the Financial Instruments Law (MIFL) and the Investment Trusts and Management Companies Law ITMCL.

150. Employees' participation in management is regulated by the Law on European Workers' Councils (LEWC),[51] the Law on Employees' Participation in Management (LEPM),[52] the Law on Employee Participation in profit (LEPP),[53] the Law on Employees' Participation in Management of a European Company (LEPMEC)[54] and the LEPM of a European Cooperative.[55]

C. The Corporate Governance Code

151. The Corporate Governance Code (the Code) was jointly adopted by the LSE, the Association of Supervisory Board Members of Slovenia and the Managers' Association of Slovenia.[56]

In addition, there is The Corporate Governance Code for Companies with State Capital Investment approved in December 2014 (The State Companies Code).

The State Companies Code is addressed to companies with State capital investment. It also applies to subsidiaries in the group, in which the position of the parent company is the State capital investment.

Both Codes are in conformity with the revised OECD Principles of Corporate Governance and were supplemented with new recommendations and principles that are the result of further development and study of best practices in corporate governance. The State Companies Code is in conformity with the OECD Guidelines/ G20 on Corporate Governance of State-owned, companies.[57]

---

51. The Law on European Workers' Councils (LEWC), Official Gazette of the RS, Nos 59/2002, 103/2007 (Slovene: ZEDS).
52. The Law on workers' participation in management (Official Gazette of RS, No. 42/93 of 22. 7. 1993), LEPM:
    - Law Amending the Law on workers' participation in management – ZSDU-A (Official Gazette of RS, No. 56/01 of 6. 7. 2001), LEPM-A.
    - Law Amending the Law on workers' participation in management of governance – ZSDU B (Official Gazette of RS, No. 26/07 of 23. 3. 2007), LEPM-B.
    - The Law on workers' participation in management of governance – official consolidated text – ZSDU UPB1 (Official Gazette of RS, No. 42/07 of 15. 5. 2007), LEPM-OCT1.
53. Law on Employee Participation in Profit (Official Gazette of RS, No. 25/08).
54. The Law on Employees' Participation in Management of a European Company (LEPSE) Official Gazette of the RS, No. 28/2006 (Slovene: ZSDUEDD).
55. The Law on Employees' Participation in Management of a European Cooperative, Official Gazette of the RS, No. 79/2006.
56. Code of Corporate Governance was jointly phrased and adopted by the Ljubljana Stock Exchange d. d., Ljubljana, Slovenia Association of Supervisors and Managers' Association of 18. 3. 2004, modified and supplemented 14. 12. 2005 and 5. 2. 2007. The Code in its current form has been renewed and approved 8. 12. 2009, and becomes effective on 1. 1. 2010.
57. According to The Law on Slovenian Sovereign Holding (Official Gazette of RS, No. 25/2014 (SDH-1) governs the status and functioning of the Slovenian Sovereign Holding (SSH, Slovene: SDH), all

Both codes contribute to better corporate governance and capital investment management, to strengthen integrity and accountability and limit the risks of corruption, to avoid conflict of interest and abuse of insider information.

152. The Code is a collection of best practice recommendations relating to corporate governance, including mandatory legal provisions and optional recommended practices for PLC. Its purpose is to encourage the setting up of a good governance system and create conditions for long-term sustainable development of PLC. At the same time, the Code prompts shareholders and important stakeholders (employees, creditors, contracting partners, the company's wider environment, etc.) to actively cooperate and exercise their rights in a responsible manner. The Code incorporates the Slovene legislation, the directives and recommendations of the EU, principles of business ethics, internal bylaws of the three institutions and internationally recommended best practices of responsible and good governance. The purpose of the Code is to define in more detail the governance and management principles of PLC, whose shares are listed on the Slovene-regulated market. The recommended practices can also be applied by other companies.

153. The statement on corporate governance has become a requisite element of the business report in companies' annual reports and is based on the 'comply or explain' principle. This principle allows companies to deviate from the Code's recommendations, thus enabling them to develop their own business practices. While the Code's provisions are not binding, companies are nonetheless obliged to disclose which provisions they do not follow and their reasons for not doing so.

§5. Private International Law

154. The law applicable to corporations and partnerships with a foreign element (i.e., place of business, place of incorporation, etc.) is Private International Law and Procedure Act (PILPA, Slovene: ZMZPP).[58] According to Article 17 of the PILPA, the legal position of a legal person shall be governed by the law of the country to which the legal person belongs. The affiliation of a legal person is determined by the law of the country under which it was established. There is only one exception: if a legal person has its actual seat in a state other than that in which it was established and has its affiliation under the law of that other state, it shall be deemed to belong to that other state.

Between the two theories – registered office of the legal entity (seat theory) and establishment (theory of registration or incorporation) – PILPA adopted the theory of incorporation. The law under which a legal person was established is therefore decisive for determining its legal and business capacity. It depends on the revoked

capital investments of the Republic of Slovenia are managed by SDH. SDH-1 in Article 32 as one of the acts investment management provides the Corporate Governance Code for Companies with State capital investment adopted by the Management Board with the consent of SSH Supervisory Board.

58. Private International Law and Procedure Act (PILPA, Slovene: ZMZPP) Official Gazette RS, No. 56/99 in 45/08 – ZArbit).

law whether it also sets a seat on its territory as a condition for the existence of a legal person. The seat of a legal person alone is not sufficient for a legal person to have the nationality of the country in which it is established. The legal order under which it is established may also take the view that it is not necessary for it to have its seat in its territory: in such a case, the seat is not relevant to the application of the conflict-of-law norm.

In only one case is the seat also important. If a legal person has its actual seat in a country other than that in which it was established and has its affiliation under the law of that other country, it shall be deemed to belong to that other country. It is therefore a situation where a legal person is established under the law of one country and has its actual seat in another. If the theory of the seat applies in this other country (and they therefore consider the legal person as their own), then Slovenian law also considers that the legal person has the nationality of the country in which it has its actual seat.

155. In Slovenia, employee involvement is based on Article 75 of the Constitution the RS which guarantees employees the right of codetermination. On this constitutional basis, the Law on the Participation of Employees in Management (LPEM)[59] was approved. The law provides a variety of participation rights, information and consultation rights and participation of employees in corporate boards for all companies including those in public utility services, in banks and insurance companies, unless otherwise provided by a special law.

LPEM determines the ways and conditions for the participation of employees in the management of companies and also sole proprietors with at least fifty employees and cooperatives. LPEM transposes Directive 2002/14/EC, establishing a general framework for informing and consulting employees in the European Community and Council Directive 2001/23/EC relating to the safeguarding of employees' rights in the event of transfer of undertakings, businesses or parts of undertakings or businesses (Article 1 of the LPEM).

According to Article 8 of the LPEM, employees have the right to elect a workers' council if the company employs more than twenty workers. In particular, the workers' council has the following powers (Article 87, LPEM): ensures that laws and other regulations adopted collective agreements and agreements reached between the workers' council and the employer are implemented; proposes measures for the benefit of workers; accepts proposals and initiatives of employees and, if justified, takes them into account when negotiating with the employer; assists in the integration into work of disabled people, the elderly and other workers who are provided with special protection.

According to Article 78 of the LPEM, employees have the right to participate in the companies' boards. The participation of employees in management in the company's bodies is realized through the representatives of employees in the company's management and supervisory bodies, namely:

---

59. The LPEM does not apply to the participation of employees in management in European Works Councils, the European Joint Stock Company and the European Cooperative Society, unless otherwise provided by a special law.

- in a two-tier management system (management board and supervisory board) through employee representatives in the company's supervisory board and/or through an employee representative in the company's management board (employee director);
- in a one-tier management system (board of directors only) through employee representatives in the board of directors and in the committees of the board of directors and/or through an employee representative among the executive directors of the company or cooperative.

At least one-third, but not more than one-half, shall be employees' representatives in the supervisory board and at least one on three members of the board of directors shall be employees' representatives. The president of the board is not permitted to be an employee representative.

Part I. Companies

Chapter 1. A Public Limited Company

§1. Characteristics of a PLC

I. Definitions and Goals of a PLC

156. There are several definitions of a PLC in the law. For example, a PLC is a company that raises the capital for its formation and for its operations from the public. Another definition says that a PLC is a company which has subscribed capital divided into shares (Article 168/1 LCC). According to the Code[60] (Article 1), the key goal of a PLC engaged in a gainful activity is to maximize the company's value. This and other goals, pursued by the company in performing its activity, should be stated in the company's Articles of Association.

II. Legal Status, Founders

157. A PLC is a legal entity. It acquires its own legal personality upon its entry in the register. A PLC is liable to creditors for its obligations with all its assets; shareholders are not liable to creditors for the obligations of the company (Article 168/2, 3 LCC).

158. Founders of a PLC may be one or more natural or legal persons (domestic or foreign) who adopt the company's Articles of Association (Article 169 LCC).

Article 10a of the Act Amending the Companies Act,[61] (LCC-1E, Slovene: ZGD-1 E) imposed restrictions on establishment of companies related to insolvency procedures. It was stipulated, that the founder or partner of the company cannot be anyone who was a member of the management or supervisory body of a company, over which one of the insolvency proceedings or compulsory dissolution was placed

60. Slovene Code of corporate governance for joint stock companies https://www.bing.com/search?q=kodeks+upravljanja+delni%C5%A1kih+dru%C5%BEb&form=WNSGPH&qs=SW&cvid=b95524898f88459a87384ef9a424ff9f&pq=kodeks+upravljanja+delni%C5%A1kih+dru%C5%BEb&cc=SI&setlang=en-GB&nclid=0399E0419BC78F24AD457A19473E463B&ts=1597397822565&wsso=Moderate.
61. Official Gazette of the RS, No. 91/2011 of 14 Nov. 2011.

under. The same restriction applied to persons who have held the offices of the management or supervisory bodies against which proceedings (insolvency or compulsory winding up) have been instituted during the last two years. (The first to the fourth paragraph of Article 10a.)[62]

This provision was overruled by the Decision of Constitutional Court of 24 May 2013.[63] The Constitutional Court decided that the first to the fourth paragraph of Article 10a of the Companies Act are repealed.

The 2015 amendment to LCC (LCC-1I) brings a new, more comprehensive regulation of this issue, which replaces the above-described provisions. LCC-1I imposes the following restrictions on the establishment of companies and entrepreneurs as well as on obtaining the status of shareholder. The founder, shareholder and entrepreneur cannot become a person, who:

(1) has been sentenced to imprisonment for criminal offence against the economy, against the employment and social security, against legal transactions, against property, against the environment and natural resources and is entered in the criminal record of the Ministry of Justice; this restriction expires in five years after the final judgment, or after the criminal records were erased;
(2) has been in the last twelve months, on the list of those, who did not propose the accounts for taxation, or on the list of tax defaulters (failure to register or to fulfil tax obligations);
(3) holds more than 25% share in the equity capital of the company (with the exception of banks and insurance companies, some State-owned companies), which has been in the last twelve months, on the list of those, who did not propose the accounts for taxation, or on the list of tax defaulters;

    Restriction from the points 2 and 3 ceases when the tax authority issue a certificate attesting that the respective person has no overdue tax obligations, and that it has complied with all the obligations relating to submission accounts for taxation, for the payment of wages and wage compensation (the certificate must not be older than fifteen days).

(4) has been fined for an offence in relation to payment for work or offence relating to illegal employment in the past three years by a final decision of the Inspectorate work or the Financial Administration at least twice; this restriction ceases within three years from the date of the final decision or judgment;
(5) holds more than 50% share in the capital of a LLC, which has been deleted from the register without liquidation under the law governing the financial operations, insolvency proceedings and forced termination; this restriction is terminated within one year from the date of the erasure of the company from the register.

The founder or shareholder of a LLC cannot become a person who has in the last three months set up a LLC or acquired a stake in a LLC, which is not older than

62. Official Gazette of the RS, Nos 65/ 09 – official consolidated text, 33/ 11, 91/11, 32/12 and 57 /12.
63. Official Gazette of the RS, No. 44/2013.

three months (with the exception of banks and insurance companies, some state-owned companies and for medium and large companies). This restriction does not apply in the case of acquisition by inheritance.

The same restriction also does not apply if a LLC, in which the person in the last three months acquired shareholding, fulfil the following conditions:

- has an account open meaning, that the company is entered in the Commercial Register of Slovenia;
- has not been in the last twelve months on the list of those, who did not propose the accounts for taxation;
- has no outstanding liabilities from the compulsory charges and other non-tax cash obligations by recoveries Financial Administration, of more than EUR 50; and
- has employed for at least one month continuously at least one person, or compulsorily insured shareholder in accordance with the law governing health insurance for at least part-time.

III. The Principle of Equality of Shareholders

159. A PLC's shares should be issued by applying the principle of 'one share, one vote' (Article 178, LCC). A PLC may not issue shares which, although of equal nominal amounts or value, carry different voting rights. In the case of shares with limited or no voting rights, a PLC should publicly disclose their type and volume and specify the rights carried by these shares.

160. The LCC stipulates the principle of equal status of shareholders; the bodies of the company must treat equal shareholders equally under equal conditions (Article 221, LCC). According to the Code, companies must treat equally all shareholders who hold shares of the same class: internal and external, minority and substantial shareholders, the State as a shareholder, and domestic and foreign shareholders. The principal obligation of shareholders is to pay the issue value of the subscribed shares to the account of the company or deliver to it non-cash contributions of such value.

IV. Business Secret

161. The new Law on Business Secret brings substantially new regulation related to business secret in Slovene legislation. Until the entry into force of the Business Secrets Act (hereinafter: BSAct, Slovene: ZPosS),[64] the definition of professional secrecy was stipulated in Article 39 and the protection of professional secrecy in Article 40 of the Companies Act (hereinafter: LCC-1, Slovene: ZGD-1). The BSAct amended the text of Article 39 of the LCC-1 by a clause providing that confidential information is considered as information that meets the requirements of

64. The Business Secrets Act – BSAct (Official Gazette of the Republic of Slovenia, No. 22/19 of 5 Apr. 2019).

professional secrecy in accordance with the law governing business secrets. Article 40 of the ZGD-1 has been deleted, which simply means that LCC-1 is not regulating business secrets anymore.

The reason for the drafting of the new regulation is the implementation of the Directive on the protection of undisclosed expertise and business information (business secrets) prior to their unlawful acquisition, use and disclosure (hereinafter: Directive 2016/943). The BSAct, adopted on the basis of Directive 2016/943, brings important innovations to this area. In particular, the BSAct redefines the concept of business secrets and stipulates that professional secrecy covers undisclosed expertise, experience and business information that are not generally known and easily accessible and that have a certain market value and for which the business secret holder has taken sufficient measures to maintain it as a business secret. As a business secret, it is not permissible to include information that does not meet all three requirements (cumulatively). In addition to the definition of business secrets, the law distinguishes between legal and unlawful acquisition, the use of business secrets and direct and indirect (noncommittal) acquirers.

The BSAct also lays down rules on legal remedies in civil proceedings against the misappropriation, use and disclosure of business secrets, as well as the rules on the preservation of confidentiality of business secrets during and after the judicial process. The law provides for prohibition and suspensive claims, as well as temporary injunctions for the immediate cessation of violations, and the right to compensation for damage.

The business secret is still regulated by the Prevention of Restriction of Competition Act,[65] which defines business secrets as data whose disclosure would cause significant damage and are known to a limited circle of persons (Article 17, paragraph 1), and the Obligation Code (OC)[66] in the chapter on damage and in a special part, within the framework of the license agreement (protection of confidentiality of the subject of the license – Article 714 of the OC), commercial agency contract or agency contract (protection of business secrets – Article 817 of the OC) and intermediary contracts (mediator's liability for damage to the principal due to the fact that, without his authorization, he informed the third party about the content of the contract, the negotiations or the terms of the concluded contract – Article 844 of the OC). Penal Code[67] determines the definition of professional secrecy in the fifth paragraph of Article 236 and includes industrial, banking and any other business secrets (issuance and unjustified acquisition of business secrets).

65. Official Gazette of the Republic of Slovenia, Nos 36/08, 40/09, 26/11, 87/11, 57/12, 39/13, 33/14, 76/15 and 23/17.

66. (Official Gazette of the Republic of Slovenia, No. 97/07 – official consolidated text.

67. (Official Gazette of the Republic of Slovenia, No. 50/12 – official consolidation) 6/16 – p., 54/15, 38/16 and 27/17.

§2. Formation of a PLC (183–220, LCC)

I. Simultaneous Formation

162. A PLC may be formed by all the founders adopting and signing the Articles of Association and acquiring all the shares themselves (simultaneous formation). A company is formed once the founders acquire all the shares. The founders must compile a written report on the forming of the company (formation report). The members of the management and the supervisory board must examine the process of the formation of the company. In addition, one or more forming auditors (appointed by the court) must review the formation:

- if a member of the management or the supervisory board acquired shares;
- if shares were acquired at the time of formation for the account of a member of the management or the supervisory board;
- if a member of the management or the supervisory board obtained a special benefit or payment for preparing the formation; or
- if the formation is carried out with non-cash contributions.

163. According to the LCC, the founders appoint the first supervisory or management board of the company and an auditor for the first full or partial financial year. The members of the supervisory or management board are appointed only until the first general meeting. The supervisory board appoints the members of the management board, and the management board appoints the first executive managers.

II. Successive Formation

A. Invitation to the Public

164. A company may also be formed through a subscription for shares on the basis of publication of an announcement containing an invitation to the public to subscribe for shares (prospectus). The founders adopt Articles of Association, publish a prospectus and acquire just some of the shares. The time limit for subscribing to and paying for the rest of the shares may not be longer than three months from the date determined as the commencement of the subscription.

165. The unsuccessful subscription is described in LCC: if within the time limit all the shares on offer are not subscribed and correctly paid for, the founders may themselves, within fifteen days of the expiry of this time limit, acquire or subscribe for the shares that have not been subscribed and paid for. According to Article 214 LCC, the Articles of Association, the reports of the founders and the auditors, and the prospectus must be made available to subscribers for inspection at the bank handling the subscription and payment for the shares.

B. The Founding General Meeting

166. Convening the founding general meeting is required in the case of successive formation. It must be held no later than two months after the expiry of the time limit set out in the prospectus for completion of the share subscription. The founders must convene the founding general meeting by way of an announcement which must be published in the same manner as the prospectus and with an interval of at least fifteen days between the date of the last publication of the prospectus and the date of the founding general meeting (Articles 214–200 LCC).

167. The founding general meeting has the following powers:

- to establish whether all shares have been subscribed for or acquired, whether the shares have been allocated and whether the payments which should have been made by the time of the founding general meeting have been made in accordance with the Act and the Articles of Association;
- to examine whether all requirements have been met in respect of non-cash contributions so that the company will be able to dispose freely of the non-cash contributions as soon as it is entered in the register;
- to establish the maximum permitted amount of formation expenses to be debited to the company; and
- to elect those bodies of the company which the general meeting is competent to elect pursuant to the law or the Articles of Association (Article 218 LCC).

III. Subsequent Formation

168. Article 188 LCC regulates so-called subsequent formations. A subsequent formation contract is a contract concluded by a company within the first two years of formation, on the basis of which the company acquires corporeal assets or rights at a price amounting to at least one-tenth of the company's subscribed capital.

169. A subsequent formation contract enters into force when the general meeting has adopted a resolution giving consent to the conclusion of the contract and the contract has been entered in the register. Legal actions taken by the company for the purpose of fulfilment of a subsequent formation contract to which a general meeting has not given consent and which is not entered in the register are null and void.

IV. The Articles of Association

A. The Components of the Articles of Association

170. The Articles of Association, which must be drawn up in the form of a notarial record, must contain (LCC Article 183) the following components:

- founders: the name, surname and address or the registered name and registered office of each founder;
- legal specificities: the registered name and registered office of the company, the activity (object) of the company.

(a) capital and shares:

- the amount of the subscribed capital;
- if the company has shares with nominal amounts, the nominal amount of the shares and the number of shares of each nominal amount, and, where there is more than one class of shares, the share class and the number of shares issued in each particular class;
- if the company has no-par value shares, the number of shares and, where there is more than one class of shares, the share class and the number of shares issued in each particular class; also whether the shares are bearer or registered shares; and
- the amount of paid in capital as at the date of the company's registration and the paid in capital at that time.

(b) management system:

- whether the management system is one or two tier;
- the number of members of the management and supervisory bodies or the manner in which this number is determined; and
- the term of office of members of the management or supervisory bodies.

(c) other matters:

- the form and method of announcements of importance for the company or for the shareholders;
- the manner of disclosure of information and communications of the company – information or communications which the management believes are important for the shareholders must be published in a publication or electronic media determined by the Articles of Association;
- the duration of the company if it is formed for a fixed period; and
- the method of dissolving the company.

B. *Different Regulation and Additional Matters*

171. It is important to emphasize that matters regulated by law may only be regulated differently by the Articles of Association where explicitly so provided by law. Additional matters may only be regulated by the Articles of Association where such matters are not comprehensively regulated by law. Other issues of importance for the company which are not regulated in the Articles of Association may be regulated in the company's other acts (bylaws) in accordance with the LCC.

172. For any amendment to the Articles of Association, a resolution passed by a general meeting is required. A general meeting may transfer authority for an amendment to the Articles of Association to the supervisory board or the board of directors in instances where such an amendment merely brings the wording of the Articles of Association into line with properly adopted resolutions; a majority of at least three-quarters of the subscribed capital represented is required for such a resolution. This does not apply to an amendment of the company's activity and instances where the law stipulates a higher majority of the represented capital. The Articles of Association may also lay down other requirements.

V. Notification

A. Notification for Entry of a Company in the Register

173. The LCC (Articles 43–48) regulates notification for the entry of a company in the register. It stipulates that the members of the management or the supervisory board must make the notification for the entry of the company in the register.

174. According to the Article 201 of the LCC, the contents of a notification for entry in the register must contain the following data:

- the amount for which shares are being issued;
- evidence from an authorized bank that the management is free to dispose of the sum paid in;
- an assurance from the founders that they are aware of the duty to provide information to the registration body and that there are no constraints or circumstances not in conformity with the provisions laid down in the LCC (circumstances that would contradict their appointment pursuant to the LCC); and
- a statement as to the scope of entitlements enjoyed by the management in representing the company.

B. Documents to Be Submitted Together with Notification

175. A notification for entry in the register must be submitted together with the following:

- the Articles of Association and the documents which formed the basis on which the Articles of Association were prepared, and the documents which formed the basis on which the founders acquired shares;
- a statement of account of the formation expenses debited to the company; in this statement of account, payments must be stated by order and amount, and recipients of payments must be stated individually;

- the documents which formed the basis of the appointment of the members of the management or supervisory bodies; and
- the formation report and the audit reports of the members of the management or the supervisory board and of the formation auditors (Article 202 of the LCC).

176. These reports must be accompanied by the documents on which the significant findings contained in the reports are based.

VI. Registration

177. Court Register Law[68] regulates the register, the information to be entered in the register, the rules of procedure, in which the court decides on the entry in the register, and the rules under which the Agency for Public Legal Records and Related Services (APLRS) operates the register. CRL implements in legal order of Slovenia the following EU directives:

- the First Council Directive 68/151/EEC of 9 March 1968 on coordination of safeguards to protect the interests of members and others, are required by Member States of companies within the meaning of the second paragraph of Article 58 of the Treaty, with a view to making such safeguards equivalent throughout the Community[69] as last amended by Directive of the European Parliament and of the Council 2003/58/EC of 15 July 2003 amending Council Directive 68/151/EEC;[70] and

68. Court Register Act (Official Gazette of RS, No. 13/94 of 10. 3. 1994), CRL:

- Law Amending the Law on the Court Register – ZSReg-A (Official Gazette of RS, No. 91/05 dated 14. 10. 2005), CRL-A.
- Court Register Act – official consolidated text – ZSReg UPB1 (Official Gazette of RS, No. 114/05 dated 19. 12. 2005), CRL-OCT1.
- Law Amending the Law on the Court Register – ZSReg-B (Official Gazette of RS, No. 33/07 dated 13. 4. 2007), CRL-B.
- Court Register Act – official consolidated text – ZSReg-UPB2 (Official Gazette of RS, No. 54/07 of 18. 6. 2007), CRL-OCT2:
- The Law amending the Law on Amendments and Supplements to the Law on the Court Register – ZSReg-C (Official Gazette of RS, No. 93/07 dated 12. 10. 2007), CRL-C.
- Law Amending the Law on the Court Register – ZSReg-D (Official Gazette of RS, No. 65/08 of 30. 6. 2008), CRL-D.
- Law Amending the Law on the Court Register – ZSReg-E (Official Gazette of RS, No. 49/09 of 29. 6. 2009), CRL-E.
- Law Amending the Law on the Court Register – ZSReg-F (Official Gazette of RS, No. 17/15 of 13. 3. 2015), CRL-F.
- Law Amending the Court Register Law – ZSReg-G (Official Gazette of the Republic of Slovenia, No. 54/17 of 29 Sep. 2017).

69. Directive 68/151/EEC, OJ No. 65/8, of 9 Mar. 1968.
70. OJ No L. 221 of 4 Sep. 2003, 13.

- the Eleventh Council Directive 89/666/EEC of 21 December 1989 concerning disclosure of branches in a Member State by certain types of company governed by the law of another State,[71] as amended.

Keeping the court register means decision-making on the entry of data in the register. The register is run by the court.

Management of the register means entering data into the general ledger of the register on the basis of the court's decision, and the maintenance and management of a centralized computerized database of the register as part of the business register. The register is administered by the APLRRS.

The registration body (the court) must verify that the company has been properly formed and reported. If this is not the case, the registration body must refuse the notification. The registration body may also reject an application if the formation auditors establish or if it is clear that the formation report or the report by the members of the management or the supervisory board is inaccurate, incomplete or do not conform with the law; the same applies if the formation auditors state, or the registration body establishes, that the value of non-cash contributions or a non-cash acquisition is significantly less than the lowest remission value of the shares or the payments which need to be provided for them. The Law on Amendments and Supplements to the Law on the Court Register/ZSReg-D/[72] CRL-D introduces so-called (OSS, Slovene: Vse na enem mestu, VEM, in 2017 by LCR-G renamed in the 'point to support business entities', PSBE); this is the system of IT solutions, ensuring that entrepreneurs or partners in one place file applications for the corresponding entries in the register and other procedures to be carried out to establish the conditions for starting a business entrepreneur or company. VEM is a computer system operated by the Ministry of Public Administration, and providing adequate information to support integrated business processes covered by the PSBE (VEM) system.[73]

178. The contents of an entry in the register are the following:

- the amount of subscribed capital and any authorized capital;
- the date on which the Articles of Association were adopted;
- the names, surnames and addresses of the members of the management board;
- the duration of the company if it is established for a fixed period; and
- the entitlements of the members of the management to represent the company.

The Law on Amendments and Supplements to the Law on the Court Register/ZSReg-E/[74] imposes a new duty to the Ministry responsible for the economy,

71. OJ L No. 395 dated 30 Dec. 1989, 36.
72. Official Gazette of the RS, No. 65/2008.
73. The information system e-PSBE (VEM) is composed on the basis of association with a central population register, the register of taxpayers or other official records, assume the data necessary to compile complete applications in the PSBE (VEM) processes.
74. Official Gazette of the RS, No. 49/2009.

namely the Ministry for Economy must prepare and submit to the Ministry responsible for public administration, the conditions laid down for the performance of specific economic activities (according to the respective amendment of legislation which lays down the conditions for the pursuit of economic activities).

Law Amending the Law on the Court Register – ZSReg-F (Official Gazette of RS, No. 17/15 of 13. 3. 2015) – CRL-F requires in relation to the founders or members of a foreign company additional data to be entered in the register, as follows: identification data, the nature and extent of liability, the date of the entry and exit and the amount of the contribution (Article 4a, new point 6).

In addition, new second and third paragraphs of Article 7/2 are amended by CRL-F, including the following:

– free access to data, on persons being a founder or member of the subject of entry, must be possible via the agency website;
– free access to data, on a specific person who represents and supervises body of the subject of entry, must be possible via the agency website.

New (amended) Article 51 of the CRL-F, stipulates, that State authorities and administrators have for the purposes of the exercise of his powers and duties the right to access and extract data on whether a particular person is a founder or shareholder in the subject of the entry and whether a particular person represents and supervises body of the subject of entry. State authorities and administrators have for the purposes of the exercise of their powers and duties also the right to access and print all documents enrolled in the register.

The right to access and extract data from the register has also a creditor with an executive document that proves the claim against this person, and another person with a legal interest.

These rights are provided with direct electronic access to the data, if they relate to the period from 1 February 2008 onwards. Access to data and documents for the period from 1 February 2008, provided on the basis of a written request to the court of registration.

Law amending the Court Register Law – CRL-G (Slovene ZSReg-G), as of 2017, implements the Eleventh Council Directive of 21 December 1989 on the disclosures of branches opened in a Member State by certain forms of companies governed by the law of another country (OJ L No. 395 of 30. 12. 1989, p. 36) and Directive 2009/101/EC of the European Parliament and of the Council of 16 September 2009 on the coordination of safeguards which, for the protection of the interests of members and others, require members of companies in the light of the second subparagraph of Article 48 of the Treaty in order to create safeguards having equivalent effect throughout the Community (OJ L No. 258 of 1. 10. 2009, page 11), as amended by Directive 2012/17/EU of the European Parliament and of the Council of 13 June 2012 amending Council Directive 89/666/EEC and Directives 2005/56/EC and 2009/101/EC of the European Parliament and of the Council as regards the integration of central, commercial and company registers (OJ L No. 156, 6. 2012).

VII. Publicity

179. In addition to the contents of an entry in the register, the following must also be published:

- the contents of the Articles of Association (rules for converting types of shares, rules on disclosure of information and communications of the company, data on special benefits and formation expenses and data on non-cash contributions and non-cash acquisitions);
- the Articles of Association or other acts on the composition of the management;
- data on the issue value of the shares;
- the name, surname and address or the registered name and registered office of the founders; and
- the name, surname and address of the members of the first supervisory or management board.

180. At the same time, an announcement must be made that the submitted documents may be inspected at the registration body, in particular the reports by the members of the management or the supervisory board and the formation auditors.

181. Pursuant to the LCC, the entry in the register has legal effect as regards third parties as of the moment of the publication of the individual pieces of information in the Official Gazette of the RS.

The Act Amending the Companies Act[75] (LCC 1-G, Slovene: ZGD-1 G (Article 11) stipulates the obligation of companies to publish certain information or communications of the company on the website of the Agency of the Republic of Slovenia for Public Legal Records and Related Services (hereinafter: 'APLRS, Slovene: AJPES'). The law stipulates which information or communications of the company must be published on the website of the agency. The website has to be managed by APLRS, ensuring everyone free access to the published data. Announcements are free of charge.

If the articles of incorporation provide that, individual data or communications of the Company must be published, they may be published either on the website of the APLRS (not necessarily free of charge) or in the newspaper or both.

VIII. Interconnection of Business Registers

182. CRL-G, 2017 explicitly ensures that everyone is provided with free access to: the Articles of Association of a PLC, LP companies, European public limited-liability companies or a company's LLC contract, including a pamphlet of the amended statute or social contract with a notarial certificate, the act of incorporation on the basis of which an entity of entry, other than the company referred to in the previous indent, was incorporated, including amendments or prudential amendments and final court decisions on the annulment of a capital company. Also the

75. Official Gazette of the RS, No. 32/12 of 4 May 2012.

minutes of the General Meeting of Shareholders which were submitted to the court register in the previous year for publication, and the documents that were attached to the proposal for the entry of a merger or division into the court register in the last year preceding the publication of the entry, if the court authorized the entry of a merger or division into the court register on the basis of this proposal must be same way accessible.

The CRL-G, 2017 requires that website of the agency must be designed in such a way that the insight of the data on the subject of entry in the court register also contains a link to the access to above information. The view of participation in related parties is displayed at the request of the user. Data connectivity is carried out automatically on the basis of a unique identification number.

Service in electronic form have to be, according to LCR-G, 2017, carried out by a notary through a secure electronic route, in accordance with the provisions of the law governing civil procedure.

In the system of interconnection of business registers, the subjects of entry are, according to LCR-G, 2017, provided public access to data and documents pursuant to the provisions of the LCR-G, 2017 and exchange of data between the court register and the system of connecting business registers, namely:

- the provision of notifications on the initiation or termination of the liquidation or deletion procedure without liquidation, compulsory settlement or bankruptcy against the entity of entry and the entry of the deletion of the subject of registration from the court register (Article 49c of this Act);
- receipt of a notice of initiation or termination of a liquidation, insolvency, eradication or winding-up procedure of a foreign company and the termination of such an undertaking by the execution of the cancellation of a branch of a foreign company from the EC;
- the transmission of a notice on the entry into the court register of a company with a registered office in the Republic of Slovenia, which is involved in a cross-border merger as a company that leaves the merger,
- the receipt of a notice on the entry of a foreign company from the EC into a register that is involved in a cross-border merger as a company that leaves the merger, in order to carry out the procedure for registering the cancellation of the acquired company from the court register.

The system of interconnection business registers also enables access to the data and documents including the annual reports required to be publicly accessible. Access may also be made to the documents on which entries of data are based, for which the law provides that they are published on the agency's website for official public announcements.

Access to data and documents must be made possible on the basis of a search request that is transmitted in accordance with the rules and technical requirements of the portal through the electronic access point on the European e-Justice portal as part of the system of interconnecting business registers. If the request refers to a document that is not yet in the computerized database it is converted into electronic form and transmitted into the system of connecting business registers.

The Law on amending the Law of Business Register of Slovenia[76] (LBR-1B 2017, Slovene ZPRS-1B) defines 'System of connecting business registers' as the system of connecting business registers of the Member States of the EU and as a European central platform and an electronic access point. LBR-1B 2017 also defines 'System for Support to Business Entities' as a set of information solutions that ensures the submission of an application, proposal or other application for entry in the court register in accordance with the law governing the court register in order to ensure the conditions for the commencement of business or in connection with subsequent changes. 'Information system for support to business entities' means a computer system managed by the ministry responsible for public administration, providing adequate information support for the integrated implementation of business processes, which includes the system for supporting business entities. 'Points for support to business entities' (former OSS, Slovene: vse na enem mestu, VEM) are local points which, through the information system for supporting business entities, implement procedures to support business entities.

The administrator of the business register assigns a single identifier for the remuneration and the transmission of data and documents and the publication of public data and documents through the system of connecting business registers to the business entities from the Member States of the EU and the European Economic Area, subject to Directive 2009/101/EC.[77] The unique identifier consists of elements enabling identification of the Republic of Slovenia and the business register, and the registration number of the business register unit.

IX. Contracts Made on Behalf of a Company in Formation

183. Prior to entry in the register, the rules governing a contract of members in civil law apply to relations between the members. If a person acts in a company's name prior to the entry of the company in the register, that person is personally

76. Business Register Law of Slovenia – ZPRS-1 (Official Gazette of the Republic of Slovenia, No. 49/06 of 12. 5. 2006):

   - Law Amending the Court Register Law – ZSReg-B (Official Gazette of the Republic of Slovenia, No. 33/07 of 13 Apr. 2007).
   - Law Amending the Business Register of Slovenia Law – ZPRS-1A (Official Gazette of the Republic of Slovenia, No. 19/15 of 20 Mar. 2015).
   - Law Amending the Business Register of Slovenia Law – ZPRS-1B (Official Gazette RS, No. 54/17 of 29 Sep. 2017).

77. Directive 2009/101 / EC of the European Parliament and of the Council of 16 Sep. 2009 on the coordination of safeguards which, for the protection of the interests of members and others, required by Member States of companies in application of the second subparagraph of Article 54 of the Treaty, in order to create safeguards having equivalent effect throughout the Community (OJ L No. 258 of 1. 10. 2009, page 11), most recently amended by Council Directive 2013/24 / EU of 13 May 2013 adapting certain Directives in the field of company law, by reason of the accession of the Republic of Croatia (OJ L No. 158 of 10. 6. 2013, p. 365), (hereinafter referred to as 'Directive 2009/101 / EC').

liable with all his assets; if there are several such persons, they are jointly and severally liable. If through such actions members acquire rights of any sort, they must transfer them to the company after its entry in the register.

184. The LCC regulates operating within the process of simultaneous formation, prior to entry in the register: if a company assumes a debt prior to its entry in the register the consent of the creditor is not necessary for the assumption of the debt to be valid, provided the company approves the assumption of the debt within three months of the entry of the company in the register and reports this to the creditor and the debtor.

185. Prior to the entry of a company in the register, the right to a share may not be transferred, and shares or interim certificates may not be issued. Shares or interim certificates issued before this time are null and void. The issuers are jointly and severally liable to the holders for damage arising from any such issue.

X. The Minimum Value of Subscribed Capital

186. The minimum value of subscribed capital for PLC is EUR 25,000 (Article 171, LCC). Shares may be paid for with money or non-cash contributions but at least one-third of the subscribed capital must comprise shares paid for with money. Only payment effected by legal means to the bank account of a company being formed is regarded as payment. Before the entry of a PLC in the register, at least 25% of the lowest issue value of each share which is paid for with money must be paid in. In respect of shares that are partly covered by non-cash contributions, the part which is not covered by a non-cash contribution must be paid for in money before the company is entered in the register (Article 191, LCC). If shares are sold above the lowest issue value (i.e., for a premium), the entire premium must be paid in before the company is entered in the register. If a company is formed by one founder, that founder must pay for the shares in full or provide appropriate collateral to the company before the company is entered in the register.

XI. Nominal or No-par Value Shares

187. According to the LCC (Article 172), shares can be either of nominal value or of no-par value shares. The company may not have two forms of shares at the same time. Shares with nominal amounts must be denominated in units of EUR 1 or multiples thereof. The proportion of the subscribed capital of each share must equal the ratio which that share bears to the total number of shares subscribed No-par value shares do not have a nominal value. The proportion of each no-par value share must equal the ratio which that share bears to the total number of shares subscribed. The value of each no-par value share related to the subscribed capital (the related value) must not be lower than EUR 1 (Article 170). Shares with a different nominal amount and no-par value shares with a related value of less than

EUR 1 are null and void (Article 172/4, LCC). The issuers are jointly and severally liable for damage arising from any such issue.

By means of an amendment to the Articles of Association and subject to unchanged subscribed capital, the shares may be split up or split into several parts. By means of an amendment to the Articles of Association and subject to unchanged subscribed capital, shares are combined into shares with a higher nominal value or fewer parts. However, such an operation is subject to the consent of all the shareholders (Article 172/4, LCC).

XII. Contributions in Kind

188. Contribution in kind can be a non-cash contribution and a non-cash acquisition. If shareholders make contributions otherwise than by paying in the issue value of the shares in money, that would be a non-cash contribution. But on the other hand, if the company acquires an existing or future establishment or other items of property, that would be a non-cash acquisition. In the case of a non-cash contribution or a non-cash acquisition, the Articles of Association must determine (Article 187, LCC):

- the subject of the non-cash contribution or non-cash acquisition;
- the person from whom the company acquires it; and
- the number of shares and, in the case of shares with nominal value, also the nominal value represented by the non-cash contribution or non-cash acquisition. Only items of property or rights whose economic value can be established may be considered a non-cash contribution or a non-cash acquisition. The duty to perform a service cannot be considered a non-cash contribution or a non-cash acquisition. In the case of non-cash contributions, a non-cash acquisition and cash payments, the company must be allowed to permanently and freely dispose of them from the time the company is entered in the register.

189. LCC-1B -The Act amending Law on Commercial Companies [Official Gazette of the RS], No. 68/08 of 8 July 2008, permits public LLC to allot shares for consideration other than in cash without a special expert valuation in cases in which there is a clear point of reference for the valuation of such consideration (the fair value is determined for a date not more than six months before the effective date of the asset contribution and the valuation has been performed in accordance with generally accepted valuation standards and principles); the right of minority shareholders to require such valuation is still guaranteed.[78]

78. Directive 2006/68/EC of the European Parliament and of the Council of 6 Sep. 2006 amending Council Directive 77/91/EEC as regards the formation of public limited liability companies and the maintenance and alteration of their capital.

XIII. Special Benefits and Formation Expenses

190. According to the LCC, special benefits for particular shareholders or third parties, stating the person entitled to these benefits, may only be determined by the Articles of Association. Only the Articles of Association may determine the costs which the company must reimburse to the shareholders or other persons as an allowance or as a consideration for attending to the formation of the company. If special benefits or costs are not provided for in the Articles of Association, any contracts or legal act granting such benefits or providing for the payment of costs have no legal effect against the company. This may not be remedied by amendment to the Articles of Association after the company has been entered in the register. The provisions regarding special benefits and costs may only be amended after five years have elapsed since the entry of the company in the register (Article 186, LCC).

§3. Essential Elements of the Legal Person

I. Legal Personality

191. According to the LCC, all companies (including of course a PLC) are legal persons The definition of legal personality is determined by law. As legal persons, companies may:

- own movable and immovable property;
- acquire rights and assume obligations; and
- sue and be sued. All companies, including PLC acquire legal personality upon their entry in the register. Prior to entry in the register, the rules governing a contract of members in civil law apply to relations between the members (Articles 3, 4, 5 LCC).

II. Liability

192. The LCC (Article 7) lays down the provisions regarding liability of companies. It is determined, that companies (including PLC) are liable for their liabilities with all their assets. Shareholders of PLC are not liable for their liabilities.

Disregard of the legal person (lifting the veil) is established for companies in general in the LCC, Article 8, as follows.

193. Notwithstanding the provision that members are not liable, the shareholders will also be liable for the liabilities of the company in the following cases:

- if they abused the company as a legal person in order to attain an aim which is forbidden to them as individuals;
- if they abused the company as a legal person, thereby causing damage to its creditors;

- if in violation of the law they used the assets of the company as their own personal assets; or
- if for their own benefit or for the benefit of some other person they reduced the assets of the company even if they knew or should have known that thereby the company would not be capable of meeting its liabilities to third persons.

III. Seat

194. The LCC (Article 29) deals with registered office generally for all companies. The registered office of a company is the location entered in the register as the registered office of the company. The location where a company pursues its activities or the location where it predominantly carries out its operations, or where its management operates, may be determined as its registered office.

195. A company may have branches which are separate from the registered office of the company. Branches must be entered in the register. Branches are not legal persons but may carry out all operations which the company may carry out.

IV. Name

A. *Principle of Exclusivity and Distinction*

196. The LCC (Articles 12–28. Of the LCC) deals with the registered name generally for all companies, including, of course PLC. The registered name is the name under which the company operates. A registered name must be clearly distinct from the registered names of all other companies (principle of exclusivity). Affiliated companies may use common elements in their registered names.

B. *Elements of the Registered Name*

197. The registered name contains at least one element distinguishing it from the registered names of other companies and a designation indicating what type of company it is. The registered name must contain:

(1) an indication of the activity pursued by the company; and
(2) additional elements which characterize the company in more detail. However, these elements may not be such as to cause misunderstanding as to the type and scope of its operations or as could lead to a confusion with the registered name or distinguishing symbol of another person or infringe the rights of other persons.

198. As for additional elements of the registered name, the following rules apply:

(1) Names of foreign countries: A registered name may not contain the names or symbols of foreign countries or international organizations.

The rule referring to the name and surname of the person has also changed by the LCC-1 J 2017. It is since then stipulated, that the name and surname or pseudonym of a historical or other famous person may be entered in the company only with its permission; if she has already died, with the permission of her spouse and relatives up to the third generation in a straight line, and her parents, if they are still alive. Permission of the minister responsible for public administration is no more required.

(2) A registered name may not contain words or symbols which:
- contravene the law or morals;
- contain trademarks or registered signs, which are protected under the regulations governing trademarks (LCC-1I of 2015); or
- contain or imitate official symbols.

C. *Use of a Registered Name*

199. The use of a registered name is compulsory. In its operations, a company must use its registered name in the form in which it is entered in the register. A company may also use an abbreviated registered name. It must contain at least an element distinguishing it from the registered names of other companies and a designation indicating what type of company it is. The abbreviated registered name must be entered in the register.

D. *Language of a Registered Name*

200. The elements of the registered name, indicating the activity and the Company must be in the Slovenian language (LCC-1I of 2015). Additional elements of the registered name, in addition to the letters of the Slovenian alphabet may also contain the letters X, Y, W and Q. An additional element of the registered name may use the words, that include other letters, if it:

- correspond to the registered names, the names and surname of the shareholders, which are an integral part of the registered name; or
- correspond to registered trademarks (LCC-1I of 2015). A translation of a registered name into a foreign language may only be used together with the registered name in Slovene.

E. *An Intended Registered Name*

201. Anyone may require the registration body to enter a registered name in the register without the company being founded at the same time (an intended registered name). An intended registered name must conform to the provisions laid down in the LCC regarding registered names. The registration body deletes an intended registered name from the register ex officio if the person who registered the intended registered name does not register a company with that name within one year of registration of the intended registered name.

F. Protection of a Registered Name

202. The registration body must ex officio reject a proposal for the entry in the court register of a registered name which:

- contravenes the provisions laid down in the LCC; or
- is not clearly distinct from registered names of companies or other legal entities (LCC-1 I, 2015) already registered in the Republic of Slovenia.

203. A company which believes that the registered name of another company is not clearly distinct from its own previously registered name, or if another company uses its registered name improperly, has the right to sue (no later than three years after the registration):

- for an order that the name not be used;
- for an order that the name be deleted from the register; or
- for compensation.

Since LCC-1 I, 2015, this protection refers to trademarks or unregistered signs, which are protected under the regulations governing the trademark. There are additional provisions contained in the regulations regarding protection of competition and other regulations for protecting registered names.

V. Objects Clause

204. According to the LCC (Article 6, activity), companies may pursue as their activity all operations other than those which, by law, may not be pursued as commercial operations. The law may provide that certain commercial transactions may only be pursued by companies as determined by law or only by certain types of companies or other organizations (e.g., banks, insurance companies, brokerage companies).

205. Companies may only pursue commercial transactions within the framework of the activity which is entered in the register. A company may also pursue all other transactions which are necessary for its existence and for pursuing its activity but which do not constitute the direct pursuit of the activity.

206. Legal transactions concluded by a company with third persons which go outside the framework of the activity entered in the register or otherwise permitted transactions are valid unless the third person knew or should have known about the transgression. Not acting in good faith is a condition of ultra vires. The fact of the activity being stated in the register does not imply that the third person knew or should have known about the transgression.

207. A company may take up and pursue its activity when it is entered in the register. If another law lays down special conditions for taking up and pursuing a particular activity, the company may take up and pursue that activity when it meets that special condition. If another law provides that a company may take up and pursue a particular activity when the competent State body has issued a decision establishing that the company meets the conditions for taking up and pursuing the activity concerned (e.g., concession), the company may take up and pursue that activity when the competent body issues a decision to that effect.

§4. Capital and Shares

I. Different Kinds and Meanings of Capital

A. Capital of a PLC: General

208. Apart from short-term borrowing, a company raises its working capital by the issue of shares or debentures. The term 'capital' has a variety of different meanings according to the context in which it is used. Generally, the expression 'capital' refers to the amount of money or consideration in kind, invested in the company so that it can carry on its activities. The capital clause in the Articles of Association must state the amount of capital with which the company is registered (under the LCC: subscribed capital), giving details of the number of shares and the type of shares of the company (Article 183 of the LCC).

209. The following different terms are used in theory to denote different aspects of share capital:

- Working capital is money and other assets raised by the company to carry on business.
- Share capital is that part of the working capital raised by the issue of shares.
- Nominal or registered capital means the sum mentioned in the capital clause of the Articles of Association. It means the amount of capital the company is authorized by its memorandum to raise by the issue of shares (this is sometimes referred to as 'authorized' capital).
- Issued share capital means that part of the nominal capital which has been issued, the balance being referred to as unissued share capital. It means that part of the nominal or registered capital, which has been offered for subscription to members and also includes shares allotted to members for consideration in kind.
- Loan capital is the term sometimes used to indicate that part of the working capital raised by the issue of debentures.

B. Rules Referring to Subscribed Capital in the LCC

210. Subscribed capital means that part of the issued capital which has been subscribed or taken up by purchasers of shares in the company and which has been allotted. The following rules of the LCC refer to subscribed capital:

(a) Among other matters, the Articles of Association must determine the amount of the subscribed capital.
(b) The subscribed capital of a PLC is divided into shares. Subscribed capital must be denominated in euros.
(c) At least one-third of the subscribed capital must comprise shares paid for with money.
(d) The amount of subscribed capital and any authorized capital must be entered into the register.
(e) The proportion of shares with a nominal value in the subscribed capital must be determined according to the ratio between its nominal value and the total value of the subscribed capital.
(f) Priority shares may not comprise more than half of a company's subscribed capital.
(g) Own shares, LCC-1B -The Act amending Law on Commercial Companies [Official Gazette of the Republic of Slovenia], No. 68/08 of 8 July 2008,[79] permits a company to acquire its own shares, either itself or through a person acting in his own name but on the company's behalf, subject to the following conditions:
   - authorization must be given by the general meeting, which determines the terms and conditions of such acquisitions, and, in particular, the maximum number of shares to be acquired, the duration of the period for which the authorization is given;
   - the nominal value including shares previously acquired by the company and held by it, and shares acquired by a person acting in his own name but on the company's behalf, may not exceed 10% of the subscribed capital;
   - the power of the company to acquire its own shares, the maximum number of shares to be acquired, the duration of the period for which the power is given and the maximum or minimum consideration are laid down in the statutes of the company;
   - the shareholders' shares in the profit for appropriation are determined in proportion to their share of the subscribed capital. If contributions to the subscribed capital are not paid in full or are not paid up for all shares in the same proportion, the shareholders' shares in the profit for appropriation are determined in proportion to the payments made;
   - different kinds of minority rights are subject to one-twentieth or one-tenth of subscribed capital (e.g., to convene a general meeting, to put items on the

79. Implemented Directive 2006/68/EC of the European Parliament and of the Council of 6 Sep. 2006 amending Council Directive 77/91/EEC as regards the formation of public limited liability companies and the maintenance and alteration of their capital.

agenda, to apply to the court, special or extraordinary audit, priority voting on electoral proposals by minority shareholders);
- rules on different kinds of qualified majorities needed for voting at general meetings for different kinds of decisions are defined in relation to subscribed capital;
- complex rules apply to measures to increase or reduce the subscribed capital;
- companies must create statutory reserves in an amount such that the aggregate of statutory reserves and capital reserves equals 10% or a higher percentage of the subscribed capital determined in the Articles of Association.

C. Called-Up and Paid in Capital in the LCC

211. Called-up capital means the total amount of called-up capital on the shares issued and subscribed by the shareholders on capital account.

For the shareholders who do not pay on time, a further period can be determined with the warning that their shares and payments made, will be withdrawn after its expiry. Extended deadline should be published and communicated to each shareholder by registered letter. If shareholder's contribution despite the repeated call is not paid, the company may withdraw his shares and payments made. Instead of withdrawn shares, the company issues new ones (LCC-1I 2015, Article 224).

212. In addition, the LCC also mentions paid in capital as the total amount of called-up share capital, which was actually paid to the company by the members. It means the amount which has actually been received by the company in payment for issued shares, the balance still to be paid being referred to as 'unpaid' or 'uncalled' capital. Among other matters, the Articles of Association must, according to the LCC, determine the amount of paid in capital as at the day of the company's registration and the paid in capital at the time.

II. Alteration of Capital Requirements

A. Measures to Increase the Subscribed Capital: General

213. A decision to increase the subscribed capital must be passed by shareholders with a majority of at least three-quarters of the subscribed capital represented in the voting. The Articles of Association may stipulate a different majority but not less than a majority of the subscribed capital represented in the voting (Articles 333–342, LCC).

214. If non-cash contributions are being invested, a resolution on the increase in the subscribed capital must determine the object of the contribution, the person from whom the company acquires that object, and the number of shares which must be provided in exchange for the non-cash contribution. An increase in the subscribed capital through non-cash contributions must be examined by one or more auditors.

215. The management and the chairman of the supervisory board must notify a resolution on an increase in the subscribed capital for entry in the register. The increase in the subscribed capital takes effect on the day it is entered in the register. Rights to the new interests may not be transferred, and new shares or interim certificates may not be issued before the increase in the subscribed capital is entered in the register.

216. In increasing the subscribed capital, LCC-1B[80] permits public LLC to allot shares for consideration other than in cash without a special expert valuation when the fair value is determined for a date not more than six months before the effective date of the asset contribution and the valuation has been performed in accordance with generally accepted valuation standards and principles.[81]

B. A Conditional Increase in the Subscribed Capital

217. A general meeting (with a majority of three-quarters or more) may only decide to conditionally increase the subscribed capital (not to exceed half the subscribed capital) for the following reasons (Article 343, LCC):

- in order for the holders of convertible bonds to exercise their right to exchange them for shares, or for the exercise of a right of pre-emption to acquire new shares;
- in order to prepare for the merger of several companies or to provide compensation to shareholders in connection with the restructuring of companies;
- in order for the company's employees to exercise their right to receive new shares in exchange for monetary claims accruing to them as their share of the profits as guaranteed to them by the company; and
- to ensure option entitlements to purchase shares which the company has provided to members of the management or supervisory body and employees of the company or an affiliated company.

For the purpose of ensuring the option rights to purchase shares, conditional increase of the share capital may amount to only 10% of the share capital which exists between the conclusion of the conditional capital increase (LCC-1I, 2015, Article 343/1).

218. The resolution must also determine the purpose of the conditional increase, the persons entitled to participate and the amount of the increase.

80. LCC-1B -the Act amending Law on Commercial Companies. Official Gazette of the RS, No. 68/08 of 8 Jul. 2008.
81. Directive 2006/68/EC of the European Parliament and of the Council of 6 Sep. 2006 amending Council Directive 77/91/EEC as regards the formation of public limited liability companies and the maintenance and alteration of their capital.

C. Authorized Capital

219. The Articles of Association (or an amendment to the articles) may authorize the management, for a maximum of five years after the entry of the company in the register, to increase the subscribed capital up to a certain value (authorized capital) by issuing new shares in exchange for contributions. In order for the resolution to be valid, a majority of at least three-quarters of the subscribed capital (the articles may stipulate a larger majority) is required. The amount of authorized capital may not exceed half of the subscribed capital existing at the time the authorization was given (Article 353, LCC).

220. New shares may only be issued with the approval of the supervisory board. New shares are issued on the basis of authorization without an extraordinary resolution by the general meeting. The authorization may determine that the management may decide on the exclusion of the priority right to new shares.

Article 356a of the LCC-1 regulates the issue of shares against contributions in kind without audit. It is laid down, that for the issue of shares against contributions in kind, which need not be inspected by the auditor, the provisions of the LCC-1 referring to establishing procedure apply (first to the fourth paragraph and the first to the third sentence of the fifth paragraph of Article 194 of the LCC-1).

Auditor to review the issue of shares for cash consideration may be, as an exception, appointed by the court at the proposal of shareholders whose total shares amount to at least one-twentieth of the share capital on the date of the resolution to issue shares auditor. Shareholders must remain holders of shares until the proposal is brought to the court (LCC-1I, 2015, Article 356a/5).

D. Increase in the Subscribed Capital from the Company's Assets

221. The general meeting may decide (only after the adoption of the annual report for the last financial year) to increase the subscribed capital by converting other capital items owned by the company into subscribed capital. Reserves (including revaluation reserves, *see* LCC-1I, 2015, Article 359/1, p. 5) and profits can be converted into subscribed capital.

222. Own capital items to be converted into subscribed capital must appear in the last annual balance sheet or interim balance sheet. An interim balance sheet for this purpose must be compiled in accordance with the provisions of the LCC concerning the compilation of an annual balance sheet.

223. It is not permitted to convert other items of capital into subscribed capital if a loss is brought forward or a net loss for the financial year is disclosed in the balance sheet which is the basis for the conversion.

224. The increase in the subscribed capital takes effect when the resolution on the increase in the subscribed capital is registered. Once the resolution has been entered in the register, it is deemed that the new shares have been fully paid up.

225. Shareholders receive new shares in proportion to their contributions to the existing subscribed capital of the company. After the entry of a resolution for an increase in the subscribed capital by issuing new shares in the register, the management must immediately publish an invitation to the shareholders to take up their new shares.

E. Measures to Reduce the Subscribed Capital: General

226. For a reduction in the subscribed capital to be valid a majority of at least three-quarters of the subscribed capital is required (the articles may stipulate a larger majority). The resolution must determine the reason and the method by which the subscribed capital is to be reduced. The reduction in the subscribed capital takes effect when the resolution on the reduction in the subscribed capital is entered in the register. The resolution must be published Articles 372–383, LCC).

227. Protection of creditors is regulated by the LCC. Creditors whose claims originated prior to the announcement of the entry in the register of the resolution for the reduction in the subscribed capital must be given security to the extent that they cannot be repaid, if they register their claims within six months of the announcement. The creditors must be informed of this right in the announcement of the entry in the register.

228. Payments to shareholders must be made on the basis of a reduction in the subscribed capital only after six months have passed since the announcement of the entry in the register and after creditors who registered in time, are guaranteed repayment or insurance. Creditors may demand insurance even if the shareholders are not paid.

LCC-1I, 2015 (new Article 376), brings here an important change; namely, it explicitly stipulates, that by merging the shares, shareholder of the company cannot be excluded. It is necessary to establish the legal community of those shareholders, resulting from the reduced share capital. Persons participating in the legal community, have to determine one of them, who will take over a share. Call for acquiring the shares must contain a warning that if the shares which will not be acquired in this way, they will be sold for the account of the persons involved in the legal community, according to the official stock price through a broker or public auction, if there are no stock market prices.

F. Simplified Reduction in the Subscribed Capital

229. A reduction in the subscribed capital which is intended to cover a loss brought forward or a net loss for the financial year or for the transfer of amounts to the capital reserves may be carried out in a simplified form. The resolution for the reduction in the subscribed capital must state the purpose of the reduction. A simplified reduction in the subscribed capital is allowed if:

- there are no profit reserves or they are released beforehand, apart from statutory reserves and capital reserves, the sum of which equals 10%, or more of the remaining subscribed capital as determined by the Articles of Association, after the reduction of capital; or
- net profit for the year and net profit brought forward no longer exist (Article 372, LCC).

G. Reduction in the Subscribed Capital by Means of a Withdrawal of Shares

230. A company may withdraw shares compulsorily (the provisions on an ordinary reduction applies) or through acquisition by the company. A compulsory withdrawal is permitted only if it was provided for or permitted in the original Articles of Association or through an amendment to the Articles of Association before the shares were acquired or subscribed to. A resolution by a general meeting is not required if a compulsory withdrawal of shares is provided for in the Articles of Association. In the application of the provisions for an ordinary reduction in the subscribed capital, a decision by the management to withdraw shares is sufficient instead of a resolution by a general meeting (Article 381, LCC).

H. Preferential Right of Subscription

231. The LCC lays down priority rights to new shares in the case of an increase of the subscribed capital. Existing shareholders have a priority right to subscribe for new shares in proportion to their contribution to the subscribed capital. The time limit for the exercise of this right must be at least fourteen days.

According to LCC-1I, 2015, Article 337/2, management must publish the issue price of new shares or the criteria by which this amount is calculated and the time limit for the exercise of this right (at least fourteen days). If the criteria are published only, management should publish the issue amount not later than three days before the deadline for the implementation of priority right.

232. Only a resolution for the increase in the subscribed capital may partly or wholly exclude a priority right. In such a case, the resolution must be passed by a majority of at least three-quarters of the subscribed capital represented in the voting (the articles may stipulate a larger majority and lay down other requirements).

233. A resolution fully or partially excluding a priority right may only be adopted if the exclusion was published. The management must submit a written report to the general meeting on the grounded reasons for the full or partial exclusion of the priority right.

I. Issues of Shares at a Discount and at a Premium

234. As far as the issue value of shares is concerned, the following rules are applied:

- The share may not be issued for an amount (issue value) which is lower than the nominal amount and in the case of no-par value share lower than the related share (lowest issue value).
- A share issued for a greater amount is always permitted.

235. Shares may not be issued at a discount. If the company agrees to issue shares for less than their nominal value and to treat the shares as fully paid, this is wholly ineffective.

236. There is, of course, no objection to the issue of shares at a premium, but any premiums received must be set aside in a separate share premium account.

III. Classes of Shares

A. Bearer-Nominative

237. According to the Article 175, LCC, shares can be made out to their bearer or to a particular party (bearer and registered shares). In some cases, shares must be made out to a party. For example, shares must be made out to a party if they are issued before full payment of the value thereof. The amount of partial payments must be stated on the share.

238. Where so provided in the Articles of Association, a bearer share may be converted into a registered share or a registered share into a bearer share upon request from the shareholder.

B. Ordinary and Priority Shares

239. Depending on the Articles of Incorporation, shares can be issued as ordinary or priority shares (Article 176, LCC). Shares are classified as ordinary or priority shares according to the rights attached to them. According to the LCC, ordinary shares are shares which grant the holder:

(a) the right to participate in the management of the company;
(b) the right to a part of the profit (dividend); and
(c) the right to a corresponding part of the residue of assets after the liquidation or bankruptcy of the company. Priority shares are shares which confer upon their holders certain priority rights, such as:
    - priority in the payment of predetermined sums or percentages of the nominal value of the shares or of profits;

- priority payment upon the liquidation of the company; and
- other rights set out in the Articles of Association of the company.

240. In accordance with the resolution passed in respect of the share issue, a cumulative priority share confers upon its holder the prior right to payment of all outstanding dividends before dividends of any sort are paid to holders of ordinary shares in accordance with a resolution for the distribution of profits. In addition to the prior right to dividends, a participating priority share also confers upon its holder the right to payment of dividends accruing to holders of ordinary shares in accordance with a resolution for the distribution of profits.

241. Voting rights may be excluded from shares which grant a prior right in respect of the distribution of profits (non-voting priority shares, LCC, Article 178). Non-voting priority shares carry all rights which a shareholder derives from shares except voting rights. If the preferential amount is not paid within one year or is not paid in full and the outstanding amount is not paid the following year, priority shareholders have the right to vote until the outstanding amount is paid. (So long as this situation exists, priority shares are taken into account when calculating the majority of the capital).

242. The consent of all the priority shareholders is required for a resolution limiting or annulling the priority to be valid. Priority shareholders must also give their consent to a resolution for the issue of priority shares which, in the distribution of profits or the assets of the company have priority over non-voting priority shares or which are equated with them.

243. Non-voting ordinary shares are not known under the LCC, but according to the LCC, the law may determine that ordinary shares are issued without voting rights.

C. Deferred Shares

244. Deferred shares are not known under the LCC.

D. Non-voting

245. Non-voting ordinary shares are not regulated in the LCC, but according to the LCC (Article 317), the law may determine that ordinary shares may be issued without voting rights. Under the Article 178 of the LCC only preferred shares can, but need not necessarily be, non-voting shares, if so provided in the Articles of Incorporation. The LCC, in regulating voting rights, stipulates the following rules:

- Each share shall confer one voting right.

– Only priority shares may be issued without voting rights. It is necessary to add that non-voting shares may not comprise more than half of a company's subscribed capital.

246. To summarize, voting rights may only be excluded from shares which grant a priority right in the distribution of profits (non-voting priority shares). Non-voting priority shares carry all rights which a shareholder derives from shares except voting rights.

247. If the preferential amount is not paid within one year or is not paid in full and the outstanding balance is not paid the following year, priority shareholders have the right to vote until the outstanding amount is paid. In this case, priority shares are taken into account when calculating the majority of the capital required by law or the Articles of Association.

248. In order for a resolution limiting or annulling their priority to be valid, the consent of all the priority shareholders is required. It must be approved by an extraordinary resolution passed at a separate meeting of priority shareholders with a majority of at least three-quarters. Priority shareholders must also give their consent (with some exceptions) to a resolution for the issuing of priority shares which, in the distribution of profits or on the liquidation of the company, have priority over non-voting priority shares or which are equated with them.

E. Multiple Voting

249. Multiple voting shares may not be issued under the LCC. It is explicitly forbidden (Article 178/2 LCC) to issue shares which would confer a different number of votes for the same proportion of subscribed capital.

F. Interim Certificate, Confirmation of Shares Issued

250. The LCC in Article 181, regulates so-called interim certificates. An Interim certificate constitutes confirmation of participation which is delivered to shareholders before the shares are issued. Interim certificates must be made out to a particular party. Bearer interim certificates are null and void. The issuers are jointly and severally liable for damage arising from any such issue. The LCC regulates confirmation of shares issued: the company can issue to shareholders confirmation of the number of their shares. In the case of shares with a nominal amount, such confirmation must clearly state the nominal amount of the shares. A confirmation may only be used as evidence in exercising the right to vote at a general meeting of shareholders.

G. Book-Entry Form, Dematerialized Securities

251. The LCC stipulates that shares must be issued in book-entry form (Article 181). In respect of shares in book-entry form, the provisions of the DSL-1[82] apply. DSL-1 transposes into the legal order of the Republic of Slovenia, Directive 98/26/EC of the European Parliament and of the Council of 19 May 1998 on settlement finality in payment and securities settlement systems (OJ L No. 166, 11. 6. 1998, p. 45), last amended by Regulation (EU) No. Regulation (EC) No. 909/2014 of the European Parliament and of the Council of 23 July 2014 on improving the organization of securities settlement in the EU and on central depot companies and amending Directives 98/26/EC and 2014/65/EU and Regulation (EU) 236/2012 (OJ L No. 257, 28. 8. 2014, p. 1) and Directive 2009/44/EC of the European Parliament and of the Council of 6 May 2009 amending Directive 98/26/EC on settlement finality in payment and securities settlement systems and Directive 2002/47/EC on financial collateral arrangements as regards related systems and bank loans (OJ L No. 146 of 10 June 2009, p. 37).

252. The DSL-1 regulates dematerialized securities, their transfer, the fulfilment of the obligations contained therein, the central register and access to data kept in the central registry.

253. A dematerialized security is a statement of the issuer thereof, entered in the central register of dematerialized securities, by which the issuer undertakes to fulfil all obligations under the security to a person who is entered into the central register as a legal holder of the security. Dematerialized security incurs when it is first entered in the central register at the account of the holder (hereinafter: the holder) and exists until it is deleted from the central registry.

254. The central register of dematerialized securities is a central electronic database into which the rights arising from dematerialized securities, holders of those rights at any given time and any possible rights of third parties to such securities, are entered. The central Register is an informatized record of dematerialized securities, rights and obligations arising therefrom, their respective holders and burdens on them, and managed by a central securities depository.

255. A central securities depository is a legal person who, in accordance with Regulation (EU) No. Regulation (EC) No. 909/2014 of the European Parliament

82. Dematerialized Securities Law – DSL-1, – DZNVP-1 (Official Gazette of the Republic of Slovenia, No. 75/15 of 8 Oct. 2015):

- Act Amending the Dematerialized Securities Law – DSL-1A, – ZNVP-1A (Official Gazette of the Republic of Slovenia, No. 5/17 of 3 Feb. 2017).
- Decision to annul the first and second sentences of the fourth paragraph of Article 48 of the Dematerialized Securities Act (Official Gazette of the Republic of Slovenia, No. 15/18 of 7 Mar. 2018).
- Act Amending the Dematerialized Securities Act Law – DSL-1B, – ZNVP-1B (Official Gazette of the Republic of Slovenia, No. 43/19 of 28.

and of the Council of 23 July 2014 on improving the organization of securities settlement in the EU and on central depot companies and amending Directives 98/26/EC and 2014/65/EU and Regulation (EU) 236/2012 (OJ L No. 257 of 28. 8. 2014, p. 1), performs the activity of a central depository company. A member of the central securities depository is a person who, in accordance with the rules of the central securities depository, has acquired the position of a member of the central securities depository.

256. The keeping of the central register by the CCDC is monitored by the SEA.

H. Debentures, Convertible Bonds and Dividend Bonds

257. A debenture-holder is a creditor of the company and his debenture is merely an acknowledgement by the company of its indebtedness.

258. Convertible debentures may be issued, giving the holder the right to convert the debentures into shares on specified terms on a fixed date.

259. The LCC in Article 371, regulates the following types of bonds and rights:

- bonds granting the holder the right to convert them into shares (convertible bonds);
- bonds granting the holder the right of pre-emption to acquire shares;
- bonds with which the rights of the bondholders are connected to the dividends of shareholders (dividend bonds); and
- special rights to participation in profits.

260. These types of bonds (rights) may only be issued on the basis of a resolution passed by a general meeting with a required majority of at least three-quarters of the subscribed capital represented at the voting. The Articles of Association may stipulate a different majority of the capital and lay down other requirements. The company's shareholders enjoy the right of pre-emption of the bonds.

261. Authorization may be given to the management to issue convertible bonds for a maximum of five years. The management and the chairman of the supervisory board must notify the resolution approving the issue of convertible bonds and a statement regarding their issue for entry in the register. The notification of the resolution and the statement must be published.

I. Acquisition of Shares by the Company Itself

262. In principle, the acquisition of its own shares is prohibited (LCC, Articles 247–252). The company cannot purchase its own shares or those of its holding company. This prohibition prevents the company from utilizing its own capital for the acquisition of its shares, even where such a purchase is authorized by its memorandum.

263. The company may not give financial assistance for the purchase of its own shares. The prohibition applies both to the making of a loan directly to the intending purchaser and to the giving of security to a third party in consideration of such a loan.

264. However, as an exemption, a company may acquire its own shares on the basis of authorization by a general meeting convened to consider the purchase of its own shares. The authorization may be valid for eighteen months and must determine the minimum and maximum purchase price for the acquisition of these shares, as well as the proportion of shares which may be purchased, which may not exceed 10% of the subscribed capital.

265. A company may also acquire its own shares in the following cases:

- if the acquisition is necessary in order to prevent serious and immediate damage being caused to the company (may not exceed 10% of the subscribed capital);
- if the shares have to be offered for sale to the employees of the company or of an affiliated company (may not exceed 10% of the subscribed capital);
- if it acquires the shares in order to provide compensation for the shareholders in accordance with the provisions of the LCC (may not exceed 10% of the subscribed capital);
- if it acquires the shares without payment;
- if a bank, insurance company or another financial organization obtains shares with the purchase committee;
- on the basis of universal legal succession; or
- pursuant to a resolution by a general meeting for the withdrawal of shares in accordance with the provisions on reduction of the subscribed capital.

266. The company may not acquire its own shares exclusively for trading purposes. The general meeting may authorize the management to withdraw the company's shares without a further decision on a reduction in the subscribed capital. Such acquisition by a company of its own shares is only permitted if the company acquires the shares by creating reserves for its own shares without reducing the subscribed capital or reserves. A legal transaction by means of which a company secures an advance or a loan for the acquisition of shares is null and void (this does not apply to the current legal transactions of financial organizations in the ordinary course of business or to transactions by means of which the employees of a company or of an affiliated company acquire shares). The company may not derive rights from its own shares.

IV. Transfer of Shares

A. *The Manner of Transfer of Shares*

267. According to the LCC (Articles 236–240), registered shares are transferred by endorsement. The regulations regarding bills of exchange apply *mutatis mutandis* to an endorsement.

268. The DL regulates the transfer of registered shares issued in book-entry form.

B. *Permission for the Transfer of Shares: General*

269. The Articles of Association may limit the transferability of registered shares by determining, that such transfer requires the company's permission for the transfer of shares.

A decision regarding permission for the transfer of shares must be made by the company's management (or, if provided by the articles, by the company's supervisory board or a general meeting).

C. *Permission for the Transfer of Shares Not Traded on the Regulated Market*

270. When registered shares are not traded on the regulated market and the Articles of Association stipulate that the company's permission is required in order to transfer its shares, the Articles of Association must lay down cogent reasons for the company to refuse permission for their transfer (i.e., in cases where such transfer could jeopardize the achievement of the company's goals or its economic independence).

271. The company may require persons seeking permission to acquire shares to state whether they intend to acquire the shares in their own name and for their own account. In such a case, the company may also refuse to give permission for the transfer of shares if persons requiring permission for their transfer do not state explicitly that they intend to acquire the shares in their own name and for their own account.

272. When the legal basis for the acquisition of shares is inheritance, division of community property of spouses or a sale pursuant to a compulsory execution procedure, the company may refuse to give permission for a transfer of shares only if it pays the market value to the shareholder who wants to transfer the shares.

273. In respect of the transfer of registered shares not traded on the regulated market, the Articles of Association may not lay down stricter conditions than those applicable to the regulated market. The effect of the requirement of permission for the transfer of shares not traded on the regulated market is that until the company grants permission for such a transfer, the acquirer of these shares does not have any rights against the company.

D. Permission for the Transfer of Shares Traded on the Regulated Market

274. The regulations for transfer of shares are different when the Articles of Association stipulate that the company's permission is required in the case of registered shares traded on the regulated market. In this case, the only circumstance which the Articles of Association may determine as a good reason for refusal of permission is that with the acquisition of these shares the transferee's shareholding would exceed a certain proportion of the voting rights or a certain proportion of the capital of the company.

275. The company may require the acquirer to state whether he intends to acquire the shares in his own name and for his own account. In such case, the company may also refuse to give permission for the transfer of shares if the acquirer does not state explicitly that he intends to acquire the shares in his own name and for his own account.

276. When the legal basis for the acquisition of shares is inheritance, division of community property of spouses or a sale pursuant to a compulsory execution procedure, the company may not refuse to give permission for the transfer of shares.

277. In respect of the transfer of registered shares traded on the regulated market, the Articles of Association may not lay down conditions stricter than those prescribed by law.

278. The effect of permission for the transfer of shares traded on the regulated market is different from those described above. An acquirer-traded shares whose transfer is refused acquires property rights derived from the shares from the moment they are acquired and the management rights only on permission from the company for the transfer of the shares.

279. Until the company issues permission for the transfer of shares, the acquirer may not, on the basis of these shares, exercise voting rights or other rights associated with voting rights but may exercise all other rights derived from the shares, including the priority right to subscribe for new shares.

E. Registration

280. The rules on entry in the share register are laid down in the LCC. It is stipulated that registered shares (also applies to interim certificates) must be entered in the share register together with the holder's designation or the name, surname and address of the holder (Article 235, LCC).

281. In relations with the company in respect of registered shares, the shareholder is taken to be the person entered in the share register as the shareholder.

282. If, in the opinion of a company, a person is wrongly entered in the share register as a shareholder, the company may only delete the entry if it advises the shareholder in advance of its intention to delete the entry and gives the shareholder a period within which to object. If the shareholder lodges an objection in time, the entry may not be deleted from the share register.

283. Every shareholder must be given access to the share register upon request.

V. Securities Market Regulation

A. The Legal Framework for Securities Market Legislation

284. The following legislation establishes Slovene securities market regulation: The Law on Markets in Financial Instruments (MIFL),[83] Investment Trusts and Management Companies Law[84] Takeover Law (TL),[85] e BL.

---

83. Law on Market in Financial Instruments – ZTFI (Official Gazette of the Republic of Slovenia, No. 67/07 of 27. 7. 2007):

- Correction of the Law on Market in Financial Instruments – ZTFI (Official Gazette of the Republic of Slovenia, No. 100/07 of 2 Nov. 2007).
- Law Amending the Market in Financial Instruments Market – ZTFI-A (Official Gazette of the Republic of Slovenia, No. 69/08 of 8 Jul. 2008).
- Law Amending the Market in Financial Instruments – ZTFI-B (Official Gazette of the Republic of Slovenia, No. 40/09 of 29 May 2009).
- Law Amending the Market in Financial Instruments – ZTFI-C (Official Gazette of the Republic of Slovenia, No. 88/10 of 5 Nov. 2010).
- Law on Market in Financial Instruments – official consolidated text – ZTFI-UPB3 (Official Gazette of the Republic of Slovenia, No. 108/10 of 30 Dec. 2010).
- Law Amending the Market in Financial Instruments Law – ZTFI-D (Official Gazette RS, No. 78/11 of 5 Oct. 2011).
- Law Amending the Law on Market in Financial Instruments – ZTFI-E (Official Gazette of the Republic of Slovenia, No. 55/12 of 20. 7. 2012).
- Law Amending the Law on Market in Financial Instruments – ZTFI-F (Official Gazette of the Republic of Slovenia, No. 30/16 of 25 Apr. 2016).
- Law Amending the Law on Market in Financial Instruments – ZTFI-G (Official Gazette of the Republic of Slovenia, No. 9/17 of 24 Feb. 2017).
- Law on Market in Financial Instruments MFIL-1, Slovene ZTFI-1 (Official Gazette of the Republic of Slovenia, No. 77/18 of 30 Nov. 2018).

84. The Investment Funds and Management Companies Law – ZISDU-3 (Official Gazette of the Republic of Slovenia, No. 31/15 of 4 May 2015):

- Law Amending the Investment Funds and Management Companies Law – ZISDU-3A (Official Gazette of the Republic of Slovenia, No. 81/15 of 30. 10. 2015).
- Law Amending the Investment Funds and Management Companies Law – ZISDU-3B (Official Gazette of the Republic of Slovenia, No. 77/16 of 2 Dec. 2016).

The Law on Markets in Financial Instruments (MFIL) regulates (Article 1 of the MIFL):

- the conditions for the offering of securities to the public and the admission of securities to trading on a regulated market;
- the obligations concerning the disclosure of information related to the securities admitted to trading on a regulated market;
- the terms and conditions for founding, operation, supervision and winding up of investment firms, market operators and settlement systems with the registered office in the Republic of Slovenia;
- the terms and conditions under which the persons with the registered office outside the Republic of Slovenia may provide investment services in the Republic of Slovenia;
- the rules of trading on regulated markets, prohibited acts of market abuse and the rules for settling transactions concluded on regulated markets;
- the rules of operation of the Securities Market Agency in the performance of its competences and responsibilities hereunder and under any other acts.

The ESMA as the European Supervisory Authority set up by Regulation 1095/2010/EC and the European Systemic Risk Board set up by Regulation 1092/2010/EC are also a part of MFIL.

According to MFIL-1, financial instruments (Article 7 of the MFIL) are:

- Law Amending the Investment Funds and Management Companies Law – ZISDU-3C (Official Gazette of the Republic of Slovenia, No. 77/18 of 30 Nov. 2018).

85. Takeover Law – TL-1, Slovene: ZPre-1 (Official Gazette of the Republic of Slovenia, No. 79/06 of 27 Jul. 2006):

- Law Amending the Takeovers Law – ZPre-1A (Official Gazette of the Republic of Slovenia, No. 1/08 of 4 Jan. 2008).
- Law Amending the Takeovers Law – ZPre-1B (Official Gazette of the Republic of Slovenia, No. 68/08 of 8 Jul. 2008).
- Decision to repeal the second sentence of the second paragraph of Article 75 and Article 63 in conjunction with the second sentence of the second paragraph of Article 75 of the Takeover Law regarding the content given by the Authentic interpretation of the second paragraph of Article 75 and Article 63 in conjunction with the second paragraph of Article 75 of the Takeovers Law (Official Gazette of the Republic of Slovenia, No. 105/11 of 23 Dec. 2011).
- Law Amending the Takeovers Law – ZPre-1C (Official Gazette of the Republic of Slovenia, No. 10/12 of 10. 2. 2012).
- Law Amending the Takeovers Law – ZPre-1D (Official Gazette of the Republic of Slovenia, No. 38/12 of 25. 5. 2012).
- Law Amending the Takeovers Law – ZPre-1E (Official Gazette of the Republic of Slovenia, No. 56/13 of 2 Jul. 2013).
- Law Amending the Courts Act – ZS-K (Official Gazette of the Republic of Slovenia, No. 63/13 of 26 Jul. 2013).
- Law Amending the Takeovers Law – ZPre-1F (Official Gazette of the Republic of Slovenia, No. 25/14 of 11 Apr. 2014).
- Law Amending the Takeovers Law – ZPre-1G (Official Gazette of the Republic of Slovenia, No. 75/15 of 8 Oct. 2015).

- transferable securities (shares in PLC, other shares equivalent to securities representing a share in the capital or members' rights of legal persons and a deposit certificate in respect of shares, bonds and other types of securities containing the issuer's monetary obligation, including a deposit certificate in respect of those securities), money market instruments and units of collective investment undertakings;
- options, futures, swaps, forward rate agreements and other securities-related transactions, currencies, emission coupons or returns as basic instruments or other derivative financial instruments, financial indices or other financial criteria, which can be settled by transferring the underlying instrument or by cash payment;
- options, futures, swaps, non-standardized futures and other derivative transactions as a basic instrument which must be settled in cash, or may be settled by cash payment at the option of one of the parties, with the exception of the failure of the other party to default or another reason for the termination of the contract;
- options, futures, swaps and other derivative transactions as commodities that can be settled by the transfer of the underlying instrument, provided that they are traded on a regulated market, with the exception of wholesale of energy products which must be settled by the transfer of the underlying instrument;
- options, futures, swaps, non-standardized futures and other derivative transactions in relation to goods as a basic instrument which may be settled by the transfer of the underlying instrument and do not have commercial purposes, but they have the characteristics of other derivative financial instruments;
- derivative financial instruments for the transfer of credit risk, financial contracts on differences;
- options, futures, exchange transactions, forward rate agreements and other derivative transactions relating to atmospheric variables, transport costs, allowances or inflation rates, or other official economic statistics that must be settled in cash, or by cash payment at the option of one of the parties, with the exception of the failure of the other party to default or another reason for the termination of the contract;
- any other business carried out in relation to assets, rights, liabilities, indices and measures which have the characteristics of other derivatives, in particular whether they are traded on a regulated market, or they are accounted for and settled through recognized clearing companies or require the required (daily) coverage in respect of them, including emission coupons consisting of any units which are found to comply with the legal requirements (trading of greenhouse gas emission allowances in the EU).

Also trading with simultaneous purchase and sale, algorithmic trading and high-frequency algorithmic trading techniques are regulated by MIFL.

MFIL-1 defines investment company, brokerage company, small brokerage company and stockbroker. A brokerage company means an investment firm with its head office in the Republic of Slovenia, which is not a bank and has been authorized by the agency for the provision of investment services and transactions. A brokerage company can only be a legal entity. A small brokerage company is a brokerage company performing the forwarding of orders in respect of transferable securities or units of collective investment undertakings to persons or to management companies or investment consulting and whose annual revenue does not exceed EUR 750,000. An investment firm is a legal entity that professionally performs investment services for other persons or investment business as its regular activity. A broker is a natural person who is authorized by the brokerage agency for brokerage and for a brokerage company or a bank on the basis of employment or on another legal basis carries out business covered by investment services and transactions carried out for its clients by a brokerage company.

There is also regulation of other issues related to operation of financial market: The Stock Exchange is an organized market whose operator is based in the Republic of Slovenia. The Stock Exchange is a stock exchange operator that has obtained the authorization of the management agency of this market. A stock transaction is a transaction with financial instruments concluded on a stock exchange market. Official stock exchange listing is a segment of the stock exchange market, which deals with securities that fulfil additional conditions that are important for protecting the interests of investors, as regards dispersal, market capitalization and the content of the rights they give to the holder and their other characteristics. The Free Market (over the counter, OTC) is the market in which it is traded outside the organized platforms. The Central Register is the register as defined by the law governing dematerialized securities; it holds the central depository position. The Central Securities Depositary (CDD) is defined in point 1 of the first paragraph of Article 2 of Regulation 909/2014/EU.

MFIL-1 also regulates so-called company with reduced market capitalization; the company with reduced market capitalization is a company listed on a regulated market and having had an average market capitalization of less than EUR 100 million on the basis of end-year quotes for the previous three calendar years.

M FIL-1 regulates small and medium-sized enterprises, saying, that they are companies which, according to its last annual or consolidated accounts, meet at least two of the following three criteria: average number of employees during the financial year is less than 250, balance sheet total does not exceed EUR 43 million, and annual net turnover not exceeding EUR 50 million.

MFIL before the change did not regulate the procedure of withdrawal of debt securities from trading on a regulated market. With the implementation of MFIL-F (eleventh paragraph of Article 101 of the ZTFI) holders of debt securities, certain securities issue at a meeting of debt securities holders accept Decision on withdrawal of debt securities from trading on a regulated market. To withdraw the *mutatis mutandis*, applicable to withdrawal of shares from trading on the regulated market (first to ninth paragraphs of Article 101 of the MFIL), MFIL-F amended MFIL Article 102, which refers to the information of listed companies on the selection of the home Member State. MFIL-1 transposes into Slovenian legislation also the provisions of Article 1.1(a) of Directive 2013/50/EU1.[86] MFIL-F (amendment

86. Directive 2013/50 / EU of the European Parliament and of the Council dated 22 Oct. 2013 amending Directive 2004/109 / EC of the European Parliament and of the Council on the harmonization of transparency requirements in relation to information about issuers whose securities are admitted to trading on a regulated market, Directive 2003/71 / EC of the European Parliament and of the Council on the prospectus to be published Having offered to the public or admitted to trading and the Commission Directive 2007/14 / EC laying down detailed rules for implementing certain provisions of Directive 2004/109 / EC.

of Article 110 of the MFIL) has extended the deadline of the public availability of the annual report to be provided by the public company of five years at least ten years after its publication.

MFIL-F has repealed the obligation to publish interim management report of listed companies. Still, quarterly reports in accordance with Article 26 of the Exchange Rules (Official Gazette of RS, No. 32/16) are the reporting obligation for companies whose shares are classified as first listing.

Based on ZTFI-F, there are several changes in the reporting obligations on significant proportions. It is also necessary to comply with the provisions of Commission Delegated Regulation (EU) 2015/7612, which entered into force on 26 October 2015 in respect of certain regulatory technical standards on major holdings.[87] Reporting duties of persons performing managerial responsibilities and persons associated with them is regulated by the Commission Delegated Regulation (EU) 2016/5224 which is binding in their entirety and apply directly.[88]

B. The Role and Tasks of the SEA

285. The supervisory authority is the authority of a Member State that is in charge of the supervision of investment firms, in accordance with the regulations adopted for the transposition of Article 67 of Directive 2014/65/EU, over the implementation of Regulation 600/2014/EU and the regulations adopted for the transposition of Directive 2014/65/EU, or designated by that Member State as a contact point on the basis of the rules adopted for the transposition of Article 79(1) of Directive 2014/65/EU, unless it is provided for by this Act that the supervisory authority responsible for another type of control. The SEA is the supervisory authority in Slovenia and the contact point in the Republic of Slovenia. All notices, exchanges of information and other cooperation with the supervisory authority of each other Member State is carried out by the agency through a contact point designated by that Member State in accordance with the rules adopted for the transposition of Article 79(1) of Directive 2014/65/EU.

The supervisory body is also the Bank of Slovenia, which in cooperation with the SEA, supervises the provision of services in relation to structured deposits referred to in this Act and Regulation 600/2014/EU.

286. According to MFIL-1, the SEA is an independent organization and acts in the public interest with a view to protecting investors and developing the securities

87. Commission Delegated Regulation (EU) 2015/761 of 17 Dec. 2014 amending Directive 2004/109 / EC of the European Parliament and of the Council concerning certain regulatory technical standards on major holdings.
88. Commission Delegated Regulation (EU) 2016/5224 of 17 Dec. 2015 amending Regulation (EU) No. 596/2014 of the European Parliament and of the Council concerning the exemption of certain public authorities and central banks of third countries, indicators of market manipulation, the thresholds for disclosure to the competent authorities for information on the suspension, admitted to trading on a closed period and type of business executives, which is to be reported.

market. The SEA is a legal entity under public law in charge of supervising the market in financial instruments. It was founded on 13 March 1994. The SEA is independent in implementing its tasks and responsibilities. It is financed from taxes and fees paid by the participants on the market in financial instruments.[89]

SEA is responsible for exercising supervision over the brokerage companies with regard to all services provided by a brokerage company in the Republic of Slovenia, a Member State and a third country in accordance with MFUL-1, Regulation 600/2014/EU and Regulation 575/2013/EU. If necessary, for the purpose of achieving the purpose of supervision of a brokerage company, SEA may carry out a business review and request appropriate reports and information from persons who are in a close relationship with a brokerage company and persons to whom a brokerage company has transferred a significant part of its business processes, and also holders of qualifying holdings in a brokerage company. For the purposes of carrying out supervision under MFIL-1, Regulation 600/2014/EU and Regulation 2016/1011/EU, SEA has all supervisory and investigative powers.

The tasks of the SEA as determined by MFIL-1 and ITMCL are to give permission for a public offer to an issuer of securities, permission for securities activities to brokerage companies, opinions regarding permission for securities activities of a bank to the Bank of Slovenia and permission for the founding of a stock exchange. SEA also supervises the operations of brokerage companies and banks, which obtain permission for their securities activities from the Bank of Slovenia. Furthermore, the SEA gives permission for a public offer to an issuer of securities, supervises the execution of the public offer, and supervises the operations of brokerage companies and banks which obtained permission for their securities activities from the Bank of Slovenia.

It gives permission for the founding of a stock exchange and supervises the business operations of the stock exchange (including insider dealing).

SEA also supervises the business operations of the central register.

287. The Stock Exchange is organized in the legal form of a joint stock company or a European joint stock company. The provisions of the Companies Act (ZGD-1) relating to PLC or European joint stock companies shall apply to the Exchange, unless otherwise provided by this Act. There is also a broad provision of the LSE rules, in terms of which the stock exchange members are obliged to observe the instructions of the SEA. The Rules of Procedure of the LSE afford the stock exchange the authority to institute disciplinary actions and impose sanctions for violations of the rules of the LSE (suspension of an LSE member from trading on the stock exchange, a broker's suspension from trading on the stock exchange, and temporary or permanent removal of a particular security from the listing).

288. SEA informs ESMA of the withdrawal of an authorization to provide investment services and transactions, about the control measures which it has issued, about the public announcement of the decision and the type of supervision measure if the agency, in accordance with the second paragraph of Article 488 of the ZTFI, publicly announces a decision or a summary of the decision on the

89. On SEA *see*: http://www.atvp.si/Eng/Default.aspx?id=1.

imposed control measures and about sanctions for a misdemeanour not published in accordance with point 3 of the sixth paragraph of Article 357 of this Act, including information on whether a judicial review procedure has been initiated against the decision and a decision on this legal remedy. By 31 March of each year, the agency must transmit aggregated data on all control measures that have been imposed in the previous year in accordance with MFIL-1.

289. SEA may conclude with the supervisory authorities of other Member States, ESMA and third-country supervisory authorities' cooperation agreements specifying the exchange of information (including personal data or another unique identifier, such as, the delegated regulation adopted pursuant to the ninth paragraph. Article 600 of Regulation (EC) No. 600/2014/EU necessary for carrying out checks on the fulfilment of the obligations laid down in Chapter 3 of this Act.

SEA informs the ESMA of the agreements concluded with the supervisory authorities of the other Member States.

C. Disclosure Requirements for Public (Listed) Companies

290. According to the MFIL-1, a public company is a company or other legal entity that is the issuer of securities, whose securities were successfully sold to the public, or which acquired the SEA's permission for organized trading. All other companies or entities are considered to be non-public.

291. A public company is obliged to immediately publish information regarding legal or business events as well as other information concerning the company or its operations, or which refer to financial instruments and which could have a significant effect on the price of the financial instrument. A public company must also immediately publish all amendments relating to published information in the same manner as it published previous information.

292. Only public companies are obliged to report on their financial and legal position and on relevant business events that could affect the price of its securities, in a manner prescribed by the MIFL. They are required to submit and publish their audited annual reports and to report promptly any events or circumstances that might substantially impact on price movements.

293. When a public company is obliged to publish relevant facts and information, it must be published in at least one newspaper widely circulated in the Republic of Slovenia, or in any other way prescribed by the SEA.

294. In addition, a company whose shares have been listed must submit semi-annual (interim) financial statements to the LSE and publish the same within two months of the end of the relevant financial period to which they relate, together with the basic data from the prospectus.

295. It must also submit an audited annual report, including audited financial statements, to the SAE and LSE within thirty days of receipt of the auditor's report, and no later than six months from the end of the relevant financial period to which they relate. The consolidated annual report should be submitted and published as required by law.

296. A public (listed) company must publish a summary of basic data from the audited report with the auditor's opinion and basic data from the prospectus attached and with the notion that the annual report is available to the public at the issuer's head office. The summary must be submitted to the SEA and LSE, and brokerage companies, together with the audited annual report. The requirement to publish the summary also applies to other (non-listed) public companies.

297. The SEA may, upon application, excuse a public company from its duty to report and disclose, when reporting on business events that would threaten the reasonable business interests of the company or be contrary to public interest, provided that the lack of information regarding business events would not be misleading for investors.

D. *Special Disclosure Requirements for Investment Companies and Mutual Funds*

298. There are special requirements for investment companies and mutual funds imposed by the LMCIF. Whenever investment companies are listed, they are required to publish monthly information on the buying and selling of securities and other assets, including prices and information regarding the book value of the company.

299. The management company must publish the following data for an investment company or investment fund:

- a prospectus on the public sale of closed-end investment coupons or an investment company's shares; the prospectus must also be submitted to the LSE, the Bank of Slovenia and the SEA;
- annual and semi-annual reports on each fund or investment company together with an investment portfolio report, along with audited financial statements, no later than eight months from the end of the relevant financial period of the issuer to which they relate; and
- the current value of investment coupons or an investment company's shares. The management company must publish the current value of the investment company's shares daily, calculated on the basis of its asset value and the last stock exchange value.

E. Notifying the SEA

300. Notifying the SEA is the duty of the Stock Exchange imposed by the MFIL-1. The Stock Exchange is obliged to notify the SEA of the following:

- securities' transactions made in the organized market;
- applications submitted for membership of the stock exchange, admissions to stock exchange membership, expired membership of the stock exchange and measures imposed on its members and/or stockbrokers;
- applications submitted for the admission of securities to listing on the Stock Exchange and applications submitted for the admission of securities to the over-the-counter market;
- any measures imposed on issuers; and
- any planned increase in the equity of the Stock Exchange and all other facts and circumstances relevant to the operation of the organized securities market.

F. Notifying the LSE

301. An issuer whose shares are listed on the LSE is required to immediately notify the LSE of any developments that could influence the price of its shares and also to attend to immediate public announcements of price sensitive information in at least one newspaper widely circulated in Slovenia. The issuer must notify the LSE of details of:

- any changes concerning its main business activities;
- planned significant change of the issuer's accounting policy;
- shareholders' meetings;
- the appointment and recall of directors;
- crucial changes in major shareholders' holdings (10%, 25%, 50% and 75% of voting rights);
- any issue of new securities;
- any decision to pay or declare any dividend or other distribution in respect of LSE securities or to withhold any dividend or interest payment on LSE securities;
- an incapability to settle liabilities arising from issued debt securities;
- the authorized share capital or issue of shares on such a basis; and
- any other price sensitive information.

302. The issuer must forward to the LSE a copy of all announcements, notices, reports and other documents as issued to the shareholders.

G. Obligation to Confirm the Prospectus Before Publication

303. No one is allowed to offer securities to the public in the Republic of Slovenia unless a prospectus has been published in connection with them in accordance with MFIL-1. Securities are not admitted to trading on the stock exchange market unless a prospectus has been previously published according to MFIL-1, unless the law specifies otherwise for the individual cases. No one shall publish a prospectus if it has not previously obtained the approval of the supervisory authority of the home Member State of the issuer for this prospectus.

H. Obligations of Public Companies

304. A public company is an issuer whose securities are admitted to trading on a regulated market in the Republic of Slovenia or in another Member State. The obligations to disclose controlled information, as defined in MFIL-1, arise from the listing of securities in regulated markets (stock exchange).

Controlled information is any information disclosed by a public company or by any other person who has asked for the listing of securities to be traded on a regulated market without the consent of the public company as internal information in accordance with Article 17 of Regulation 596/2014/EU or, in accordance with the provisions of another Member State adopted for the purpose of transposing Directive 2004/109/EC into the legal system of that Member State or pursuant to Article 3(1) of Directive 2004/109/EC.

Prohibited actions, market abuse and other obligations for prevention and detection of market abuse are regulated by MFIL-1 in detail. The competent agency to monitor the implementation of Regulation 596/2014/EU is SEA. When carrying out the supervision, SEA processes personal data in accordance with the law governing the protection of personal data. SEA supervises the prevention and detection of prohibited practices of market abuse and verifies that the addressees of the obligations act in accordance with Regulation 596/2014/EU. SEA is responsible for monitoring compliance with Regulation 596/2014/EU by monitoring, collecting and verifying published information and reports and notifications by persons reporting to the SEA, by obtaining information and carrying out business checks in accordance with MFIL-1 and Regulation 596/2014/EU and by issuing control measures under this Act and Regulation 596/2014/EU. The SEA may order a temporary freezing of funds, deprivation of assets, a temporary ban on the exercise of a professional activity.

I. Market Manipulation

305. There are a number of provisions to ensure fair dealings in the MIFL-1. A brokerage company may not conduct such business with securities such as might endanger the stability of the securities market (inconsistent conduct). In particular, brokerage companies may not execute fictitious transactions in securities with the intention of misleading investors regarding the value of securities. It may generally not directly or indirectly execute transactions in listed securities with the intent to adjust or stabilize the prices of securities.

306. There is a general prohibition against insider dealing, market manipulation and other violations of the provisions enacted by the MIFL-1, BL and other related laws, following EU Regulations 596/2014/EU, 2016/1011/EU, 575/2013/EU, 600/2014/EU, 909/2014/EU. Under this rule, nobody is allowed to trade or act as a broker when trading in securities or commit other acts with the intention of providing false or misleading information with regard to either the volume of sales of a security or the price of an individual security.

307. The operations and acts regarded as manipulation are, for example, fictitious transactions with regard to securities. Manipulation would also be the publishing or dissemination of false and/or misleading information regarding the financial standing of the issuer and/or business events.

308. It is thus prohibited to create a false or misleading impression for other parties on the financial instrument market regarding (market manipulation):

- the supply or demand, price or volume of sales of an individual or several financial instruments;
- the properties of an individual or several financial instruments; or
- the issuer of an individual or several financial instruments.

309. Market manipulation is:

(1) conduct or actions, including transactions or the issuing of orders for the purchase or sale of a financial instrument or instruments, which:
  - create or could create a false or misleading impression of supply or demand, price or volume of sales of a financial instrument; or
  - enable a specific natural or legal person or several natural or legal persons acting in collaboration to price individual or several financial instruments at abnormal or artificial levels.

(2) fictitious transactions to purchase or sell financial instruments or issuing fictitious orders for such transactions or any other form of fraud or deception; or

(3) disseminating information via the media including the Internet, or in another manner, that creates or could create a false or misleading impression about one or more financial instruments or their issuers, including the dissemination of unsubstantiated rumours and false or misleading news, if the person who has disseminated the information knows or could know that the information is false or misleading.

J. Insider Dealing

310. Inside information is deemed any information of a precise nature relating to one or several securities which has not been made public and which, if it were to be made public, would be likely to have a significant effect on the price of the security or securities in question. Information is deemed to be of a precise nature if it states:

- existing facts or circumstances;

- facts or circumstances which is reasonable to believe that they will come into being; or
- an event that has happened or can be reasonably expected to happen.

311. There is a general prohibition imposed by EU Regulations and sanctioned by the MIFL-1 on the use of inside information. No one is allowed to acquire securities or dispose of them on the basis of inside information. Insider dealing is a criminal act under the Criminal Act (Article 243).

312. Persons with direct access to inside information are the holders of qualifying holdings of a legal entity and the Management and/or Supervisory Board members of a legal entity.

313. Persons with direct access to inside information are not allowed to disclose this information to third parties or recommend, on the basis of such information, to third persons that they acquire or dispose of certain securities.

314. Inside information is any precise information that refers directly or indirectly to one or more issuers or to one or more financial instruments and that has not yet become available to the public or which has not yet been published, which, if it became known to the public, would probably have a significant effect on the price of those financial instruments relating to them. The information is considered precise if it states the following:

- existent facts or circumstances, or facts or circumstances which may reasonably come into being; or
- an event that has happened or can be reasonably expected to happen, and could affect the price of the financial instrument.

315. Information which could have a significant effect on the price of the financial instrument is information that an intelligent investor would take into account when making an investment decision, if the information were available to the public.

316. Nobody is allowed to acquire financial instruments or dispose of them on the basis of inside information. This prohibition also applies to attempts to acquire or dispose of a financial instrument.

317. The prohibition also applies to all persons who have directly acquired inside information or to whom it was directly available due to:

- membership in the management or supervisory board, or power of attorney for a public company that issues financial instruments;
- participation in the capital of a public company that issues financial instruments; or
- executing tasks and professional work or duties.

318. Nobody in possession of inside information is permitted to:

- reveal this inside information to a third party, unless this disclosure is part of the execution of normal working or professional tasks or duties; or
- recommend or in any other manner albeit a third party in the acquisition or disposal of any financial instrument to which this information relates, on the basis of the information.

K. Reporting Duties for Company Insiders

319. The SEA may determine reporting duties for company insiders for transactions of securities for their own account. Substantial shareholder reporting duties are required by the TOL and the MIFL.

320. For example, those employed with the Stock Exchange and members of the bodies of the Stock Exchange are obliged to report to the Stock Exchange each purchase or sale of securities performed, stating the number of securities bought and/or sold, the date of purchase and/or sale and the price at which securities were bought and/or sold. That also applies to their close relatives and the legal entities controlling them.

321. An issuer whose security has been listed on the stock exchange must inform the stock exchange and the public as soon as possible in certain determined cases (material changes in the issuer's trading, activities, accounting policy, dividend payouts, rights issues, shareholders' meetings, capital changes, etc.).

322. The Stock Exchange's employees are bound to report securities transactions for their own account. Under the MFIL-1, the SEA may require banks or brokerage companies to establish so-called restricted lists.

323. Reporting on transactions is, under the MIFL, the duty of those persons with direct access to inside information. They are obliged to report to the SEA any securities transactions which are a subject of reporting.

324. A subject of reporting is any transaction involving securities traded on the organized market, regardless of whether the person concerned made such a deal for their own or someone else's account and regardless of whether the transaction was made in or outside the organized market.

325. A person who directly or indirectly acquires 5% of the shares (a qualified share) or other securities issued by a particular company has to notify an issuer and the SEA within at least three days from the date in which the person was notified or should have known that they had obtained a qualified share. The issuer who received the notice must publish it within at least three days from receipt of the notice. The same rule applies to any further increase of ownership by 5% points.

L. *Supervision of Violations*

326. Supervision of violations of the prohibition of the use of inside information is carried out by the SEA. In order to prevent or uncover such violations, the SEA may request relevant explanations and data from the following persons:

- persons with direct access to inside information;
- issuers of securities traded in the organized markets;
- individuals and legal entities accepting orders and/or performing individual tasks relating to the transactions;
- individuals and legal entities which might be familiar with individual violations of the prohibition on the use of inside information; and
- employees and Management Board members of the legal entities referred to in the preceding items.

327. These people are obliged to respond to the SEA's request and provide it with relevant oral explanations and to disclose the identity of the person for whose account the transaction in question was made. In addition, they are obliged, upon the SEA's request, to present all documents relating to the particular transaction.

VI. Stock Exchange Introduction Requirements

A. *Admission Requirements to the LSE*

328. A company desiring to be admitted to the LSE listing must first file with the LSE a listing application and supporting documentation showing that it meets all legal and the LSE's listing requirements. The Admission Board decides on the admission of securities to the LSE listing on the basis of the application filed by or on behalf of the issuer. The whole listing process from the moment the listing application is filed with the LSE takes an average of one month.

329. Securities meeting the following conditions may be admitted to individual listings on the Stock Exchange:

- that none of the restrictions against trading apply to them; and
- that they are fully paid up, are freely transferable and issued in dematerialized form.

330. The Articles of Association of the issuer of the securities must satisfy the conditions laid down by the Stock Exchange, in particular as to:

- the capital of the issuer;
- the time period of the issuer's dealing;
- the overall nominal and market value of the issued securities; and
- the number of persons holding securities to which the application for listing in the Stock Exchange refers (securities spread).

331. The subjects of transactions on the LSE are freely transferable securities – mostly shares (ordinary and preferred) and bonds (government, municipal, corporate) and other financial instruments.

B. The Listing Prospectus

332. One of the most important documents that must be attached to the application is the listing prospectus. The company is required to publish a prospectus that meets all legal requirements.

333. It must contain all such information as investors would reasonably require, and reasonably expect to find there, for the purpose of making an informed assessment of the assets and liabilities, financial position, profits and losses, and prospects of the issuer of the securities and the rights attaching to those securities.

334. Once a listing has been approved, the company must promptly provide the LSE and the general public with all relevant information relating to its business and circumstances important for investors.

C. Stock Exchange Transactions

335. Stock exchange transactions may only be conducted by the LSE's members (brokerage companies and banks). The highest daily price movement allowed is 10%.

336. Trading on Ljubljana's Stock Exchange is performed completely electronically via the LSE's electronic trading system, called BIS. Stock exchange members may enter into the BIS a market order or limit orders. The securities listed on the LSE are traded in different market segments, depending on which LSE requirements are met by the companies or banks applying to be listed on the LSE.

337. There are two kinds of organized securities market (open to public approach, and regulated and supervised by public authorities) under the SML: Stock Exchange, trading in listed securities admitted under specified procedures and the free securities market, trading in all other, non-listed securities.

VII. Protection of Shareholders in Case of a Tender Offer

A. Public Offerings of Securities

338. A public offering of securities is a published invitation addressed to an undefined circle of persons to subscribe for securities. The offering of securities may only be carried out on the basis of a public offering and according to the procedure laid down in MFIL.

339. No public offering is required for the initial offering of securities, for example, in the following cases:

- the establishment of a PLC through a simultaneous subscription of all the shares by the incorporators;
- an offering of shares intended for a maximum of fifty previously known persons who oblige themselves to buy the entire series;
- issuing of shares in order to increase capital out of new stakes in a company other than a public company if all the shares are taken by the existing shareholders;
- issuing of shares in order to increase capital out of new stakes if the entire issue of shares is paid in assets in kind brought in; or
- in other cases if the issuer obtains approval from the SEA to carry out an initial issue without the public offering of securities.

340. The SEA grants the approval if the issuer proves that the issue is intended for previously known well-informed investors.

B. The Prospectus for a Public Offering

341. The prospectus for a public offering of shares is compulsory according to the MIFL. It is a written document containing information to enable a prospective purchaser of securities (investor) to make an assessment of the issuer's legal status, its financial standing, prospects and the rights attached to the securities offered. The prospectus must be drawn up and published in the Slovenian language. Details of the contents of the prospectus and abstracts from the prospectus are stipulated by the agency.

342. If the prospectus or abstracts from the prospectus contains information which is untrue, the persons publishing and/or participating in the publishing of the prospectus (a person made responsible by the issuer, an auditor and other persons who might affect the contents of the prospectus) are jointly and severally liable to the holders of the securities in question for any loss, if they knew or should have known about the nature of the said data.

343. These persons are also liable for any loss arising from omissions from the prospectus or abstracts from the prospectus with regard to crucial information about either the issuer or the securities, capable of affecting the investor's decision regarding the purchase of the said securities.

344. The persons referred to above can be absolved from liability if they can prove that, at the time of acquiring the securities, the investor was familiar with the inaccuracies contained in the prospectus or abstracts therefrom.

345. The SEA is not liable for the truthfulness and accuracy of the data contained in the prospectus.

C. Takeovers

346. The Takeover Act,[90] adopted on 14 July 2006, transposed Directive 2004/25/EC of the European Parliament and of the Council of 21 April 2004 on takeover bids[91] into the law of the Republic of Slovenia (Slovene: ZPre-1) lays down the methods, conditions and procedures relating to takeover bids. The TL-1 was several times amended as follows:

- The Law on Amendments and Supplements to the Law on Takeover TL-1A, Slovene: Zpre-1A.[92]
- The Law on Amendments and Supplements to the Law on Takeover TL-1B, Slovene: Zpre-1B.[93]
- The Law on Amendments and Supplements to the Law on Takeover TL-1C, Slovene: Zpre-1C.[94]
- The Law on Amendments and Supplements to the Law on Takeover TL-1D, Slovene: Zpre-1D.[95]
- The Law on Amendments and Supplements to the Law on Takeover TL-1E, Slovene: Zpre-1E.[96]
- The Law on Amendments and Supplements to the Law on Takeover, Zpre-1F – Takeover Act 1F.[97]
- The Law on Amendments and Supplements to the Law on Takeover, Zpre-1G – Takeover Act 1G.[98]

In addition, the following Constitutional Courts' decisions and authentic interpretations are relevant:

(a) Decision finding that the second sentence of the second paragraph of Article 75 Article Takeover Act is not inconsistent with the Constitution.[99]
(b) Decision to remove the second sentence of the second paragraph of Article 75 and Article 63 Art in conjunction with the second sentence of the second paragraph of Article 75 of the Law on Takeover of content that they made it authentic interpretation of the second paragraph of Article 75 and Article 63 Articles in conjunction with paragraph 75 of the Law on Takeover.[100]

90. Official Gazette of the RS, No. 79/2006.
91. OJ L No. 142, 30 Apr. 2004, 12.
92. Official Gazette of the RS, No. 12/2008. TA-1A.
93. Official Gazette of the RS, No. 68/2008. TA-1B.
94. Official Gazette of the RS, No. 10/2012. TA-1C.
95. Official Gazette of the RS, No. 38/2012, TA-1D.
96. Official Gazette of the RS, No. 56/2013. TA-1E.
97. Official Gazette of RS, No. 25/14 dated 11. 4. 2014), TA-1F.
98. Official Gazette of RS, No. 75/15 dated 8. 10. 2015), TA-1G.
99. Official Gazette of the RS, No. 22/2012.
100. Official Gazette of the RS, No. 105/2011.

(c) Decision on the temporary suspension of the implementation of the second sentence of the second paragraph of Article 75 and Article 63 Article with respect to the second sentence of the second paragraph of Article 75 of the Law on Takeover.[101]
(d) Authentic interpretation of the second paragraph of Article 75 and Article 63 Articles in conjunction with paragraph 75 of the Law on Takeover/ORZPre75/ Official RS, No. 35/2011 TA-1 applies in the case the transferee company is a listed company, and its shares with voting rights are admitted to trading on a regulated market. TA-1 also applies in the case the transferee company is a PLC, the shares of which are not admitted to trading on a regulated market (non-publicly traded company), if such company has (TA-1 C, Slovene: Zpre-1 C):
   - at least 250 shareholders on the last day prior to the year relevant for the assessment of application of this Act; or
   - more than EUR 4 million of the total equity as shown in its most recent annual, report published in compliance with the act governing companies.

According to TA-1, the takeover is a situation where the offeror alone or together with persons acting in concert achieves the takeover threshold. The takeover threshold in the target company was 25% of the voting rights in that company until TA-1 D; since 15 May 2012, when the Law on Amendments and Supplements to the Law on Takeover, Zpre-1D (Slovene: Zpre-1 D)/Official RS, No. 38/2012, came into force, the takeover threshold is not anymore 25% but one-third of the voting rights of the target company.

347. Persons acting in concert are persons who cooperate on the basis of an agreement, either express or tacit, either oral or written, aimed either at acquiring or enhancing control of the offeree company or at frustrating the successful outcome of a bid.

In order to determine whether the persons acting in concert have achieved the takeover threshold, for each of them the proportion of voting rights must be assessed and their shares must then be totalled.

According to TA-1 C (Slovene: Zpre-1 C), a person or persons acting in concert who achieve or exceed the takeover threshold in the offeree company without having achieved or exceeded the final takeover threshold, have to make a takeover bid if this results in the increase of their proportion of voting rights in the offeree company.

An important exception, related to insolvency procedures, was made by amending Article 22 with a new paragraph 3 in TA-1 C; namely, a person who, as a creditor, reaches the takeover threshold of the offeree company in insolvency proceedings under the law governing the financial operations, insolvency proceedings and forced termination is not required to make a takeover bid. The obligation to make a takeover bid of the person occurs at the first subsequent acquisition of securities of the offeree company outside of insolvency proceedings.

101. Official Gazette of the RS, No. 55/2011.

Another exception was made by amending Article 22 by new Article 22a of the TA-1 C (Acquisition of securities on the basis of security realization) which stipulates, that a bank is not obliged to make a takeover bid if it had achieved the takeover threshold by the acquisition of the offeree company's securities following a realization of a security, the subject of which was the offerec company's securities.

The Law on Amendments and Supplements to the Law on Takeover TA-1E SloveneZpre-1E)[102] brings another exception of the duty to make a takeover bid in order to ensure capital adequacy of the target company (new Article 22 b). Namely person who has made the takeover threshold in the target company for the execution of the financial restructuring of the target company in order to ensure its long-term capital adequacy or solvency before the commencement of insolvency proceedings is not obliged to make takeover bid, provided that for such acquisition of securities prior consent of the SEA was acquired. The exemption is valid for five years from the date of acquisition of securities.

Article 22.c of the TA-1 E (Slovene: Zpre-1E) brings the possibility to exercise of voting rights in order to protect the public interest to the person (or persons acting in concert), who were prohibited by a decision of the agency to exercise of voting rights in the target company. These persons may, subject to the prior approval of the SEA, exercise voting rights at the general meeting of the target company on the decisions that are necessary to protect the public interest (e.g., security or national defence, public safety, the safety of life, health and property, the operation of the economic system).

TA-1 A (Slovene: ZPre-1A),[103] brings more stringent provisions, for the payment of the securities. Namely, the SEA may from then on issue the certification for takeover bid only provided, that the following new condition is met (Article 32/7 TL): if the offeror has provided evidence to the SEA that (for the payment of the securities), he did not in any way give or pledge as collateral or insurance securities or any other form of property of the offeree company, that are not the property of the offeror.

TA-1B (Slovene ZPre-1 B)[104] brings new element of the mandatory prospectus which needs to be published, in order to allow the holders of the securities all information for the informed decision on acceptance of the takeover bid; namely, if the offeree is the non-public traded company, in addition to existing 12 elements of the prospectus the new 13th element of the prospectus is stipulated (Article 28/2 p. 13); namely, a written report of the auditors of the appropriateness of the price in the takeover bid, prepared by one or more auditors appointed by the court at the proposal of the offeror (respective articles of LCC-1 apply here *mutatis mutandis*). In addition, a written report in which the offeror explains the appropriateness of the price in the takeover bid and if necessary reasons for the price in case the price had not been found appropriate in the auditor's written report.

102. Official Gazette of the RS, No. 56/2013.
103. Official Gazette of the RS, No. 12/2008.
104. Official Gazette of the RS, No. 68/2008.

348. According to the TA-1, the takeover represents a situation in which the offeror, alone or together with persons acting in concert with him, obtains the takeover threshold (one-third share of voting rights in this company).

349. According to the TA-1, a takeover bid must be made by the offeror achieving the takeover threshold (mandatory takeover bid). A renewed takeover bid must be made by the offeror after having acquired a 10% share of voting rights (additional takeover threshold) after the completed successful takeover bid procedure.

350. The obligation of making a renewed takeover bid ceases when an offeror that has already made a successful takeover bid acquires at least 75% of the offeree company's all voting shares (final takeover threshold).

351. The SEA monitors the implementation of the TA-1. The SEA may request reports and information or carry out a review of operations of persons suspected of having acted in concert or having acted together with the offeror, and so on.

352. The TA-1 obliges a person who achieves, exceeds or ceases to exceed a 5%, 10%, 15%, 20% and 25%, one-third, 50% and 75% share of voting rights (qualifying holding) to notify the fact thereof to the issuer of securities and the agency.

D. Acting in Concert

353. The most important novelty of the new law is the regulation of the institution 'acting in concert' (together achieving the takeover threshold) and mandatory takeover bid made by persons acting in concert.

354. According to the TA-1, persons acting in concert are jointly and severally liable to make a takeover bid, unless they reach an agreement that only one or some of them will make the takeover bid.

355. According to the TA-1, persons acting in concert are persons that act in concert on the basis of an explicit or implicit oral or written agreement and whose aim is to acquire or consolidate their control of the offeree company or to prevent the offeror from making a successful takeover bid.

E. Persons Deemed to Act in Concert

356. According to the TA-1, the following persons are deemed to act in concert:

– persons linked merely by circumstances associated with the acquisition of securities (the time period in which the securities were acquired, amount of securities acquired or other circumstances that indicate a common intention of these persons);

- members of the management or the supervisory board of the persons acting in concert;
- persons interconnected as immediate family members (a person's spouse or a person with whom they live in a long-term relationship, or with whom they live in a registered same-sex civil partnership, that person's children or adoptive children and other persons who are under such a person's guardianship); and
- persons that proposed the adoption of a resolution by the offeree company at a general meeting for the appointment or discharge of members of the management or supervisory boards or the adoption of any other resolution which must, according to the LCC, be adopted by at least a three-fourths' majority, and who have achieved the adoption of this resolution.

F. Persons Who Are Incontestably Deemed to Act in Concert

357. One of the important novelties of the TA-1 is the listing of the persons who are incontestably deemed to act in concert (the opposite proof is not possible). The following persons are incontestably deemed to act in concert:

- a controlled company (in which another person has the majority of voting rights or the right to appoint or discharge the majority of board members or of which another person is a shareholder and alone controls the majority of voting rights) and the controlling entity;
- companies controlled by the same controlling entity; or
- the management company and investment funds managed by such a company.

The amendment of the Takeover Act (TA-1G), of October 2015, adjusts the takeover regulation to the new Law on Dematerialized Securities (ZNVP-1, October 2015). The amendment to the Takeover Act-1 is introducing better protection of minority shareholders. It also establishes legal framework to be able to introduce TARGET2-Securities (T2S-Eurosystem technical platform for settlement of securities).

There are more novelties, introduced by TA-1G), 2015 as for example, a minimum threshold for the successful mandatory takeover bid (at least 50% of the total shares plus one (not in the case of voluntary takeover bid). If the threshold is not reached, the acquirer will not be able to exercise voting rights, unless they will not alienate shares under the takeover threshold or the additional takeover threshold. By definition, successful bid threshold is the lowest percentage of securities by the offeror, together with securities already in his possession, on the basis of the takeover bid to be binding (Article 21, TA-1G).

§5. Shareholders, Management and Control

I. Shareholder Control Mechanisms

A. *The Shareholders' Meeting: General*

358. As is said in the Code,[105] shareholders exercise their rights at the shareholders' meetings (also referred to as general meetings), where they exercise their voting rights. The Code recommends that companies provide timely and correct information regarding the convening of meetings and encourage active exercise by shareholders of their voting rights. If attendance at a general meeting and exercise of voting rights depend on a prior notification of the shareholders' attendance, companies are recommended to enable shareholders to do so by mail or by use of information technology.

359. Each shareholder must, according to the Code, have the right to attend a general meeting and there to present their opinions on the items on the agenda, as well as ask appropriate questions and provide suggestions. At a general meeting, the company's management must provide the shareholders with reliable data on company matters relevant for an evaluation of the items on the agenda, unless otherwise stipulated by law.

360. According to the Code, companies should encourage:

- all shareholders to actively and responsibly exercise their rights and warn them against exercising their rights in a manner which could damage the company or other shareholders of the company;
- a greater representation of shareholders at general meetings indirectly, through financial and other organizations and by proxy (organized collection of proxies, publication of information on proxies); and
- substantial shareholders, institutional investors and the state, to publicly reveal the company's investment policy, for example, its voting policy, the level of activity of corporate governance and the manner of the latter, the mechanisms and frequency of communication with the management or supervisory bodies.

B. *Powers of the General Meeting*

361. Powers of the general meeting, determined by the LCC, are the following:

(1) The adoption of the annual report, but only:
   - if the supervisory board (in two-tier systems) or the board of directors (in one-tier systems) has not confirmed the annual report;

105. Code of Corporate Governance (Ljubljana Stock Exchange d. d., Association of Supervisors and Managers' Association, renewed and approved 8 Dec. 2009, and becomes effective on 1 Jan. 2010.

- if the management board or the supervisory body leaves the decision on the adoption of the annual report to the general meeting; or
- if so provided by the Articles of Association of a company that selected a one-tier management system.

In this case, the relevant resolutions of the management or the supervisory body must be stated in the report submitted by the management or the supervisory body to the general meeting. An adopted annual report must not be amended by a resolution on the use of profits for appropriation.

In a two-tier system, the management board must submit to the supervisory board the annual report (audited) immediately after it has been drafted; together with an auditor's report (if necessary).

The management board must attach to the annual report any proposal for the use of profits for appropriation which it will submit to the general meeting.

(2) A general meeting is not bound in its decision on the use of profits for appropriation by the proposal of the management or supervisory body.
(3) The appointment and recall of members of the supervisory board and the board of directors, the appointment of an auditor and the issue of a discharge for the members of the management or supervisory bodies (by issuing a discharge, the general meeting confirms and approves the work of the management or supervisory body in the financial year; however, claims based on liability for damage may also be pursued against discharged persons).
(4) Amendments to the Articles of Association, measures to increase or reduce the capital and the dissolution of the company or its restructuring.

362. Other matters where so provided by the Articles of Association in accordance with the law or other matters determined by law. When making the decision on the distribution of profits, general meeting also decides on the discharge to the management and supervisory board members. The discharge of the general meeting confirms and approves the performance of the governance and oversight for the financial year. If the general meeting votes no discharge to the board or the individual member, this is not to be deemed as the vote of non-confidence.

363. The shareholders meeting, which decides on the use of distributable profit, should be informed by the boards on remuneration that the boards' members (management and supervisory) have received in the previous financial year. This information includes the remuneration for each member of both boards (management and supervisory) and has to be broken down, at least on the basis of fixed and variable remuneration, participation in profit-sharing, options, and other bonuses, reimbursement of expenses, insurance premiums, commissions and other extra payments. The information should also contain the benefits that the members of the boards gained through the performance of the duties of the affiliated companies. This information should be recorded in the business report along with the policy for the remuneration, determined by a general meeting of shareholders. The general meeting may (but not must) determine the remuneration policy for the members of the management and supervisors bodies; in that case, that the remuneration of the boards' members shall be in accordance with the remuneration policy. In determining the policy of remuneration and also if no remuneration policy is determined by general meeting, the law stipulates the following principles: the remuneration policy encourages long-term sustainability of the company and ensures that the benefits are provided in accordance with the results and the financial condition of the company; the total remuneration may consist of a fixed and a variable component; the variable part of the remuneration should depend on the pre-determined and measurable criteria (the general meeting may determine the maximum amount of the variable part of remuneration); severance payment shall be payable only in the event of an early termination of the contract; severance payments shall not be paid, when the board member is recalled for cause, or, if the member terminates the contract by himself (the general meeting may determine the maximum amount of the severance payment).

364. A general meeting may not decide issues concerning the conduct of business except where so requested by the management and except of the transfer of at least 25% of the company's assets.

As it is stated in the LLC-1A,[106] for the validity of a contract by means of which an LLC undertakes to transfer at least 25% of the company's assets, provided that no other provisions of this act concerning status changes apply, a resolution must be passed by the general meeting (this limitation does not affect third parties).

365. The majority of at least three-quarters of the subscribed capital represented in the voting is required. The articles of association may stipulate a different majority of the capital but not less than a majority of the subscribed capital represented in the voting if at least one-half of the subscribed capital is represented in the voting.

366. The contract by means of which the company undertakes to transfer at least 25% of the company's assets must be concluded in the form of a notarial record. At least one month prior to a session of the general meeting that is to decide on consent to the transfer of the company's assets, the contract must be made available for inspection by the shareholders at the registered office of the company. All shareholders must be given a copy of the contract free of charge on request by the following working day at the latest.

367. The contract by means of which the company undertakes to transfer at least 25% of its assets must be submitted at the general meeting. At the start of the debate in the general meeting, the management must give an oral explanation of the contents of the contract. The contract must be attached to the minutes as a supplement.

368. If, due to the transfer of at least 25% of the company's assets such company is dissolved, the original contract or a notarized copy must be attached to the proposal for the registration of the dissolution.

---

106. LCC-1A – The Act amending Law on Commercial Companies (Official Gazette of the RS), No. 10/08 of 30 Jan. 2008.

C. The Code's Recommendations on the General Meeting Decisions

369. According to the Code, the general meeting decides predominantly on:

- the corporate restructuring of the company, measures directed at increasing or decreasing the share capital, amendments to the Articles of Association;
- distribution of accumulated profits, adoption of the annual report;
- adopting management or supervisory bodies discharges, the appointment and recalling of members of the supervisory board or the board of directors, the appointment of an auditor;
- the validity of an agreement on the transfer of at least 25% of the company's assets, where the transfer is not related to corporate restructuring;
- the authorization to purchase the company's own shares;
- the withdrawal of shares from the regulated securities market;
- the squeeze out of minority shareholders;
- matters defined by the law on takeovers; and
- the winding up of the company.

D. Convening a General Meeting

370. There is no difference between ordinary and extraordinary general meetings under the LCC.

A general meeting is convened in cases determined by law or by the Articles of Association, and whenever it is in the interest of the company. The management decides on whether to convene a general meeting (in cases determined by law or by the Articles of Association, and whenever it is in the interest of the company).

371. According to the Code, the company's management must convene a general meeting and publish its agenda at least once a year. The company's management also convenes a general meeting if this is in the company's best interest.

372. The convening of the general meeting must be announced (together with the registered name and registered office of the company, the time and place of the general meeting and the conditions applying to participation at the general meeting and the exercise of voting rights). The general meeting must be convened at least one month before the session of the general meeting. Unless otherwise provided by the Articles of Association, the general meeting must be held at the registered office of the company.

E. Convening a General Meeting by Minority Shareholders

373. Amendments of 2009 to LCC-1 (LCC-C)[107] stipulates, that a general meeting must be convened, if shareholders whose total interest accounts for one-twentieth of the subscribed capital (or smaller interest defined by the articles) make a written request (accompanied in writing by an agenda with a proposed resolution for each suggested item on the agenda) to the management to convene a general meeting.

374. Upon the request, the general meeting must meet as soon as possible but no later than within two months of receipt of the request.

375. The court may authorize the shareholders who made the request, or their authorized persons, to convene the general meeting. The court issues its decision without obtaining the statements of the other parties.

376. The articles of association may enable minority shareholders to send requests to convene the general meeting via electronic means.

F. Content and Publication of Convocation

377. The amendments to LCC-1 (LCC-1C)[108] require the convocation of the general meeting to include at least the following information:

- the registered name and registered office of the company, time and place of the general meeting and proposed agenda;
- cut-off date (the general meeting may be attended and the voting rights exercised solely by those shareholders who are registered as holders of shares in the central register of book-entry securities at the end of the fourth day prior to the general meeting) together with an explanation that the general meeting can only be attended and voting rights exercised by shareholders holding shares on that day, and other conditions relevant for participation at the general meeting and exercise of voting rights;
- the deadline or day by which the shareholders may request to amend the agenda (request must be sent to the company within seven days at the latest following the publication of the convocation of the general meeting);
- the deadline or day by which the shareholders may notify the company of a proposal for publication (seven days of the convocation of the general meeting);
- proposed resolutions of the management or supervisory bodies (for each agenda item, the management or supervisory bodies must specify proposed resolutions, unless the general meeting is not adopting a resolution);

107. LCC-1C – The Act amending Law on Commercial Companies (Official Gazette of the RS), No. 42/09 of 5 Jun. 2009.
108. LCC-1C – The Act amending Law on Commercial Companies (Official Gazette of the RS), No. 42/09 of 5 Jun. 2009.

- where and how the full texts of documents and proposals (the management must at the company's registered office provide shareholders with access to proposed resolutions and explanations of individual agenda items);
- that at the general meeting a shareholder may exercise his/her right to information (information may be provided in a joint answer to shareholders' questions with the same content);
- the procedure for exercising the voting right by electronic means if provided by the company (the Articles of Association may stipulate that shareholders can participate in the general meeting or vote prior to the general meeting or at the general meeting via electronic means without being physically present, and regulate the procedure to this effect);
- the procedure for exercising the voting right by mail if provided by the company (the Articles of Association may enable shareholders to vote by mail before the general meeting).

378. The convocation of a general meeting must be published at least thirty days (or shortest period defined by the articles) before the actual session of the general meeting. The Articles of Association may stipulate as a condition for participating in the general meeting or exercising voting rights that the shareholders notify their participation prior to the general meeting. In this case, it is sufficient if shareholders notify their participation no later than at the end of the fourth day prior to the general meeting.

379. Notwithstanding the provisions of the act governing book-entry securities, the general meeting may be attended and the voting rights exercised solely by those shareholders who are registered as holders of shares in the central register of book-entry securities at the end of the fourth day prior to the general meeting (hereinafter: 'cut-off date').

G. Convocation When Companies' Shares Are Traded

380. A company whose shares are traded on the organized market must, according to the LCC-1C the Act amending LCC-1C[109] requires convocation, also specify the following information:

- the company's website address where the following information will be available: convocation of a general meeting, the total number of shares and voting rights on the day of convocation, full texts of documents and proposals, forms used for voting and information on how these forms may be acquired, information on shareholders' rights, and so on;

109. LCC-1C – The Act amending Law on Commercial Companies (Official Gazette of the Republic of Slovenia), No. 42/09 of 5 Jun. 2009.

- that exhaustive information on the shareholders' rights (minority shareholders' supplements to the agenda, shareholders' proposals, electoral proposals by shareholders, shareholder's right to be informed) is available on the company's website;
- information on the procedure for exercising voting rights by an authorized person, in particular information on forms to be used for this purpose and the manner of notifying the company of the appointment of an authorized person by electronic means, the method of exercising voting rights must be regulated by the Articles of Association; the Articles of Association must lay down that a company may or must establish a connection between the authorized person present at the general meeting and the represented shareholder through electronic or other comparable media;
- the method of sending additional agenda items via electronic means (a company whose shares are traded on the organized market must offer its shareholders at least one method for sending additional agenda items from the previous paragraph via electronic means);
- the method of sending proposals via electronic means (a company whose shares are traded on the organized market must offer its shareholders at least one method for sending proposals from the previous paragraph via electronic means).

381. From the publication of the convocation of a general meeting to the day of the session of the general meeting, at least the following information must according to the LCC-1C[110] be available on the website of a company whose shares are traded on the organized market:

- convocation of a general meeting;
- the total number of shares and voting rights on the day of convocation of the general meeting, including separate data on each class of shares;
- full texts of documents and proposals; the management must at the company's registered office provide shareholders with access to proposed resolutions and explanations of individual agenda items;
- forms used for voting by an authorized person or by mail, or if these cannot be published on the website due to technical reasons, information on how these forms may be acquired free of charge in physical form upon a shareholder's request;
- exhaustive information on shareholders' rights;
- the shareholders' proposals (like supplements to the agenda, shareholders proposal for resolutions for each agenda item, electoral proposals by shareholders).

110. LCC-1C – The Act amending Law on Commercial Companies (Official Gazette of the Republic of Slovenia), No. 42/09 of 5 Jun. 2009.

H. Participating and Voting in the Shareholding Meetings via Electronic Means

382. As it is stipulated, in the LCC-1C,[111] the Articles of Association may stipulate that shareholders can participate in the general meeting or vote prior to the general meeting or at the general meeting via electronic means without being physically present, and regulate the procedure to this effect.

383. But it is explicitly stipulated by law, that participation and voting can depend solely on the requirements and limitations required for identification of shareholders and secure electronic communication, and to an extent commensurate with the implementation of this objective.

384. The Articles of Association may authorize the management to regulate in detail this Procedure.

I. Information to Shareholders

385. According to LCC-1C,[112] for each agenda item to be decided upon by the general meeting, including the election of members of the board, the management or supervisory bodies must specify proposed resolutions in the agenda, unless the general meeting is not adopting a resolution.

386. From the publication of the convocation of the general meeting to and on the day of the actual session of the general meeting, the management must at the company's registered office provide shareholders with access to:

- proposed resolutions from the previous paragraph, specifying the company body which submitted the proposal;
- explanations of individual agenda items; the explanation of the agenda item involving the general meeting's decision on the appointment of members of the supervisory board or board of directors must include at least the first name and surname, education, relevant work experience and current employer of the proposed member, and an explanation of the agenda item involving the decision on the appointment of an auditor with at least the auditor's registered name, registered office and key references;
- when the convocation refers to the debate on issuing a discharge which must be linked to the debate on the use of the profit for appropriation, the annual report and the report of the supervisory board or the board of directors; the shareholder must be provided (at his/her request) free of charge with a copy of reports on the next working day at the latest, unless the reports are published on the company's website;

111. LCC-1C – The Act amending Law on Commercial Companies (Official Gazette of the RS), No. 42/09 of 5 Jun. 2009.

112. LCC-1C – The Act amending Law on Commercial Companies (Official Gazette of the RS), No. 42/09 of 5 Jun. 2009.

– if the general meeting is to decide on an amendment to the Articles of Association: the text of proposed amendments.

J. Minority Shareholders' Supplements to the Agenda

387. LCC-1[113] stipulates, that shareholders whose total interest accounts for one-twentieth (or smaller interest defined by the articles) of the subscribed capital may request in writing that an additional item be placed on the agenda.

388. The request must be accompanied in writing by a proposed resolution to be decided upon by the general meeting or an explanation of that item. The request must be sent to the company within seven days at the latest following the publication of the convocation of the general meeting.[114]

A company whose shares are traded on the organized market must publish a clean copy of the agenda in the same manner as it published the convocation.

389. Immediately upon the expiry of the deadline from the first paragraph of this article, the management must publish additional agenda items to be discussed at the general meeting. An additional agenda item may be discussed at the general meeting only if it was published no later than fourteen days prior to the general meeting; otherwise, it must be discussed at the next general meeting.

K. Notifying Shareholders and Members of the Supervisory Board

390. At the latest on the fourteenth day before the general meeting, the management must according to LCC-1[115] notify the financial organizations and associations of shareholders which exercised voting rights at the last general meeting of the convocation of the general meeting and of shareholders' proposals and electoral proposals by shareholders.

391. If the agenda has changed, the amended agenda must also be forwarded. The same applies to other financial organizations and associations of shareholders if the management receives their request no later than on the sixteenth day before the general meeting.

392. Any member of the supervisory board may request that the management send him/her the above notification. Any shareholder who is entered as a shareholder in the share register and any member of the supervisory board may require

113. LCC-1C – The Act amending Law on Commercial Companies (Official Gazette of the RS), No. 42/09 of 5 Jun. 2009.
114. A company whose shares are traded on the organized market must offer its shareholders at least one method for sending additional agenda items via electronic means.
115. LCC-1C – The Act amending Law on Commercial Companies (Official Gazette of the RS), No. 42/09 of 5 Jun. 2009.

that the management inform him/her in writing of resolutions adopted at the general meeting. If the company has published data on its website, it is sufficient to give the address of the website where this data is available. The company must not charge its shareholders any costs related to the notifications.

L. Shareholders' Proposals

393. Shareholders according to LCC-1C,[116] may propose resolutions in writing for each agenda item. Shareholders' proposals must be published and notified in a manner defined by the rules on the publication of convocation only if within seven days of the convocation of the general meeting the shareholder sends the company a reasonably substantiated proposal, giving notification that he/she will oppose the proposal of the management or supervisory body and that he/she will prevail upon other shareholders to vote for his/her counterproposal.[117]

394. The management is obliged to publish a shareholder's proposal and its substantiation (need not be published if it contains more than 3,000 characters):

- if publication of the proposal would constitute a criminal offence or a minor offence;
- if the proposal would lead to a resolution by the general meeting that would be in conflict with the law or the Articles of Association;
- if the substantiation of a proposal in essential points contains clearly incorrect or misleading information or insults;
- if a shareholder's proposal with the same content has already been reported to the company's general meeting;
- if during the last five years the same shareholder's proposal containing essentially the same substantiation has already been reported to at least two general meetings of the company and less than one-twentieth of the subscribed capital represented at the general meeting voted in favour of it;
- the shareholder makes it known that he/she will not attend the general meeting and will not be represented at it; or
- if during the last two years the shareholder has not presented his/her proposal to the general meeting or has not had it presented.

395. The management may publish as a summary the proposals and their substantiations of several shareholders on the same subject. Shareholders' proposals which have not been sent to the company by the deadline set in the first paragraph of this article and have been submitted no later than at the general meeting itself are discussed at the general meeting.

---

116. LCC-1C – The Act amending Law on Commercial Companies (Official Gazette of the RS), No. 42/09 of 5 Jun. 2009.
117. A company whose shares are traded on the organized market must offer its shareholders at least one method for sending proposals from the previous paragraph via electronic means.

M. List of Participants and Minutes

396. At the general meeting, a list must be compiled of the shareholders present or represented and of the representatives, which shall contain the name, surname and address and for each shareholder the number and class of shares and, in the case of shares with nominal value, also their nominal value.

397. If a financial organization or an association of shareholders has been authorized to exercise a voting right the amount and the class of the shares and also their nominal value (in the case of par value shares) for which authorization was obtained must be entered in the list.

398. The amount and class of shares and also their nominal value must also be entered in the list for the person authorized by the shareholder to exercise the voting right in his own name on behalf of the shareholder.

399. Each resolution passed by the general meeting must be confirmed by a notary in a notarial record. The record must state the place and date of the session, the name and surname of the Notary Public, the result of the voting and the chairman's summary of the adoption of resolutions.

400. The results of voting at the general meeting of a company whose shares are traded on the organized market must specify at least the following information:

- number of shares for which votes were duly cast;
- stake of these shares in the subscribed capital;
- total number of votes duly cast; and
- number of votes cast in favour and against, and the number of abstentions.

Within twenty-four hours of the conclusion of the general meeting, the management must send a copy of the record and the supplements, verified by a notary, to the register (LCC-1C).[118]

N. Decision-Making at the General Meeting

401. It is recommended by the Code that companies use information technology while conducting the general meeting. It is also recommended that general meetings be attended by a majority of the members of the management or supervisory bodies.

It is also recommended by the Code that a general meeting should elect members of the supervisory board and members of the board of directors individually and pass separate resolutions on the adoption of management or supervisory body discharges for each body.

118. LCC-1C – The Act amending Law on Commercial Companies [Official Gazette of the RS], No. 42/09 of 5 Jun. 2009.

O. Public Announcement of the Resolutions Adopted

402. It is recommended by the Code that the company's management publish the resolutions adopted at the general meeting and information as well on any challenging or void actions against the general meeting's resolutions, announced at the meeting, as soon as possible. In its public announcement, as recommended by the Code, a company's management should also include the following:

- the total number of shares and voting rights represented at the meeting, and the number of represented shares and voting rights from individual classes;
- the results of voting on each proposal, including at least the number of shares relating to the vote, the number of votes cast, and the 'in favour' and 'against' votes, given in percentages;
- a clear identification of the five largest shareholders present or represented at the meeting, together with the number of shares held by each of them and the number of their voting rights; voting rights should also be expressed as a percentage of all the voting rights in the company and of the voting rights in the respective class of shares;
- a notice regarding the distribution of accumulated profits, as well as data on the dividend amount, the record date when those entitled to dividend payments are to be identified, and the date when they will be paid; and
- a detailed account of the rights and obligations attached to new serial securities (shares, bonds, etc.) when the adopted resolutions refer to such securities.

P. The Shareholders' Right To Be Informed

403. At a general meeting, the management must give the shareholders reliable information on matters concerning the company which are important for an assessment of the agenda.

According to the LCC, the right to be informed also applies in respect of the company's legal and business relations with affiliated companies. The Code also recommends that the right to be informed also applies to legal and business relations of the company with associated companies.

The company's management should prepare in advance for the questions of shareholders and should ensure the requisite support of the general meeting.

404. The management is not obliged to provide data:

- if reasonable business judgment suggests that the provision of information could cause damage to the company or an affiliated company;
- on the method of compiling the balance sheet and of making estimates, if stating these methods in a supplement is sufficient for an assessment of the property and the financial and profit position of the company which conforms with the actual circumstances; or
- if disclosure of the information would constitute a criminal offence or an economic infringement or would be in breach of good business practices.

405. If a shareholder is given information outside a session of a general meeting, that information must be passed on to every other shareholder upon request even if it is not necessary for an assessment of an item on the agenda.

If a shareholder is not given information, he may require that his question and the reason why the information was refused be entered in the record. In the instance of a shareholder, the court decides whether the management must provide information.

Q. Corporate Governance Code on Information for Shareholders and Disclosure

406. The Code recommends that the company's management ensure that the company, upon convening a general meeting, uses information technology that will allow information to be disseminated uniformly to all shareholders and for their rights to be exercised effectively. When releasing data and material and publishing them on the company's official website, the company's management should abide by the rules of uniform information dissemination. When publishing the convening of a general meeting, then, according to the Code, the company's management should also provide the company's official website address.

407. The company's management should publish the reports and material stipulated by law on the company's official website, together with the notice convening the general meeting, and the agenda, for resolutions to be adopted and their substantiation.

If the general meeting is to decide on amendments to the Articles of Association, the company's management should publish the text of the proposed amendments and substantiate them, on the company's official website.

In addition, the Code recommends that the company's management should also publicly disclose, on the company's official website, the total number of shares and voting rights, together with the number of shares and voting rights for a particular class of shares, according to the situation at the time of convening the general meeting.

R. Voting Rights

408. Shareholders exercise their voting rights according to the proportion of shares they hold in the subscribed capital.

In principle, a majority of votes cast by shareholders (a simple majority) is required to adopt resolutions at a general meeting. However, the law or the Articles of Association may require a larger majority or lay down other requirements.

The Articles of Association may provide for restrictions on voting rights such that:

- the number of votes which an individual has, based on the number of shares held by him may not exceed a certain number or a certain percentage; and

- shares belonging to another person for the account of the shareholder also count as the shareholder's shares (this restriction may not be laid down for individual shareholders and may also not be laid down for voting rights deriving from shares traded on the regulated market).

409. If the shareholder is a company, the Articles of Association may determine that shares belonging to a dependent company or a company controlling it or a company affiliated with it in a group of companies or to a third person for the account of such companies also count as its shares.

Voting rights may only be acquired once the entire contribution has been paid in (the Articles of Association may determine otherwise).

Persons related to the shareholder by blood in direct line up to three removes or the shareholder's spouse may exercise the voting right.

Exclusion of voting rights is stipulated for involved shareholders; a shareholder may not participate in a vote on whether he should be exempted from certain obligations or on the pursuit of a claim by the company against him. In such cases, no other person may exercise the voting rights applicable to the shares held by that shareholder.

A contract under which a shareholder undertakes to vote in accordance with instructions from the company, the management or supervisory body or in accordance with instructions from a dependent company, is null and void. In addition, a contract under which a shareholder undertakes to vote for every proposal of the management or the supervisory board is also null and void.

410. Amendment to LCC-1 of 2009 (LCC-C) stipulates that a shareholder who is entitled to participate in the general meeting has the right to authorize a natural or a legal person with the legal capacity to participate in the general meeting on his/her behalf and exercise his/her voting right. Such authorization must be given in writing.

The authorization must be submitted to the company and must be kept by it. At the general meeting, an authorized person enjoys the same rights to speak and ask questions as the shareholder he/she represents.

Shareholders of a company whose shares are traded on the organized market may, via electronic means, appoint an authorized person in accordance with the previous paragraph. The Articles of Association must specify at least one method for using electronic means to transfer such proof of the authorized person's appointment.

S. Corporate Governance Code on Elections of Corporate Bodies

411. If a general meeting is to elect members of the supervisory board or the board of directors, as proposed by the supervisory board or the board of directors, the Code proposes that the motivation for such proposals for resolutions to be adopted should include – along with the data required by law (name and surname, education, appropriate work experience and current employment) – at least information on the proposed nominee's membership in other management or supervisory bodies and any potential conflicts of interests.

412. The management should, according to the Code, also express their view on whether the proposed nominee is independent in relation to the company (whether he or she is economically, personally or in any other way closely linked to the company or its management).

It is also recommended by the Code that this information be made public and available to the proposed nominee for a member of a management or supervisory body from the time when the general meeting has been convened.

T. Authorization to an Individual Financial Organization

413. Voting rights can be exercised through financial and other organizations and other persons on the basis of an authorization. A financial organization may only exercise or verify the exercising of a voting right for registered shares if it has written authorization to do so.

Authorization may be given to an individual financial organization for a maximum of fifteen months and may be revoked at any time. The authorizing certificate must be submitted to the company and must be stored by it.

414. According the 2009 amendment of the LCC-1 (LCC-1C), a financial organization must call upon shareholders to provide it with instructions for exercising voting rights and advise the shareholders that if they do not give instructions for exercising voting rights, these are going to be exercised under its own proposals of which the shareholders were informed, unless it can presume that the shareholders would approve of a different decision if they were aware of the actual state of affairs.

415. Financial organizations, an association of shareholders and other persons planning to implement their voting rights, at a general meeting, on the basis of an organized collection of proxies (any collection of proxies intended for more than fifty shareholders), must have a written authorization (authorized person). The authorization only applies for one general meeting. It must contain the proposed resolutions, the nomination of an authorized person to vote on individual proposed resolutions, a request to the shareholder to give instructions on how to exercise the voting right and indicate to the shareholder that if the shareholder does not provide different instructions, it will exercise the voting right in accordance with its own judgment which must be explained in the proxy, and the indication that the shareholder may revoke such a proxy at any time.

416. A person or a group, intending to use a voting right on the basis of the organized collection of voting authorizations at a shareholders' meeting must notify the SEA of their intentions, the reasons for them and the means of collecting the authorizations in advance.

Any collection of authorizations from more than fifty shareholders of a PLC which has a voting right is considered an organized collection of voting authorizations. The authorizations obtained are only valid for one shareholders' meeting. It must contain the voting proposals, the name of the proposed voter and call on the shareholders to provide their voting instruction (with a statement that in the absence thereof the authorized voter will vote according to the proposals stated in the authorization proposal).

A financial organization must call upon shareholders to provide it with instructions for exercising voting rights and advise the shareholders that if they do not give instructions for exercising voting rights, these must be exercised under its own proposals of which the shareholders were informed, unless it can presume that the shareholders would approve of a different decision if they were aware of the actual state of affairs.

U. The Corporate Governance Code on Collection of Proxies

417. The proxy statement should, according to the Code, include at least the following:

- a request to the shareholder to give his proxy holder precise instructions for exercising the voting right;
- a statement of proposals on which the proxy holder will vote and how he will vote, unless otherwise instructed by the shareholder;
- a statement of any potential conflict of interests; or
- a statement of caution to the effect that the shareholder may revoke the proxy and attend the general meeting in person.

When the collection of proxies is paid for by the company, it is recommended by the code that the invitation for the granting of proxies be addressed to all shareholders.

418. Should a person or financial institution that has undertaken an organized collection of proxies notify the company thereof in a timely manner, it is recommended by the Code that the company publish this information on its official website, together with a list of such persons or financial institutions.

II. A General Meeting and Minority Shareholders

419. A general meeting must be convened if shareholders whose total interest accounts for at least one-twentieth of the subscribed capital make a written request to the management for the convening of the general meeting, stating the purpose and reasons for it.

The Articles of Association can also regulate the right to convene a general meeting in another manner, in which case the total interest of the shareholders requesting the convening of the general meeting may not be set at more than one-tenth of the subscribed capital.

Upon such a request, a general meeting must take place as soon as possible but no later than within two months, or the court may authorize the shareholders who requested the meeting, or their authorized representatives to convene a general meeting and to publish the subject which the general meeting should decide.

420. Shareholders whose total interests account for at least one-twentieth of the subscribed capital may require the publication at the general meeting of the subject regarding which resolutions are to be submitted upon their proposal.

If, after a general meeting has been convened, shareholders holding at least one-twentieth of the subscribed capital request the publication of a subject on which the general meeting is to decide, it is sufficient that the subject be published within ten days of the notice to convene the general meeting.

According to the Code, the company's management must convene a general meeting upon a request of the shareholders, if so provided for by law, who together represent 5% of the company's share capital or another percentage, if so stipulated by the company's Articles of Association, whereby the total stake cannot be set at more than 10% of the share capital.

A. Disclosure of Conflicts of Interests in Representation

421. According to amendments to LCC-1 of 2009 (LCC 1-C), any person who offers an unspecified group of shareholders without being authorized by them for the purposes of representation to represent them at the general meeting must disclose to the shareholders in writing any circumstances which may be of relevance to the shareholders in their assessment of risks in order for the authorized person to act in an interest different from the interests of the shareholder (hereinafter: 'conflict of interests').

422. A conflict of interests may primarily arise when the authorized person is:

- the majority shareholder of the company or a person controlled by him/her;
- a member of the management or supervisory body of the company or the majority shareholder or a person controlled by him/her;
- an employee or an auditor of the company or the majority shareholder or a person controlled by him/her; or a close family member of persons from the preceding indents.

423. The following are deemed close family members of the person from the previous paragraph:

- the person's spouse or a person with whom they live together in a long-term relationship that, under the act governing marriage and family relations, has the same legal consequences as marriage, or with whom they live in a registered same-sex civil partnership;
- children and adoptees who lack full legal capacity; and
- other persons who lack full legal capacity and were placed under the person's guardianship.

The person must send information in writing on a conflict of interests or a statement that there is no conflict of interests to shareholders prior to being granted authorization.

424. The provision, that person who does not represent more than ten shareholders at the general meeting and more than 1% of the subscribed capital is not obliged to disclose information is in accordance with LCC-1I, 2015 (Article 308/5) not any longer in power. That means that also the mentioned group of shareholders is subject to disclose information.

III. Annual Reports: Profits and Dividends

A. General Accounting Rules

425. Companies (also sole traders) must keep books of account and render year-end accounts once a year in accordance with the Slovenian Accounting Standards or International Financial Reporting Standards (IFRS), unless otherwise stipulated by the law.

The financial year may differ from the calendar year. Annual financial statements must be compiled every financial year based on the closed books of account within three months of the end of the financial year.

426. Books of account must be kept in accordance with the double-entry bookkeeping system. The books of account, the balance sheet, the profit and loss account, the annual report and the business report must be stored permanently. Accounting documents need to be stored for a specific period only.

More detailed rules on accounting are defined by the Slovenian Accounting Standards, which were adopted by the Slovenian Institute of Auditing in agreement with the ministers responsible for economy and finance. Slovenian Accounting Standards transpose the contents of European Community Directives 76/660/EEC and 83/349/EEC.

427. Companies whose securities are listed on one of the organized securities markets in the European Community Member States and which are subject to consolidation must compile consolidated financial statements in accordance with the IFRS. Besides listed companies as set out above, financial reports in accordance with the IFRS must also be compiled by:

- banks;
- insurance companies; and
- other undertakings if so decided by the assembly of the undertaking.

428. According to LCC-1B, the members of the management and supervisory bodies of the company have the duty to ensure that the annual accounts, the annual report and the corporate governance statement are in conformity with law.[119] LLC-1 I 2017 requires that the annual reports (including consolidated annual reports) of large- and medium-sized capital companies and DP are reviewed by the auditor who must audit the financial report and review the business report and also verify that the business report contains corporate governance statement and a statement on non-financial operations and examine their formal completeness (amended Article 57/1 LCC-1).

B. The Annual Report

429. The annual report of companies must contain:

- a balance sheet (setting out the balance of assets and liabilities at the end of the financial year);
- a profit and loss statement (setting out the income, expenses and operating results for the financial year);
- a cash flow statement (setting out changes in receipts and disbursements, or inflows and outflows for the financial year and explain changes in the balance of cash);
- a capital flow statement (setting out changes in the individual elements of capital during the financial year, including the use of net profit and the covering of losses);
- annexes with notes to the financial statements; and
- a business report (setting out at least a fair presentation of the development and results of the company's operations and its financial position, including the description of essential risks and uncertainties the company is exposed to).

The members of the management and supervisory bodies of the company must jointly ensure that the annual reports with all the components, including the corporate governance statement and the statement of non-financial transactions, are compiled and published in accordance with the Law, Slovenian Accounting Standards or IFRS. In doing so, they act in accordance with the competencies, diligence and responsibilities that the law provides for the individual form of company. The annual report and its components must be signed by all the members of the management of the company.

The above-listed accounting statements and the annex with notes to accounting statements form an accounting report. Companies must submit the annual reports and the consolidated annual reports to the Agency of the Republic of Slovenia for Public and Legal Records and Services (hereinafter: 'APLRS, Slovene: AJPES') within eight months after the end of the financial year due to public disclosure,

119. Directive 2006/46/EC of the European Parliament and of the Council of 14 Jun. 2006, amending Council Directives 78/660/EEC on the annual accounts of certain types of companies, 83/349/EEC on consolidated accounts, 86/635/EEC on the annual accounts and consolidated accounts of banks and other financial institutions and 91/674/EEC on the annual accounts and consolidated accounts of insurance undertakings.

together with the auditor's report. Amended Article 57 (LCC-1 J 2017) requires that companies must also submit a revised annual report or a consolidated annual report or changes to the auditor's report. Companies must also submit a proposal for allocating profits or dealing with a loss and distribution of profits or dealing with a loss, if this is not apparent from the annual report in the time limits set by the law regulating tax procedure. APLRS (AJPES) informatizes the received documents and makes them publicly available free of charge on their websites, so as to indicate the reason.

In case of termination (liquidation, bankruptcy, etc.) companies and entrepreneurs have to make a balance sheet and income statement and the final report in accordance with the deadlines laid down by the law governing the tax procedure. LCC-1I (Article 59/3) requires these documents to be submitted in electronic format for further processing of data for national statistics and other analytical information, research and tax purposes. LCC-1 I in the same article also stipulates, that AJPES must sent that data in appropriate electronic form to State bodies and legal persons who are authorized by law to obtain and use this information for registration, information-analytical, research and tax purposes. State authorities, the Bank of Slovenia and members of the Economic and Social Council are entitled to get this information free of charge; other legal persons pay the actual costs of handling or placing data.

Specific rules for companies which are engaged in financial economic sectors, especially banks and insurance companies, are determined by the relevant Sectoral Law.

430. A fair presentation must be a balanced and comprehensive analysis of development and operating results of the company and its financial position corresponding to the extent and the complexity of its operation.

LCC-1I (Article 67) brings an extensive new regulation of general rules for the valuation of items in the financial statements; the general rules are the following:

(1) Assuming a continuation of the company as a going concern.
(2) The use of valuation methods are not to be changed without compelling reasons from fiscal year to fiscal year (consistent valuation).
(3) It is necessary to take into account the precautionary principle as laid down by Slovenian Accounting Standards or IFRS, in particular:
   - only profits made at the balance sheet date can be recognized;
   - all obligations incurred during the financial year, even if they become apparent only between the balance sheet date and the date of preparation of the balance are recognized;
   - all the negative value adjustments, regardless of whether it is a result of the financial year the profit or loss are recognized.
(4) The principle of original value must be observed; this is the initial measurement of the purchase price or production cost, as determined by the Slovenian Accounting Standards or IFRS.

   The company may, in accordance with the LCC-1I and the Slovenian Accounting Standards and IFRS value:
   - tangible fixed assets at revalued amounts; and

- financial instruments, including derivatives, and investment property at fair value in the manner specified by Slovenian Accounting Standards or IFRS.

(5) The amounts recognized in the balance sheet and income statement are accounted for on an accrual basis.

(6) The components of assets and liabilities should be valued separately.

(7) The opening balance sheet of the financial year must correspond to the closing balance sheet of the previous financial year.

(8) The financial statement items are accounted for and presented having regard to the content of events and not only in terms of their legal form.

(9) The requirements for the presentation and disclosure need not be met where the impact of their performance is immaterial.

There are numerous and very detailed technical rules in the LCC-1I2015 (Article 67) explaining general rules for the evaluation, referring to tangible fixed assets, revaluation reserve, fair value, profit or loss from the change in fair value, financial investments, long-term and short-term assets, fixed assets with limited useful life, biological assets, current assets, reservations, etc. (LCC-1I2015, Article 67/1-12).

New Article 69 of the LCC-1I2015 in a very detailed and comprehensive way stipulate the mandatory elements of the annex to the financial statements (balance sheet and income statement), which must be presented and disclosed in addition to those defined by the Slovenian Accounting Standards or IFRS (*see* for ex.LCC-1I 2015, Article 69/2, 1-10 or Article 69/3, 1-19).

C. Business Report

431. LCC stipulates that the business report must contain at least a fair view of the development and results of the company's operations and its financial position, including a description of the essential risks and uncertainties that the company is exposed to (LCC-1, Article 70). A fair presentation must be a balanced and comprehensive analysis of the company's development and outcomes and its financial position, which corresponds to the scale and versatility of its operations. The analysis must, to the extent necessary for understanding the development and outcomes of the company's operations and its financial position, include key accounting, financial and, if necessary, and other indicators that also include information related to environmental protection and workers. The analysis must include an appropriate reference to the amounts in the financial statements and the requisite additional clarifications.

The business report should also show all major business events that occurred after the end of the financial year, the expected development of the company and the company's activities in the field of research and development. There is a special regime for micro companies (new Article 70a of the LCC-1I, 2015).

In addition, LCC-1I 2015 imposes completely a new regulation (new Article 70.b of the LCC-1I) referring to report on payments to governments from large companies, whose activities span exploration, search, discovery, development and extraction of minerals, oil, natural gas or other materials and from companies engaged in the activities in the logging of old-growth forests. The article also applies to large companies, not engaged in the above activities referred, carried out by any of its subsidiaries.

The company referred to, must prepare and publish in accordance with LCC-1 a report on all payments to the national, regional or local authorities of the Member States or third countries in relation to the activities referred to (for each country. as consolidated report if needed, but not necessary, if several individual payments do not exceed EUR 100,000).

To the extent necessary to understand the development and operating results of the company and its financial position, the analysis must contain the key accounting, financial and, where necessary, other indicators, ratios and factors also including information concerning environmental protection and employees. The analysis must include the appropriate reference to the sums provided in financial statements and necessary additional clarifications.

D. A Consolidated Annual Report

432. LCC-1I, 2015, Article 56, brings here important changes and additional more comprehensive regulation. It is stipulated, that the company located in the Republic of Slovenia, which is the controlling one or more companies established in the Republic of Slovenia or outside (the subsidiary), shall prepare a consolidated annual report, if the parent company or one of its subsidiaries organized as a LLC, as a double company or other such legal form by the law of the country of residence of the company.

LCC-1I, 2015, Article 56 is explaining in detail, what is the controlling company; it is the company which is controlling another company if it has a majority of the voting rights in another company or if it has the right to appoint or remove a majority of the members of the management or supervisory board of another company. The company is also controlling another company if it has the right to a dominant influence over another company on the basis of a business contract or through agreement with other shareholders of that company controls the majority of voting rights in that company. The company is also controlling another company if it has a dominant influence over another company, actually carried out subordinating management of the company.

The voting rights or rights of appointment and removal, whose owner is the parent company are added to the voting rights or rights of appointment and removal, held by another company, which depends on controlling company. Likewise are added those rights held by persons acting on behalf of the parent company to its other subsidiaries.

However, rights from holding shares on behalf of a person who is not the parent company or its subsidiary and rights to shares held by way of guarantee, for loans, do not count.

The parent company, which together with its subsidiaries does not meet the conditions for large companies, whereby the criteria of net sales revenues and asset value increases by 20%, is not obliged to prepare consolidated annual report. This does not apply if the parent company or any of its subsidiaries is PIE.

The parent company, whose securities are not traded on a regulated market and is also a subsidiary company of a Member State, is not obliged to prepare consolidated annual report (exempted company), if the company in a Member State holds all the shares in the exempted company or it owns more than 90% of the shares and the remaining shareholders have approved the exemption. An exempted company must be included in the consolidation of the parent company of a Member State.

An exempted company must, within one month of the publication of the consolidated annual report of the Member State, publish a translated annual consolidated report and the auditor's report of the parent company.

Notwithstanding the possibility of an exemption, exempted company should provide information from the consolidated annual financial statements or consolidated management reports, if they are required to inform employees or their representatives, or if requested by the administrative or judicial authorities for their needs.

The consolidated annual report must reflect the true and fair view of the financial position, income statement, cash flows and changes in equity of companies included in the consolidation taken as a whole. If the composition of the companies included in the consolidation during the financial year significantly changed, the consolidated annual report shall include information enabling the comparison of successive annual consolidated reports.

The consolidated annual report shall be prepared on the same reporting date as the annual report of the parent company. In preparing the consolidated annual accounts, the same measurement bases as those used in the annual financial statements of the parent company shall be used.

The consolidated annual report consists of the consolidated financial report and consolidated management report of the group of companies included in the consolidation. Consolidated financial report consists of the consolidated balance sheet, consolidated income statement and consolidated statement of comprehensive income, the consolidated statement of cash flows and consolidated statement of changes in capital and the annex to the consolidated financial statements.

In an annex to the consolidated financial statements to be disclosed, the transactions between related parties between companies included in the consolidation may be excluded. In disclosing the amounts of emoluments and advances and loans to members of management and supervisory board, only the amounts of members of the management and supervisory boards of the parent company are disclosed.

In the Corporate Governance Statement of the consolidated financial report, only the main features of the internal control and risk management at the level of groups of companies is shown.

E. Statement on the Corporate Governance

433. According to LCC-1 B,[120] companies whose securities are admitted to trading on a regulated market are obliged to disclose an annual corporate governance statement as section of the annual report. That statement provides shareholders with

120. Directive 2006/46/EC of the European Parliament and of the Council of 14 Jun. 2006 amending Council Directives 78/660/EEC on the annual accounts of certain types of companies, 83/349/EEC

information about the corporate governance practices actually applied. The statement includes a description of the risk management systems and internal controls in relation to the financial reporting process.

Corporate governance statement, according to the amended Article 70 (LCC-1J 2017), must, except for small and medium-sized companies, contain a description of the policy of diversity that is carried out in relation to representation in the management and control bodies of the company from a gender perspective and other aspects, such as age or education and professional experience, and an indication of the objectives, the manner of implementation and the results of the policy of diversity in the reporting period. If the policy of diversity in the company is not implemented, that should be explained in the corporate governance statement.

434. The corporate governance statement should make clear whether the company applies any provisions on corporate code to which the company is subject or in any corporate governance code which the company may have decided to apply.

435. Furthermore, companies may also provide an analysis of environmental and social aspects necessary for an understanding of the company's development, performance and position.

436. In addition, Slovene Corporate Governance Code for listed companies requires the business report to contain the statement on the management of the company, together with a statement whether the company uses any codes for its operations.

437. If so, the statement must contain the indication of such a code, its public availability and an indication of individual provisions of such a code with which the company has not complied, with appropriate justification.

F. A Statement of Non-financial Operations

438. LCC-1 J 2017 brought an important novelty concerning non-financial reporting, based on the Directive 2013/34/EU concerning the disclosure of non-financial information and information on the diversity of certain large enterprises and groups (OJ L No. 330 of 15. 11. 2014, page 1) and Directive 2014/95/EU of the European Parliament and of the Council of 22 October 2014 amending Directive 2013/34/EU concerning the disclosure of non-financial information and information on the diversity of certain large enterprises and groups (OJ L No. 330 of 15. 11. 2014, page 1). It stipulates that in a statement of non-financial operations, LCC-1, Article 70. C, contains at least information on environmental, social and staff matters, respect for human rights and in matters relating to the fight against corruption and bribery, including a brief description of the company's business model, a

---

on consolidated accounts, 86/635/EEC on the annual accounts and consolidated accounts of banks and other financial institutions and 91/674/EEC on the annual accounts and consolidated accounts of insurance undertakings.

description of the company's policies on those matters and the results of these policies. A statement of non-financial business must also contain the main risks associated with those matters that relate to the activities of the company, including its business relationships, products or services, where appropriate and proportionate, which could lead to serious adverse effects in these areas, and the ways in which the company manages these risks. A statement of non-financial business also explains key non-financial performance indicators relevant to individual activities. If a company does not pursue any of these policies, it has to explain that in a non-financial statement clearly.

Where possible, the statement of non-financial operations has to include an appropriate reference to the amounts in the financial statements and the necessary additional clarifications.

The company may prepare a declaration on non-financial operations as a separate report. In this case, a separate report has to be published together with the business report, or a separate report must be published on the company's website within a reasonable period of time not exceeding six months after the balance sheet date and the business report is referred to.

The LLC-1 2017 also stipulates that a consolidated business report of a public interest entity whose average number of employees in the financial year is more than 500 on the balance sheet date at the group level also includes a consolidated statement of non-financial operations.

G. *Use of Net Profit and Profit for Appropriation*

439. If a company discloses a net profit in the financial year, it must first use it for the following purposes and in the following order (Article 230, LCC):

- to cover a loss brought forward;
- to create statutory reserves;
- to create reserves for its own shares; and
- to create reserves under the Articles of Association.

440. When adopting an annual report, the management or the supervisory board may use the amount of net profit remaining following its use for the purposes to create other profit reserves, but may not use for this purpose more than half of the amount of net profit remaining following the use of the profit.

The Articles of Association may authorize the management or the supervisory board to use a part which is greater than half of the amount of net profit (if shares are not traded, the part may be less than half). The general meeting may decide to create other profit reserves from the net profit remaining but may not use more than half of the net profit.

441. When the general meeting is deciding on the use of the profit for appropriation, the management must, according to 2009 amendments to LCC-1

(LCC1C),[121] inform the shareholders of income of the members of the management or supervisory bodies which they received in the past financial year for performing tasks in the company. Information must include income per member of the management or supervisory body and must be broken down into at least fixed and variable income, participation in the profit, options and other bonuses, reimbursement of costs, insurance premiums, commissions and other additional payments. Information must also include income acquired by the members of the management or supervisory bodies for their performance of tasks in controlled companies.

442. This information must also be disclosed in the annual report together with the income policy for the members of the management or supervisory bodies if defined by the general meeting.

443. The general meeting may define an income policy for the members of the management or supervisory bodies. All income of the members of the management or supervisory bodies must be in accordance with such income policy. In defining the income policy for the members of the management board and executive directors, the general meeting has to follow the legally defined principles.[122]

H. Distribution of the Profit for Appropriation to the Shareholders, Interim Dividends

444. The shareholders' share in the profits (dividends) for appropriation must be determined in proportion to their shares in the subscribed capital. The company must not pay dividends out of capital. A dividend is only payable out of the trading profits of the current year and undistributed reserves carried forward from previous years which have not been capitalized. Dividend distributions are made as provided by the articles. Normally they take place once a year; an interim dividend may be paid, followed by a final dividend at the end of the company's financial year, if so provided for in the articles.

If contributions to the subscribed capital are not yet paid up in full or are not paid up for all shares in the same proportion, the shareholders' shares in the profit for

121. LCC-1C – The Act amending Law on Commercial Companies (Official Gazette of the RS), No. 42/09 of 5 Jun. 2009, (Slovene: ZGD-1C).

122. *See* page 119:

- income policy for the members of the management board and executive directors must foster the long-term sustainability of the company and provide that income is in accordance with the results achieved and the financial position of the company;
- total income may be composed of a fixed and a variable part; the variable part of the income must depend on measurable criteria defined in advance; the general meeting may determine the maximum amount of the variable part of the income;
- severance pay may be paid only in the case of early termination of a contract; it may not be paid if a member of the management board or executive director has been recalled for serious reason (if he is in serious breach of obligations, if he is incapable of business conduct, or if the general meeting passes a vote of no confidence in him, except where the vote of no confidence was passed for clearly unsubstantiated reasons).

appropriation must be determined in proportion to the payments made. Contributions paid in during the financial year must be taken into account in proportion to the period from when they were paid until the end of the financial year (Article 23, LCC).

445. In accordance with the Articles of Association, the management may be authorized to pay an interim dividend based on the anticipated profit after the end of the business year.

The management may only pay an interim dividend if the accounts for the previous business year show a net profit.

446. A maximum of half the amount remaining from the anticipated net profit after profit reserves have been set aside in accordance with the law or the Articles of Association may be paid out as an interim dividend. Moreover, the amount of interim dividends must not exceed half of the balance sheet profit from the previous year. The payment of interim dividends must be approved by the supervisory board.

IV. Corporate Governance

A. Corporate Governance: General

447. Corporate governance can be identified with the conduct of a company and the managerial instruments associated with the control exerted by management (e.g., reporting, auditing). Other definitions state that corporate governance consists of rules regulating the composition, competences, duties and responsibilities of corporate organs.

A more complex approach is the principal-agent (investors-managers) relationship problem, concerned with ways of bringing the interests of the two parties into line and ensuring that firms are run for the benefit of investors.

More generally, corporate governance has been defined as the relationship between various participants (shareholders, directors, creditors, employees, etc.) in determining the direction and performance of companies.

448. The main existing corporate system involves two models in particular: a market-oriented model represented by the US, and a bank-oriented model, represented by Germany and continental Europe (mainly France and Italy). The distinction between the two models relates to the different financial system structures, which is then reflected in corporate governance structures.

B. Corporate Governance Systems: General

449. Slovenian company law (LCC, 1993) at the beginning introduced a mandatory two-tier system for larger companies, while leaving it up to the shareholders to opt for a one or two-tier system in smaller companies and in closely held companies. The definition of what is a small and what is a large company for this purpose was stated precisely in the LCC (less than SIT 300 million in share capital, less than an average of 500 employees, less than 100 registered shares if a corporation is not listed on the stock exchange, if the corporation was founded simultaneously).

450. Selection of the management system is now (since 2006), according to LCC-1 (Article 253), left to the shareholders. They may choose either a two-tier management system by appointing a management board and a supervisory board or a one-tier management system by appointing a board of directors.

451. The two-tier system of management of public companies is, for now, still far predominant in Slovenia, due to the fact that the free option for the one-tier system was only introduced in legislation in 2006. The two-tier system also prevailed in Slovenia due to the fact that the great majority of companies transformed themselves through the processes of privatization and legal transformation from former social enterprises to property rights-based legal forms. Before 2006 (LCC-1), the two-tier system was compulsory for all public companies of a larger size.

452. There are two bodies that run public companies in the two-tier system of corporate governance: the management board which conducts the company (managerial function) and the supervisory board which monitors the management of the company (supervisory function). On the other hand, there is only one body that runs both the managerial and supervisory functions in the one-tier system, and that is the board of directors.

453. The LCC uses the term 'management and supervisory bodies' for the management board and the supervisory board in the two-tier system and 'board of directors' in the one-tier system.

C. *The Composition and Number of Management and Supervisory Body Members*

454. The composition and the number of members of the management and supervisory bodies are determined by law and the Articles of Association. The articles need not define the number of members; they can only authorize the bylaws in which the number will be identified.

The management or supervisory bodies are composed of at least three members, unless otherwise provided by law (exemption: the management board of a PLC using the two-tier system may be composed of less than three members). If a management or supervisory body has more members, one of them is appointed president (Article 254, LCC).

D. Appointment and Term of Office of Management and Supervisory Body Members

455. The members of the management and supervisory boards are appointed for a period determined in the Articles of Association which may not be longer than six years, with the possibility of reappointment.

456. Any natural person with legal capacity may be a member of a management or supervisory body, other than a person (Article 255, LCC):

- who is a member of another management or the supervisory body of such a company;
- who has been finally convicted of a criminal offence involving the economy, labour relations and social security, legal transactions, property, or the environment, space and natural resources;
- against whom a security measure has been passed prohibiting the pursuit of a profession, for the duration of the prohibition; or
- who, acting as a member of the management board of a company against which bankruptcy proceedings were instituted, has been pronounced liable to repay damage to the creditors in accordance with the law regulating the financial operations of companies.

Article 10a of the Law Amending the Companies Law[123] (LCC-1E, Slovene: ZGD-1 E) imposed restrictions on management and control of companies, related to insolvency procedures. By this amendment, it was stipulated, that the member of the management or supervisory body of a company cannot be anyone who was a member of the management or supervisory body of a company, over which one of the insolvency proceedings or compulsory dissolution was placed under. The same restriction applied to persons who have hold the offices of the management or supervisory bodies against which proceedings (insolvency or compulsory winding up) have been instituted during the last two years (The first to the fourth paragraph of Article 10a.[124]

These provisions were overruled by the Decision of Constitutional Court of 24 May 2013.[125] The Constitutional Court decided that the first to the fourth paragraph of Article 10a of the LCC-1 are repealed.

However, the first to the third paragraph of Article 10b were not declared inconsistent with the Constitution. The quoted paragraphs stipulate, that the court has, in insolvency or compulsory dissolution proceedings, ex officio the jurisdiction to withdraw the authorization or entitlement to conduct business or to recall members of the supervisory body to legal or natural person who was a member of the management or supervisory body of the company, over which insolvency proceedings or compulsory winding up was initiated (first paragraph of Article 10b).

123. Official Gazette of the RS, No. 91/2011 of 14 Nov. 2011.
124. (Official Gazette of the RS, No. 65/ 09 – official consolidated text, 33/ 11, 91/11, 32/12 and 57/12).
125. Official Gazette of the RS 44/2013.

As explained in 217, LCC-1I, 2015 brings here a new solution, which replaces the above-described provisions. LCC-1I imposes the conditions and the restrictions on the establishment of companies and entrepreneurs as well as on obtaining the status of shareholder.

It is additionally said in the LCC-1I, 2015, Article 255, that the registry authority ex officio examine whether the circumstances described in the new Article 10.a. of the LCC-1 2015, exist.

457. New members of the management or supervisory bodies must submit a written statement regarding the non-existence of circumstances that would contradict their appointment pursuant to the LCC. If for any reason one or more of the members of the management or supervisory body are not appointed, that member can be appointed by the court in cases of urgency upon a proposal from interested persons.

Article 38a (conflicts of interest) of the Law Amending the Companies Act[126] (LCC-1G, Slovene: ZGD-1 G) imposed directors the duty to avoid conflict of his or her personal interests against his interests, duties or obligations as a director of the company. Directors means management and supervisory board members in the two-tier system and members of board of directors in the one-tier system. In the event that a conflict of interest arises, director has the duty, not later than three working days to notify in writing to the authority of which he is a member, and supervisory body. If the company has no Supervisory Board, director has the duty to inform the shareholders at the next General Meeting.

Article 38a (LCC-1G, ZGD-1 G) lays down the definition of the conflict of interest: Conflict of interest of directors exists where the impartial and objective performance of the tasks or decision-making within the function is jeopardized because of the influence from personal economic interests, family members or from a special affection or any other interests associated with other natural or legal entity.

In addition Article 38a (LCC-1G, ZGD-1 G) stipulates, that directors may enter into a transaction with another company in which he or his family owns a share of at least one-tenth of the share capital (or anyhow participates in the profits) only with the consent of the Supervisory Board or the Management Board.

On the other hand, Article 38a (LCC-1G, ZGD-1 G) stipulates, that, director who enters into a transaction with another entity in which he himself or his family owns less than one-tenth of the share capital (or anyhow participates in the profits) must notify in three days the Supervisory Board or the Management Board.

Above provisions do not apply, if the directors or their family members hold, at least three-quarters of the share capital. This provisions also do not apply in cases where the amount of each transaction does not exceed EUR 2,000 and the aggregate amount of all transactions with another company in the current financial year do not exceed the amount of EUR 24,000.

126. Official Gazette of the RS, No. 57/2012 of 27 Jul. 2012.

E. Adoption of Decisions, Rules of Procedures, Convening Sessions

458. The management or supervisory body must be convened at least once in each quarter or a shorter period, as stipulated by the Articles of Association.

Each member of the management or supervisory body has one vote.

The management or supervisory body has a quorum to pass resolutions if at least half of its members are present when a decision is taken, unless otherwise provided by the Articles of Association.

A majority of the votes cast is required for a resolution by the management or supervisory body to be valid, unless otherwise provided by law. In the event of an equal number of votes, the president of the management or supervisory body has the casting vote, unless otherwise provided in the Articles of Association. A member of the management or supervisory body may not participate in decision-making on matters referring to him (Article 257, LCC).

459. Members of the management or supervisory body or their authorized representatives are entitled to participate in the adoption of decisions by delivering written ballots to another member of the management or supervisory body.

A management or supervisory body may adopt decisions through correspondence, via telephone, electronic media or otherwise, if this is agreed by all the members of the management or supervisory body, unless otherwise provided by the Articles of Association or the rules of procedure.

The management or supervisory body adopts the rules of procedure with the majority of votes cast by its members.

460. If requested by any member of the management or supervisory body who must also state the purpose and reasons for the convocation, the president or chairperson is obliged to convene a session immediately. A session must be held within two weeks of being convened. If the president does not convene the session, at least two members of the management or supervisory body may themselves convene a session of the management or supervisory body and propose the agenda.

F. Approval of a Loan Contract with a Member

461. A company may only approve loans to members of the management or supervisory body and the procurators on the basis of a resolution passed by the management or supervisory body (Article 261, LCC).

A separate resolution must be passed for each loan or for each type of loan and must state the manner in which interest is charged and the time limit for repayment of the loan (this also applies to cases where a loan is approved by a dominant company or a dependent company, and in cases where the recipient of the loan is a family member of the member of the management or supervisory body or the procurator).

A loan contract based on a resolution must be concluded no later than three months after the adoption of the resolution. Such a contract must be approved by the management or supervisory body; otherwise, the member of the management or supervisory body must return the benefits arising therefrom.

G. *Liability of the Management and Supervisory Body Members (Diligence and Responsibilities)*

462. The LCC prescribes for Management and Supervisory Board members the duty of care, using the standard of a conscientious and fair manager. It is laid down in the LCC that in performing their tasks on behalf of the company, the members of the management or supervisory body must act with the diligence of a conscientious and fair manager and protect the business secrets of the company.

The members of the management or supervisory body are jointly and severally liable to the company for damage arising as a consequence of a violation of their tasks, unless they demonstrate that they fulfilled their duties fairly and conscientiously (Articles 263, 264 LCC).

Members of the management or supervisory body need not reimburse the company for damage if the act that caused damage to the company was based on a lawful resolution passed by a general meeting of shareholders. However, the liability for damages of the members of the management board is not excluded on the basis that an act was approved by the management or supervisory body.

463. The company may only refuse compensation claims or offset them three years after the claims arose, provided the agreement of a general meeting is obtained and provided no written objection is made by a minority holding at least one-tenth of the subscribed capital.

464. A compensation claim of the company against members of the management or supervisory body may also be pursued by creditors of the company if the company is unable to repay them.

LCC-1I, 2015 brings important changes related to liability of the management and supervisory boards members. The following two basic rules (due diligence and opposite burden of proof) remain the same:

- member of the management or supervisory body must carry out their duties to act in good company with due care and diligence and to protect the trade secret of the company.
- the members of the management or supervisory body are jointly and severally liable for the damage that has occurred as a result of the breach of their duties, unless they can prove that they honestly and conscientiously fulfil their duties.

However, new provision (LCC-1I, 2015, Article 263) refers to insurance of liability; namely, if the company concludes insurance contract members of management or supervisory bodies against risks from performing their functions in the company, it must be fixed deductible of at least 10% damage, but not more than the 1.5 times their fixed annual remuneration.

New provision (LCC-1I, 2015, Article 263) also refers to companies' compensation claim against members of the management or supervisory body pursued by creditors of the company. Namely waiver or compensation claim against creditors have no legal effect, and so it is also not possible to refer that action based on the decision of the general meeting of shareholders.

If such a company initiated bankruptcy proceedings, the claim for damages against members of the management or supervisory board is exercised on behalf of all creditors entitled to payment of their claims in the bankruptcy proceedings against the company. The responsible persons have to pay damage compensation to the company as a debtor in bankruptcy.

The claim for damages is entitled to assert the trustee on behalf of the company as bankrupt and any creditor, which is in accordance with the law governing the insolvency proceedings, is entitled to carry out procedural actions in the bankruptcy proceedings against the company.

Claims for compensation lapse within five years, whereas claims in companies where both the Republic of Slovenia and local government exercises a dominant influence expire in ten years from the occurrence of the damage.

H. Liability for Damage Arising from the Influence of Third Persons

465. In addition to liability for damage on the part of the members of management and supervisory bodies, the LCC lays down the rules on liability for damage arising from the influence of third persons (Article 264, LCC).

The LCC stipulates that persons who use their influence on a company to induce a member of the management or supervisory body, the procurator or a proxy, to act in a manner which causes damage to the company or its shareholders must reimburse the company for the resulting damage. In addition, shareholders are reimbursed for damage if they suffered damage, apart from the damage that was caused to them through the damage caused to the company.

466. In addition to the members of the management or supervisory body anyone who derived benefit from the damaging action, if such action was committed intentionally, is also jointly and severally liable.

467. A compensation claim of the company may also be pursued by the company's creditors if the company is unable to repay them.

468. The duty of care and liability of Supervisory Board members and members of the Board of Directors is subject to the appropriate application of the LCC's provisions on the duty of care and liability of Management Board members.

V. The Two-Tier System of Management

A. Composition of the Management Board

469. In the two-tier system, the management board, as an exemption from the general rule for management and supervisory bodies (at least three members), may have one or more members (directors, managers) (Article 264, LCC).

470. If the management board has more than one member, the members must reach decisions unanimously, unless otherwise provided in the Articles of Association (which may not provide that in the event of a difference of opinion, the vote of a particular member or particular members prevail over the majority).

B. Duties of the Management Board

471. The management board is fully authorized by law to manage the company's business for the good of the company, independently, on its own responsibility. It needs no supervisory board authorization to represent and bind the company (Article 265 LCC).

The management of the business may not be transferred to the supervisory board. However, the Articles of Association of the company or the supervisory board can stipulate that certain business activities may only be performed with the supervisory board's consensus. A shareholders' meeting is not authorized to take managerial decisions, unless expressly required by the management board in cases where the supervisory board declines its consent.

472. Pursuant to the LCC, the management board is obliged to prepare any matters that are within the competence of a shareholders' meeting, at the request of a shareholders' meeting. That applies to the preparation and execution of agreements that only become effective with the consent of a general meeting of shareholders.

473. In addition, under the LCC, the management board must report to the supervisory board on the planned business policy and other matters of principle concerning business operations, company profitability (in particular profitability of its equity capital), the course of business, especially the turnover and financial situation of the company, and any transactions which could significantly influence the corporation's profitability or solvency. The supervisory board may also require reports on other matters of importance to the company's business operations.

474. The management board must submit the annual report to the supervisory board within two months after the end of the business year. The supervisory board must revise the annual report and the proposal for the distribution of profits, submitted by the management board.

475. The wording related to the management board managing the company on its own responsibility means that the management board has the competence to make all decisions, except those expressly defined as being within the competence of a general meeting or the supervisory board.

In addition, the responsibility for decisions within the competence of the management board cannot be transferred to a third party through the delegation of authority. Exceptions to the rule that the delegation of power is not possible are those provisions that enable the management board to require a general meeting to decide on management issues.

C. Powers of Management and Representation in a Two-Tier System (Articles 265–267 LCC)

476. Management in the two-tier system is in the hands of the management board which has the power to manage a company independently and on its own responsibility.

In respect of a general meeting, the powers and obligations of the management board are to prepare measures within the competence or at the request of a general meeting, further on to prepare contracts and other acts which require the consent of a general meeting and to carry out resolutions adopted by the general meeting.

477. The management board represents the company. If the management board has more than one member, the members represent the company jointly, unless (which is far more frequent) otherwise provided in the Articles of Association.

In addition to the management board members as representatives, the company may grant power of representation to one or more persons under the procedure laid down in the articles of incorporation (procurators). Procuration authorizes to represent the company for any acts which fall within the legal capacity of the company, except for the disposal of immovable property, for which the procurator must be specifically authorized.

It is now explicitly stipulated, that procurator represents the company before courts and other authorities (LCC-1I 2015).

478. The Articles of Association (or even the supervisory board itself where so envisaged by the articles), may provide that the following persons are authorized to represent the company:

- individual members of the management board;
- at least two members of the management board acting together; or
- a single member of the management board together with the procurator.

479. The main duty of the management board is to manage the business of the company. Besides managing the business, the duty of the management board is to represent and act as the agent of the company.

The LCC does not define matters considered to mean ‘managing the company’; however, it provides in different places the steps to be taken by the management board.

480. Thus, the management board is bound to convene a general meeting, propose decisions to be accepted in relation to each separate item on the agenda and perform particular duties relating to the convening of the meeting and the shareholders' rights to be informed.

481. The LCC also identifies several other management board duties. Thus, the management board is bound to enter the company into the register and register all other subsequent changes.

Furthermore, the management board members have to audit the founding proceedings of the company, and request that the stockholders pay up their shares. Also, management board duties relating to different modes of increasing the capital stock are separately defined.

482. The functions and competencies of the management board in relation to nullity and disputes are also specified in the LCC. If the management board does not adopt a resolution relating to confirmation of the annual report under the Articles of Association of the company, then this resolution is contestable.

D. Appointment and Recall of the Management Board in a Two-Tier System (Article 268 LCC)

483. The members of the management board are appointed by the supervisory board. A reappointment may not be made earlier than one year prior to the expiry of the term of office of the management board.

484. The supervisory board may recall a particular member of the management board or the president for the following reasons only:

- he is in serious breach of obligations;
- he is incapable of conducting business;
- the general meeting passes a vote of no confidence in him, except where the vote of no confidence was passed for clearly unsubstantiated reasons; or
- other economic and business reasons (significant changes in shareholder structure, reorganization, etc.).

E. Remuneration of Members of the Management Board and Participation in Profits (Article 270 LCC)

485. In determining the total remuneration of a particular member of the management board (salary, profit share, reimbursement of costs, insurance premiums, commissions and other additional payments), the supervisory board must ensure that the total income is proportional to the tasks carried out by members of the management board and the financial position of the company.

486. If, after the remuneration has been determined, the operations of the company deteriorate to an extent that threatens the economic situation of the company or could cause damage to the company, the supervisory board may lower the remuneration. Any such lowering of income does not affect the other provisions of the contract; a member of the management board has the right to terminate a contract at the end of the following quarter with two months' notice.

487. The Articles of Association may provide that members of the management board share in profits in exchange for their work. As a rule, the level of the share in the profit must be set as a percentage of the annual profit of the company.

A member of the management board may not pursue an activity for profit in the area of the company's activity without the consent of the supervisory board, or conclude operations for his own account or for the account of another person.

488. According to the 2009 amendment to the LLC-1 (LCC-1C),[127] the supervisory board must in determining the total remuneration of a particular member of the management board (salary and reimbursement of costs, perks, bonuses for business performance – shares and options remuneration program, participation in profit, etc., severance pay and other income) ensure that the total income is commensurate with the tasks of the members of the management board and the financial position of the company.

489. In addition, the supervisory board must ensure that the total remuneration of a particular member of the management board is in accordance with the remuneration policy defined by the general meeting under the LCC-1 (*see* more on boards' members remuneration policy in the chapter on the powers of the general meeting).

490. If the general meeting does not define the income policy for the members of management bodies, the supervisory board must, when determining the remuneration of a particular member of the management board, follow the following legal principles:

- remuneration policy for the members of the management board and executive directors must foster the long-term sustainability of the company and provide that income is in accordance with the results achieved and the financial position of the company;
- total remuneration may be composed of a fixed and a variable part; the variable part of the income must depend on measurable criteria defined in advance; the general meeting may determine the maximum amount of the variable part of the income;
- severance pay may be paid only in the case of early termination of a contract; it may not be paid if a member of the management board or executive director has been recalled for serious reason (if he is in serious breach of obligations, if he is

127. LCC-1C – The Act amending Law on Commercial Companies (Official Gazette of the RS), No. 42/09 of 5 Jun. 2009, (Slovene: ZGD-1C).

incapable of business conduct, or if the general meeting passes a vote of no confidence in him, except where the vote of no confidence was passed for clearly unsubstantiated reasons).

491. Severance pay may also not be paid if the member of the management board or executive director terminates a contract; the general meeting may determine the maximum amount of severance pay.

492. Amendments of 2009 (LCC-1C)[128] add the following rules, as regards incomes of the management board members:

- The supervisory board may also request that an already paid bonus for business performance or a proportional part of it be returned, if there is a final finding that the annual report is null and void, or on the basis of a special auditor's report which establishes that criteria for determining the bonus were not used properly or crucial accounting, financial and other data and indicators were not properly defined or considered; the return of an already paid bonus may be requested within three years of the day of payment of the full bonus or part of it.
- Members of the supervisory board who fail to act in accordance with the above rule are liable for damages under the general rules of the law of damages; action for compensation of damage suffered by a company due to unjustified payment of a bonus may be filed by shareholders in their own name and for the account of the company.

F. Reporting to the Supervisory Board (Article 270 LCC)

493. The management board must report to the supervisory board at least once every quarter on:

- planned business policies and other general questions concerning operations;
- the profitability of the company, and particularly the return on capital;
- the progress of operations, and particularly the turnover and the financial position of the company; and
- operations which may have a significant impact on the profitability or solvency of the company.

The supervisory board may also require a report on other issues. The management board must inform the supervisory board about issues concerning the operations of the company and affiliated companies.

128. LCC-1C – The Act amending Law on Commercial Companies (Official Gazette of the RS), No. 42/09 of 5 Jun. 2009, (Slovene: ZGD-1C).

494. The supervisory board may at any time require from the management board a report on issues relating to the operations of the company which have an important impact or which can be expected to have an important impact on the position of the company. The reports must conform to the principles of conscientiousness and reliability.

G. Duties of the Supervisory Board: General

495. In brief, the supervisory board supervises the management of the business of the corporation as performed by the management board, appoints management board members and the president of the management board, removes them and fixes their compensation package. The Articles of Incorporation or the supervisory board itself may subject certain business transactions of the management board to its consent (Article 281 LCC).

The supervisory board supervises the conduct of the business of the company. In exercising this duty, the supervisory board may inspect and verify the company's books and documentation, its treasury, the deposited securities, the supply of goods and other matters.

496. The supervisory board may convene a shareholders' meeting.

497. The duties of the supervisory board originate from supervision of the management of the company's business. The supervisory board may also examine the company's books, documentation, funds, and so on. The supervisory board may convene a general meeting, but may not transfer the management of business to the supervisory board itself.

498. The supervisory board should not be satisfied with the supervision of past business, but should, as a means of prevention, supervise the future business policy of the company, by giving its opinion on pertinent matters.

The supervisory board also constitutes, in some ways, the management board's consultancy body. However, this does not signify that the supervisory board is superior to the management board; in fact, the latter is bound to manage the company independently and its members take full responsibility. Therefore, the supervisory board may not give strict orders to the management board.

H. Election and Recall of the Members of the Supervisory Board

499. Members of the supervisory board representing the interests of shareholders are elected at a shareholders' meeting.

The Act Amending the Companies Act[129] (LCC-1G, Slovene: ZGD-1 G) in amended Article 274 stipulates that the nominated candidates for the Supervisory

129. Official Gazette of the RS, No. 57/2012 of 27 Jul. 2012.

Board members present their previous professional training and work currently being carried out, and all the circumstances that might lead to a conflict of interest or a bias, prior to the election of the Assembly.

According to LCC-1G, (ZGD-1 G) the Assembly may vote on all members of the Supervisory Board at the same time only if agreed upon by the majority of shareholders who cast their votes. The decision at the General Meeting of the company whose securities are traded on a regulated market must be taken on each member of the Supervisory Board in particular.

500. The Articles of Association may provide that a maximum of one-third of the members of the supervisory board, representing the interests of shareholders, must be appointed by the holders of registered shares whose transfer requires the permission of the company. Such shares do not constitute a separate class of shares.

501. A general meeting may recall the members of the supervisory board that it elected before the expiry of their term of office. A majority of at least three-quarters of the votes cast (the Articles of Association may stipulate a larger majority) is required in order to pass a resolution recalling a member of the supervisory board.

502. A member of the supervisory board who has been appointed to the supervisory board by qualified shareholders may at any time be recalled by the shareholders and replaced by another member. A general meeting may recall such a member by ordinary majority of votes if the right to appointment is terminated.

503. The management board must submit a proposal for the appointment of a new member of the supervisory board to the court immediately after it establishes that the number of members is insufficient and does not guarantee a quorum.

504. Where good reasons exist, the court may recall a member of the supervisory board on the motion of the supervisory board or shareholders whose shares account for at least 10% of the subscribed capital.

I. Special Conditions for Members of the Supervisory Board

505. According to the LCC, a member of a supervisory board may not be (Article 271, LCC):

- a member of the management board or board of directors of a dependent company of the company;
- a procurator or authorized person of the same company;
- a member of the management board of another company with share capital in which a member of the management board of this company is on the supervisory board;
- a person who is a member of a supervisory or management board in three other companies; or
- a person not fulfilling the conditions laid down in the Articles of Association.

J. Competences of the Supervisory Board

506. The supervisory board supervises the company's business conduct. It may examine and verify the books and documents of the company, its cash box, stored securities, stocks of goods and other matters. For the exercise of these rights, supervisory board may authorize individual members, commission or for specific tasks also special expert. In the conclusion of the contract with the experts, the president of supervisory board represents the company. President of the supervisory board represents the company as at the conclusion of the contract with the auditor of the annual and consolidated annual report (LCC-1I, 2015, Article 281).

507. The supervisory board may request from the management board any information needed for implementing supervision. Any individual member of the supervisory board may also request such information, and the management board must submit the required information to the supervisory board as a body, if so provided by the Articles of Association.

The supervisory board may convene a general meeting.

508. The conduct of business may not be transferred to the supervisory board. The Articles of Association or the supervisory board may, however, determine that certain types of operations may only be carried out with its consent. If the supervisory board refuses to give its consent, the management board may require a general meeting to determine whether to give consent by a majority of three-quarters of the votes cast.

K. Powers of the Supervisory Board in Connection with the Annual Report (Article 282 LCC)

509. The supervisory board must examine the annual report and the proposal for use of the profits for appropriation submitted to it by the management board. Each member of the supervisory board or the audit committee has the right to review and verify all the bases used for compiling the annual report, which must be submitted to him on request unless the supervisory board decides otherwise.

510. The supervisory board must compile a written report for the general meeting on the findings of the examination referred to above. The report must state the method used and the extent of the examination of the management of the company during the financial year.

511. If an audit report is also attached to the annual report, the supervisory board's report must also include an opinion on the audit report. At the end of its report following the completion of its examination, the supervisory board must state whether it has any comments in relation to the annual report and whether it confirms the annual report. If the supervisory board confirms the annual report, it is thereby adopted.

512. The supervisory board must deliver its report to the management board within one month of the submission of the annual report, failing which the management board must give the supervisory board an additional period to do so which may not be longer than one month. If the supervisory board still fails to deliver its report within this additional period, it is deemed that the supervisory board has not confirmed it.

L. *Operations of the Supervisory Board*

513. The supervisory board operates within and outside meetings. During these times, the supervisory board acquaints itself with the management board's reports and gives initiatives for supervisory functions. Furthermore, election of the president is compulsory. Besides nominating the president, it is compulsory to elect the president's substitute (deputy) from among its members, who assumes the rights and obligations of the president only if the latter is incapacitated from exercising them.

514. Besides heading meetings, the president has the following additional duties:

- signing the minutes of the supervisory board meetings;
- representing the company vis-à-vis the management board members, meaning that he or she signs related contracts;
- calling supervisory board meetings; and
- chairing the supervisory board meetings.

515. The president of the supervisory board represents the company vis-à-vis the management board.

516. Minutes must be kept of sessions of the supervisory board and must be signed by the chairman or the deputy.

517. The supervisory board does not take decisions related to issues concerning the management of business. As already mentioned, the exception is the giving of consensus.

518. In fact, the supervisory board can also work with the help of committees elected to formulate and execute resolutions. The supervisory board may authorize experts or officers to make an analysis of technical issues and invite them to supervisory board meetings.

M. *Decisions of the Supervisory Board*

519. The main function of the supervisory board is to supervise the management of the business of the company. As already mentioned, apart from such supervising, the supervisory board performs some other activities.

However, it is not possible to transfer decisions relating to the management of business to the supervisory board. The exceptions are approval in cases specified by the Articles of Association or when resolutions in this respect are adopted by the supervisory board.

520. The supervisory board expressly decides on issues relating to:

- appointing and recalling of the management board;
- the income levels of the management board members and their eventual decrease;
- giving consensus that the management board members are performing a profit generating activity within the activity of the company itself;
- giving approval of loans to management board members;
- the approval of management board reports and demands for additional reports;
- consensus for certain types of activities that are determined by the Articles of Association or the resolutions of the supervisory board;
- approval of the contracts stipulated between the supervisory board members and the company; and
- approval of loans to supervisory board members.

N. Consent of the Supervisory Board for Management Board Decisions

521. Under the LCC, certain management transactions executed by the management board are only permitted with the prior consent of the supervisory board. Management responsibilities may not be conferred on the supervisory board; however, the Articles of Association or the supervisory board may determine that specific types of transactions may only be entered into with the consent of the supervisory board (Article 281/5. LCC).

522. The LCC does not list types of transactions that are subject to prior supervisory board consent. Such instances are quite often spelled out in the management board's internal rules, and can include:

- the acquisition, sale or mortgage of real property or rights in or to real property;
- the formation or closing of subsidiaries and branches;
- the starting of new lines of business and closing down of existing lines of business;
- the acquisition or sale of equity interests in companies;
- the borrowing or lending of money;
- the entering into of employment contracts with employees with a salary exceeding a designated amount;
- the appointment of procurator;
- the promise of a bonus or pension or introduction of change in pension plans; and
- other transactions exceeding a specific amount of money.

523. It is very important to avoid in practice that this possibility of abuse by the supervisory board of its power of consent to the extent that, in practice, the management board no longer conducts the business and accordingly, no longer has responsibility for managing the company. In any event, the more comprehensive the list is of matters made subject to the prior consent of the supervisory board, the less dependent and responsible for the conduct of business is the management board.

524. According to Slovenian practice, the supervisory board is usually empowered to give its consent for decisions that are, as a rule, deemed to be of greater importance. These include decisions related to extensive purchases or investment, borrowings made outside the course of the current business, larger write-offs, sale of larger capital assets, patents, trademarks, and so on.

525. The dependence of the management board's decisions on the consent of the supervisory board is to certain extent a contradiction of the principle that the management board is directly responsible for management of the company. This, in fact, hinders the clear division of responsibility, that is, the boundary between management and supervisory functions. That is why extensive use of these legal possibilities is not advisable.

O. Conflicts Between the Management Board and Supervisory Board

526. Conflicts between the management board and the supervisory board concerning approval of proceedings are solved by a general meeting, but only if so required by the management board.

527. In fact, if required by the management board, a shareholders' meeting may give its consent to an issue not approved by the supervisory board. In this case, however, a qualified majority is necessary.

528. If a management board member does business with the company, a conflict of interest can become an issue. In this case, it is necessary to prevent the management board member from being part of the same contract twice, once as a representative of the company and the second in his personal capacity.

529. Consequently, the law specifies that in these cases, the authority of representing the company is taken away from the above-mentioned member and given to the supervisory board president.

P. Committees of the Supervisory Board

530. The supervisory board may appoint one or more committees, for example the audit committee, the appointment committee, the remunerations committee, who review the proposed resolutions of the supervisory board and take care of their implementation, in addition to performing other expert tasks. In the company, which is a public interest entity, the supervisory board must establish an audit committee (LCC-1I, 2015, Article 279). A committee may not decide on issues which are within the competence of the supervisory board.

531. A committee must be composed of a president and at least two members. The supervisory board appoints a president from among its members. The committee reports on its work to the supervisory board. If the supervisory board appoints an audit committee, at least one member must be appointed from among independent experts in the field of accounting or finance. Besides them, only the members of the supervisory board can be appointed members of the audit committee.

532. The tasks of the audit committee are (amended Article 280 of the LCC-1I 2015):

- monitors the financial reporting process and make recommendations and proposals to ensure its integrity;
- monitors the effectiveness and efficiency of the internal control of the company, internal audit where applicable, and risk management systems;
- monitors the statutory audit of annual accounts and consolidated accounts, in particular the performance of the statutory audit, taking into account any findings and conclusions of the competent authority;
- reviews and monitors the independence of the auditor of the annual report of the company, in particular as regards the provision of additional non-audit services;
- is responsible for the selection process of auditor and propose to the supervisory board the candidate for the auditor of the annual report of the company;
- supervises the integrity of the financial information provided by the company;
- assesses the composition of the annual report, including the proposal for the supervisory board;
- participates in determining the main areas of auditing;
- participates in the preparation of the contract between the auditor and the company; all contractual provisions which restrict the choice of the general meeting in the appointment of the auditor are null and void;
- reports to the supervisory board on the outcome of the statutory audit, including an explanation of how the statutory audit contributed to the integrity of financial reporting and what was the role of audit committee in this process;
- performs other duties determined by the statute or decision of the supervisory board;
- cooperates with the auditor in auditing the company's annual report, in particular by exchanging information on major issues relating to audit, and
- cooperates with the internal auditor, in particular by exchanging information on major issues relating to the internal audit.

533. The statutory auditor or audit firm report to the audit committee on key matters arising from the statutory audit, and in particular on material weaknesses in internal control in relation to the financial reporting process.[130]

534. A new Article 281a, amended with LCC-1I, 2015 regulates internal audit; it stipulates, that the annual report on internal audit (if a company has), have to be submitted to the management and supervisory board and auditors within three months after completion of the financial year. The supervisory board may require the internal auditor's additional information.

The supervisory board gives its consent to the appointment, dismissal and salaries of the head of internal audit and to the act, which govern the internal audit function, as well as the annual and multi-annual work plan of the internal audit.

If the internal audit services are outsourced, the supervisory board decides upon the consent to the conclusion of a contract between a company and external contractor, its modification and termination.

Q. Payment for Work and Extension of Loans to Supervisory Board Members

535. Members of the supervisory board may receive payment for their work as determined by the Articles of Association or the general meeting. According to the amendment to LCC-1 of 2009 (LCC-1C), members of the supervisory board may not participate in the profit any more.

Payment must be in proportion to the work performed by the supervisory board members and the financial position of the company.

536. Under the LCC, a company may approve loans to supervisory board members only after the decision of the supervisory board. Such decisions are adopted for each loan or each kind of loan separately and define the interest and manner of repayment of the loan. Loans also include other legal transactions that in commercial terms correspond to providing credit (Article 284, LCC).

R. Relationship Between the Supervisory Board and Management Board

537. In analysing the relations between the supervisory board and the management board, the most important provisions of the LCC are those that cover the management board's competencies and the provisions on the reports to the supervisory board.

538. The said provisions give us a basis from which to extract the following basic rules regarding the relationship between the two bodies in Slovenian law:

---

130. Directive 2006/43/EC of the European Parliament and of the Council of 17 May 2006 on statutory audits of annual accounts and consolidated accounts, amending Council Directives 78/ 660/EEC and 83/349/EEC and repealing Council Directive 84/253/EEC.

- The management board manages the company, whereas the supervisory board supervises management.
- The management board adopts all decisions relating to the management of the company, except those that the Articles of Association of the company has reserved for shareholders' meetings.
- The supervisory board, on the other hand, is not permitted to adopt resolutions regarding the management of business. Accordingly, the management function cannot be transferred to the supervisory board.
- Certain types of activities can only be performed with the consensus of the supervisory board if such consensus of the supervisory board is required for certain types of activities stipulated in the Articles of Incorporation, or if the supervisory board resolves that certain activities may only be performed with its consent.

539. The supervision of management of the company is performed by the supervisory board in one of two ways:

- on the basis of management board reports addressing planned business policy and other principal operating issues, company profitability, equity capital, the course of business, especially the turnover, the financial situation of the company, business that has a significant influence on the profitability and liquidity, or reports related to other significant issues that can be required by the supervisory board at any time; or
- directly through the examination of books and documentation, funds, securities, stored goods, and so on.

540. Characteristic of the LCC corporate governance system is the primary and prevailing supervisory function and the prohibition against interference in management decisions. The supervisory board may not give compulsory instructions to the management board. If approval is necessary for certain activities, it must be specifically defined in the Articles of Association; however, the need for compulsory consensus or approval of certain types of activities can, according to law, be decided through the supervisory board's own resolutions.

VI. The One-Tier System of Management

A. *Competences of the Board of Directors*

541. The board of directors in the one-tier system both manages a company and supervises its operations. Both managerial and supervisory functions are within the competence of a single corporate governing body (board of directors, 285, LCC).

542. Provisions regarding the powers and obligations of the management board in respect of general meetings apply *mutatis mutandis* to the board of directors. The powers and obligations of the board of directors in respect of general meetings are:

- to prepare measures within the competence of a general meeting at the request of a general meeting;
- to prepare contracts and other acts which require the consent of a general meeting in order to be valid; and
- to carry out resolutions adopted by a general meeting.

543. The following provisions referring to the competences of the supervisory board apply, *mutatis mutandis*, to the board of directors:

- supervising the company's business conduct;
- examining and verifying the books and documents of the company, its cash box, stored securities, stocks of goods and other things;
- convening a general meeting;
- verifying and approving the annual report by applying mutatis mutandis the provisions referring to the relevant competences of the supervisory and management boards in a two-tier system. However, it can be stipulated by the Articles of Association that the annual report must be passed by a general meeting.

B. Presentation and Representation

544. The board of directors represents the company. But if the board of directors appoints executive directors from among themselves, they present and represent the company (unless otherwise provided in the Articles of Association).

545. The provisions laid down for management board representation also apply *mutatis mutandis* to the representation by the board of directors, as follows:

- The members of the Board of Directors represent the company jointly, unless otherwise provided in the Articles of Association.
- In the case of joint representation, an expression of will given to any of the members of the Board of Directors takes effect as if it were given to all the members together.
- The Articles of Association may provide that individual members of the board of directors, or at least two members of the board acting together, or a single member of the board together with the procurator are authorized to represent the company.

C. Special Conditions for Members, Elections and Recall

546. The following conditions referring to members of a supervisory board apply *mutatis mutandis* to the members of the Board of Directors. A member of a Board of Directors may not be:

- a person who is a member of the supervisory or management board of three other companies; or

- a person who does not meet the conditions laid down in the Articles of Association.

547. The provisions referring to supervisory board apply *mutatis mutandis* to the election and recall of the members of the board of directors, as follows:

- members of the board of directors representing the interests of the shareholders are elected by a general meeting;
- the Articles of Association may provide that a maximum of one-third of the members of the board of directors representing the interests of shareholders are appointed by the holders of registered shares whose transfer requires the permission of the company;
- a general meeting may recall the members of the board of directors elected by it prior to the expiry of their term of office; a majority of at least three-quarters of the votes cast is required in order to pass a resolution recalling a member of the board of directors; and
- the board of directors must submit to the court a proposal for the appointment of a member of the board of directors immediately after it establishes that the number of members is insufficient and does not guarantee a quorum.

D. Operations of the Board of Directors

548. The following provisions apply to the operations of the board of directors and its committees:

- The president of the board of directors may not be an executive director of the company (this rule does not apply to small companies).
- The board of directors must elect a president (chairman) and at least one deputy from among its members (the deputy assumes the rights and obligations of the president only if the latter is incapacitated from exercising them).
- Minutes must be kept of sessions of the supervisory board and be signed by the president or the deputy.
- The board of directors may appoint one or more committees (an audit committee, appointment committee, remunerations committee.
- The provisions referring to the supervisory board committee apply *mutatis mutandis*).
- The board of directors must form an audit committee in a company the securities of which are traded on the regulated market, or in which the employees exercise their right to representation in the company's bodies (the members of the audit committee may not be those members of the board of directors who are executive directors).

E. Remuneration of the Members of the Board of Directors

549. The provisions regulating payment to the supervisory board members apply *mutatis mutandis* to the remuneration of the members of the board of directors.

550. Accordingly, members of the board of directors may receive payment for their services, as determined by the Articles of Association or a general meeting. Members of the board of directors may receive participation in profits.

551. Payment must be in proportion to the tasks carried out by the members of the supervisory board and the financial position of the company (see more on boards' members remuneration policy in the chapter on the powers of the general meeting).

F. Executive Directors

552. The board of directors may appoint one or more executive directors. The members of the board of directors may, but not necessarily, be appointed executive directors. The appointment of executive directors is not compulsory; the board of directors can act without executive directors if the articles so provide.

553. Nevertheless, there is an exception: the board of directors of a company, the securities of which are traded on the regulated market, must appoint from among its members at least one executive director but not more than half of the members of the board of directors may be appointed executive directors.

554. Non-executive directors are not mentioned in the LCC, but they are certainly not prohibited.

555. The following rules apply to executive directors (290, LCC):

- Executive directors are appointed for a period determined in the Articles of Association which may not be longer than six years, with the possibility of reappointment; the board of directors may recall an executive director at any time.
- Any natural person with legal capacity (other than a person who has been finally convicted of a certain criminal offence, or against whom a security measure has been passed prohibiting the pursuit of a profession, or who, acting as a member of the management board, has been pronounced liable to repay damage to the creditors) may be an executive director.
- The board of directors may assign the following tasks to the executive directors: management of regular operations, applications for registration and submission of documents to the registry, taking care of keeping the books of account, compilation of the annual report.
- If there are several executive directors, they conduct business together, unless otherwise provided in the Articles of Association or the rules of procedure of the board of directors. If there are several executive directors, they can adopt rules of

procedure for their work unless the Articles of Association stipulate that such rules of procedure must be adopted by the board of directors or if they have already been adopted.
- When signing documents for the company, the executive directors must add the note 'Executive Director' to the registered name of the company and their signature.

G. *Differences and Similarities Between the Members of the Management Board and Executive Directors*

556. Probably the most important distinction between the legal position of members of the management board and executive directors in the two-tier system is as follows: The executive directors, in performing their tasks, must comply with the instructions and restrictions imposed by a general meeting, the board of directors, the Articles of Association and the rules of procedure for executive directors.

557. On the other hand, management board members act independently on their own responsibility.

558. In the LCC, Article 290, the provisions regarding the following matters apply, *mutatis mutandis*, to executive directors:

- approval of a loan;
- contract with an executive director;
- diligence and responsibilities;
- damage liability arising from the influence of third persons;
- participation by executive directors in profits;
- income of executive directors;
- ban on competition; and
- reporting of executive directors to the board of directors.

VII. Auditors (Appointment, Powers, Duties)

A. *Auditors: General*

559. According to the LCC, an auditor is an audit company or an independent auditor holding a license to perform audit services under the law regulating auditing. There are several types of auditors, such as an annual reports auditor, a formation auditor, a special auditor, an extraordinary auditor, an acquisition auditor and a division auditor.

560. In cases defined by the LCC, certain types of auditors are decided by the court in a non-litigious civil procedure (Article 194, second paragraph of Article 318, first paragraph of Article 322, second paragraph of Articles 360, 386, 583 and 627).

561. The Slovenian Institute of Auditors (SIA) was founded under the law regulating auditing in the Republic of Slovenia. Slovenian Accounting Standards were adopted by the SIA in accordance with the LCC and IFRS (standards determined as international accounting standards by Regulation 1606/2002/EC and Regulation 1725/2003/EC).

562. The auditor is liable to the company and to its shareholders for damage caused to them through a violation of the rules on auditing (up to an amount of EUR 150,000 for small companies, up to EUR 500,000 for medium companies and up to EUR 1,000,000 for big companies).[131] The limit on such liability does not apply if the damage was caused intentionally or through gross negligence. Auditor must cooperate and provide with information to auditing committee.[132]

B. Annual Reports Auditor

563. In the LCC-1j 2017 (Article 57), there are numerous changes and additional regulations of auditing. It is stipulated that the annual reports of large- and medium-sized capital companies and DP are reviewed by the auditor in the manner and under the conditions laid down by the law governing the audit. The auditor must audit the financial report and review the business report to the extent necessary to verify that its content complies with the other components of the annual report. The auditor must verify that the business report contains a corporate governance statement and a statement on non-financial operations and examines their formal completeness. All this also applies to consolidated annual reports. The management board must submit the audited annual report or the audited consolidated annual report to the body of the company responsible for adopting the report (supervisory board in the two-tier system and the board of directors in the one-tier system), together with the audit report, no later than eight days after receipt of the audit report.

564. Annual reports must also be submitted for the purpose of publication, together with the auditor's opinion, to the Agency of the Republic of Slovenia for Public and Legal Records and Services (AJPES) within eight months of the end of the financial year.

565. The auditor must also audit the accounting report and examine the business report to an extent sufficient to verify whether its contents are in conformity with the other elements of the annual report. All these provisions also apply to consolidated reports.

131. Change was made by LCC-1B -The Act amending Law on Commercial Companies [Official Gazette of the RS], No. 68/08 of 8 Jul. 2008, (Slovene: ZGD-1B).
132. Addition was made by LCC-1B – The Act amending Law on Commercial Companies [Official Gazette of the RS], No. 68/08 of 8 Jul. 2008, (Slovene: ZGD-1B).

566. The components of the auditor's report are much more extensively by LCC-1I (Article 57); it is laid down, that the auditor's report must contain:

(1) the definition of a company whose annual or consolidated financial statements are subject to a statutory audit, a statement of the annual or consolidated accounts and the date and period covered by, and the definition of the financial reporting framework used in their preparation;
(2) a description of the scope of the audit, which shall identify at least auditing standards in accordance with which the statutory audit was conducted;
(3) the audit opinion which could be: unqualified, a qualified or adverse and in which it clearly states the auditor's opinion on whether the annual financial statements give a true and fair view in accordance with the applicable financial reporting framework, and, whether the annual accounts comply with statutory requirements. If the auditor cannot express an audit opinion, there is a disclaimer of opinion;
(4) reference to any other matters to which the auditor draws particular attention, without audit opinion therefore changed;
(5) opinion on whether the business report is consistent with the financial statements for the same financial year and whether the financial report is prepared in accordance with applicable legal requirements;
(6) indication of whether the reference to the knowledge and understanding of the company and its environment, which the auditor has obtained during the audit, found essential misstatements in the financial report, stating the nature of any such claims;
(7) the statement of any material uncertainty related to events or conditions that may cast significant doubt about the company's ability to continue its business;
(8) indication of the establishment auditor or audit firm;
(9) date and auditor's signature.

The auditor carries out an investigation of the annual accounts and its opinion in accordance with international auditing standards also in those small capital companies that measure tangible fixed assets at revalued values, or values of the financial instruments for which no quoted prices on the regulated market (including derivatives and investment property).

The investigation of the annual accounts must be made within six months after the end of the year.

567. When, in adopting an annual report, a general meeting has amended a compiled annual report, the annual report will be null and void if, within two weeks, the amendments to the annual report have not been reviewed by an auditor or if the auditor has not given a positive opinion in respect of these amendments.

568. The appointment of an annual reports auditor is one of the powers of the general meeting. The proposal for the election of the auditor must contain at least the registered name, the registered office and key recommendations.

C. Founding (Formation) Auditor

569. One or more forming auditors (appointed by the court) must review the formation:

- if a member of the management or the supervisory board acquired shares;
- if shares were acquired at the time of formation for the account of a member of the management or the supervisory board;
- where a member of the management or the supervisory board obtained a special benefit or payment for preparing the formation; or
- if the formation is carried out with non-cash contributions.

570. The formation auditor must establish in particular:

- whether the founders' data concerning the acquisition of shares, contributions to the subscribed capital, special benefits and non-cash contributions and non-cash acquisitions are correct and complete; and
- whether the value of non-cash contributions and non-cash acquisitions equal at least the issue value of the shares or the value of payments which have to be provided for this purpose.

571. A written report must be drawn up for each audit which describes the subject of a non-cash contribution or a non-cash acquisition and states the methods of assessment used. The formation auditor must deliver one copy of the report to the registration body and one copy to the company's management. The report must be available for public inspection at the registration body.

572. The registration body may reject an application if the formation auditors establish that the formation report or the report by the members of the management or the supervisory board are inaccurate, incomplete or do not conform with the law; the same applies if the formation auditors state that the value of non-cash contributions or a non-cash acquisition is significantly less than the lowest estimated value of the shares or the payments which need to be provided for them.

573. Any disagreement between the founders and the formation auditors as to the scope of explanations and evidence which must be provided by the founders is decided by the court.

574. The formation auditors have the right to reimbursement of their expenses and payment for their work (in accordance with the tariff adopted by the SIA).

D. Special Auditor

575. A general meeting may appoint, by a simple majority of votes, a special auditor with the aim of verifying the foundation procedures and the management of individual operations of a company, including the increase and decrease of the subscribed capital in the last five years.

Shareholders, who are promoters of special audit shall remain holders of shares up to a decision on the proposal, otherwise it is considered that the proposal is withdrawn (LCC-1I, 2015, Article 318/3).

576. A person who audited the company's annual report in the last five years cannot be appointed special auditor.

577. If the general meeting rejects the proposal for the appointment of a special auditor, such auditor can be appointed by the court on application filed by minority shareholders (whose holdings total not less than one-tenth of the subscribed capital or a nominal amount or the pertaining amount of the subscribed capital totalling at least EUR 400,000), provided that a reason exists to believe that serious fraud or violations of the Articles of Association or the law have occurred in the conduct of business and procedures.

578. The management is obliged to enable the special auditor to review the books of account and the company's documents as well as its property items and especially its cash register, stocks, securities, goods and other property. The special auditor may request that the members of the management or supervisory bodies provide all the necessary explanations and evidence for conducting a detailed review of procedures.

579. The law regulating auditing applies *mutatis mutandis* to the verification of the foundation procedures and the management of individual operations of a company in respect of the auditing procedure and conditions.

580. The special auditor must draw up a written report on the findings of the audit (special auditor's report) containing facts, the publication of which could cause serious damage to the company or an affiliate company, provided that these are important for a general meeting to appropriately evaluate the procedures and operations subject to the audit.

E. Extraordinary Auditor

581. The court will appoint, on an application by minority shareholders (not less than one-tenth of the subscribed capital or a nominal amount of at least EUR 400,000), an extraordinary auditor, on the following grounds:

- Individual items of financial statements that are a constituent part of an adopted annual report are considerably underestimated.

– The notes to financial statements which are a constituent part of the adopted annual report do not contain the prescribed notes, or they are incomplete and the management failed to provide the missing notes to the shareholders at a general meeting (even though they requested such additional notes and also asked that their questions be recorded in the minutes).

582. The application can be submitted by the shareholders to the court within thirty days of the general meeting at which the annual report was contested.

Shareholders who propose extraordinary audit must prove that they have been holders of the shares for at least three months before the convening date of the meeting at which it was contested annual report. They must also remain holders of shares until a court decides on the proposal, otherwise it is considered that the proposal is withdrawn (LCC-1I, 2015, Article 322/3).

583. The extraordinary auditor must draw up a written report on the findings of the extraordinary audit (extraordinary auditor's report). If the extraordinary auditor finds out, during the auditing, that individual items in the accounting statements were considerably overestimated or that the provisions in respect of the contents of the annual report have been violated, the extraordinary auditor's report must contain these findings.

In the case of challenging the findings of a special audit reports, shareholders must prove that they have been holders of the shares for at least three months before the convening date of the meeting at which it was contested annual report. They must also remain holders of shares up to the decision of the court, otherwise it is considered that the objection is withdrawn (LCC-1I, 2015, Article 325/2).

In the case of bringing the action on behalf of the company at the request of minority shareholders, they must prove that they have been holders of the shares for at least three months before the date of the Meeting, which had rejected their proposal. They must also remain holders of shares till the court decision on the claim, otherwise it is considered that the lawsuit is withdrawn (LCC-1I, 2015, Article 328/2).

F. Merger by Acquisition Auditors

584. A merger by acquisition contract must be audited by one or more auditors for each of the companies participating in the merger by acquisition.

585. The merger by an acquisition auditor for a company participating in the merger must be appointed by the supervisory board (or board of directors) of that company.

586. The same merger auditor or auditors may carry out the audit of the merger by acquisition for all the companies participating in the merger, provided that the supervisory boards or the boards of directors of all the participating companies agree. In this case, the merger by an acquisition auditor or auditors must be appointed by the court upon a joint application from the supervisory boards or the boards of directors.

587. The auditors must draw up a written report on the audit of the merger by acquisition. The report on the audit of the merger by acquisition may also be drawn up jointly for all the companies participating in the merger. The report on the audit of the merger must contain an opinion from the auditor or auditors as to whether the provision of shares in the acquiring company at the exchange ratio proposed in the merger by acquisition contract and the amount of any cash payments or compensation offered are suitable recompense for the shares being acquired.

588. It is necessary to explain in particular:

- the appraisal methods used to determine the exchange ratio proposed in the contract and the reasons why the use of such methods in the particular case is appropriate for determining the exchange ratio; and
- if several methods were used for the determination of the exchange ratio, what value was established by the use of each of the methods. At the same time, an opinion must be issued on the relative significance attached to such methods in calculating the value to be decided. Moreover, any specific problems in evaluating the participating companies must be described.

589. For the merger by an acquisition auditor or auditors, an audit report must be submitted to the management or supervisory bodies of the company for which they carried out the audit. The provisions of the law regulating the auditing of annual reports apply *mutatis mutandis* to the procedure and the conditions for an audit of a merger by acquisition. The merger by acquisition auditors are liable for damage to all the companies participating in the merger by acquisition and to all the shareholders of these companies.

G. Division Auditor

590. The draft terms of division must be reviewed by an auditor (division auditor). The provisions referring to the audit of a merger by acquisition apply *mutatis mutandis* to the audit of division.

591. In a division where the capital ratios are not preserved, the report on the audit of the division must contain an opinion from the division auditor as to whether the provision of shares in the new companies at the exchange ratio proposed in the draft terms of the division, together with any cash payments and compensation offered, are appropriate recompense for shares in the new companies.

592. An audit of a division is not required if all the holders of shares in the transferring company submit a statement in the form of a notarial record declaring that they waive the application of the provisions of this Act relating to an audit of a division. Shareholders may also make a waiver statement orally at the session of the general meeting of the transferring company, which decides on the division. In this case, the statement must be included in the minutes of the general meeting.

H. Other Auditing

593. Auditing is also prescribed as compulsory in the following cases:

- An increase in the subscribed capital through non-cash contributions must be examined by one or more auditors.
- The resolution on an increase in the subscribed capital from the company's assets must be based on the balance sheet once it has been reviewed and given a favourable opinion without reservation by an auditor.
- In the event that minority shareholders are excluded from a company (squeeze out), the appropriate amount of monetary compensation offered by the principal shareholder must be reviewed by one or more auditors appointed by the court on a motion by the principal shareholder; an auditor's report is not required if it is waived by all minority shareholders in the form of a statement (in the form of a notarial record).
- The appropriateness of the amount of monetary compensation offered in a proposal on the transfer of an SE registered office must be verified by an auditor (must contain an opinion on whether the monetary compensation offered is an appropriate compensation for the acquired shares).
- In the case of conversion of a PLC into an SE and an SE into a PLC, the conversion plan must be examined by an auditor; pursuant to Regulation 2157/2001/EC. The auditor must also examine whether the total asset value of the company reduced by the liabilities is at least equal to the amount of the subscribed capital increased by the sum of reserves which the company is obliged to create.
- A merger contract must be audited by one or more auditors for each of the companies participating in the merger by acquisition.
- A report on relations with affiliated companies must be submitted to the auditor at the same time as the financial statements and the business report are submitted.
- Supervision of the business conduct of a grouping, must be entrusted to an auditor.
- If the grouping issues bonds, the supervision must be carried out by one or more auditors appointed by a general meeting, whose powers and term of office are determined in a separate contract.
- Supervision of the books of account of a grouping which has more than 100 employees must be carried out by auditors in the manner and under the conditions applying to companies.

VIII. Employee Participation in Management

A. Legal Regulation of Employee Participation in Slovenia

594. The basic regulation of employee participation in Slovenia is set out in the LEPM, which comprises the rules referred to the participation of employees in the companies' bodies as in the supervisory and management boards and in the board of directors.[133] The LEPM also covers companies performing the activities of commercial public services, organized in the legal form of a public enterprise.[134]

595. The legal position of workers concerning the organization, elections and powers of workers' councils is regulated by the LEWC.[135]

596. In addition, there are two separate laws regulating employee participation in SE and cooperatives, as follows: the LEPM of an SE LEPMEC[136] and the Law on Employees' Participation in Management of a European Cooperative (LEPMEC).[137]

---

133. The Law on Employee's Participation in Management (LEPM), Official consolidated text, Official Gazette of the RS, No. 42/2007 of 15 May 2007 (Slovene: ZSDU-UPB-1) The Act amending The Law on employee's participation in management, Official Gazette of the RS, No. 26/07 of 23 Mar. 2007.
134. The Law on Commercial public services, LCPS, Official Gazette of the RS, No. 32–1350/93/1994 (Slovene: ZGJS).
135. The Law on European Workers' Councils (LEWC), Official Gazette of the RS, Nos 59/2002, 103/2007 (Slovene: ZEDS).
136. The Law on Employees' Participation in Management of a European Company (SE) LEPMEC, Official Gazette of the RS, No. 28/2006 (Slovene: ZSDUED).
137. The Law on Employees' Participation in Management of a European Cooperative, Official Gazette of the RS, No. 79/2006, LEPMEC (Slovene: ZSDUEZ).

    LEWC transposes into Slovenian legal system the Directive of the European Parliament and Council Directive 2009/38 / EC of 6 May 2009 on the establishment of a European Works Council or a procedure for informing and consulting employees in undertakings or associated companies within the Community (OJ L No. 122 of 16 May 2009, p. 28). LEWC regulates the establishment of European Works Councils, composed of representatives of workers (hereinafter: 'employees'), and editing procedures for informing and consulting employees in corporations or associated corporations which are established in the Member States of the EU and operate in at least two Member States.

    LEPMEC, in accordance with Council Directive 2001/86 / EC of 8 Oct. 2001 supplementing the Statute for a European company with regard to the involvement of employees (OJ L No. 294 dated 10. 11. 2001, p. 22), the forms of involvement of workers in the management of a European company (Societas Europaea). The objective of LEPMEC is that, in reaching agreement on the participation of workers in the management of the SE, which provides workers' rights to transnational information, consultation and participation.

    If no agreement is reached, the workers' participation in management IS assured by LRPMEC.

    LEPM stipulates the terms and conditions for the participation of workers in management of all companies (irrespective of the form of ownership), sole proprietors with less than fifty workers and cooperatives in accordance with Directive 2002/14 / EC of the European Parliament and of the Council of 11 Mar. 2002 establishing a general framework for informing and consulting employees in the European Community (OJ No. 80 of 23 Mar. 2002, p. 29) and Council Directive 2001/23 / EC of 12 Mar. 2001 on the approximation of the laws of the Member States relating to the safeguarding of employees' rights in the event of transfers of undertakings, businesses or parts of undertakings or businesses (OJ L No. 82 of 22 Mar. 2001, p. 16).

B. The Two-Tier System with Obligatory Employee Participation

597. In the two-tier system, the law provides that at least one-third and not more than one-half of the supervisory board's members must be the employees' representatives. Before 2001, the rule for public companies with more than 1,000 employees was that at least half of the members must be the employees' representatives.[138] Employee representatives are chosen by the workers' council. As already described, the remaining supervisory board members are elected by the shareholders' meeting.

598. As already mentioned, the two-tier model used to be compulsory for large companies (*see* Chapter 2 in the introduction for the historical background; and Part 1, Chapter 5 on the two-tier system). In smaller companies (fewer than 500 employees and 100 named shareholders, not listed on the stock exchange), the shareholders might have prescribed in the Articles of Association whether to adopt the two-tier model.

599. LCC-1, enacted in 2006, brought a significant change, by granting freedom of choice to shareholders as regards the decision on one or two-tier systems. Nonetheless, the two-tier system still prevails in Slovenia since the great majority of privatized corporations were large enough to be subject to the two-tier system.

C. Employee Participation in the One-Tier System

600. Employee participation in companies operating under the one-tier system is slightly different from those under the two-tier system. In accordance with the LEPM, unless this is contrary to a separate law (e.g., the BL, the IL, and the FMIL), the employees appoint:

- at least one representative to the board of directors, for every three members of the board of directors; and
- at least one representative to each committee of the board of directors.

601. Employee representatives appointed to the board of directors in accordance with the previous rule cannot be president of the board of directors.

602. In addition, if a PLC has more than 500 employees, the board of directors can appoint an employees' representative as an executive director on the motion of the workers' council (employees' executive director).

LEPP governs the involvement of employees in the company's profit and participation in the ownership of the company, contract profit participation, the procedure for the conclusion of the contract, cash bonus and share scheme and the conditions for obtaining relief from taxes and social security contributions (the tax concessions).

138. Before 2001, the law stipulated workers' representatives making up half the board members for companies with more than 1,000 employees. This rule was judged a breach of the constitutional principle of equality by the Slovenian Constitutional Court, however, and was therefore changed.

603. In this capacity, an employees' executive director can, in the scope of the general rights and obligations applicable to all executive directors, carry out the tasks of representing and presenting the interests of the employees in respect of personnel and social issues in accordance with the law regulating employee participation in the management of companies.

604. These provisions do not apply to small companies.

D. The Labour Director

605. The LEPM provides for employee representation on the management board (labour director) in the two-tier system (comparable to the workers' executive director in the one-tier system; *see* above). In companies with 500 or more employees, a so-called labour director, as a representative of employee interests, responsible for personal and social issues, is mandatory.

606. The labour representative on the management board is nominated by the employees through their workers' council, although he or she is formally elected by the supervisory board. In other respects, however, the labour member's legal responsibilities are the same as those of the other management board members.

607. There are several questions regarding implementation of this law, for instance whether it refers to public companies with a sole manager, or what happens if the articles, according to a resolution of shareholders are not changed to enable the nomination of a labour director, and so on. In any case, the labour director must be nominated by the supervisory board like all other management board members but upon the proposal of the workers' council.

608. There is a general understanding that this law refers only to PLC, although the law is not entirely clear on this point. It is generally understood that the law refers only to public companies, because only the managerial body of that type of company is called a management board, as opposed to the private company type which is conducted by a managing director (in German: Geschäftsführer).

609. According to a special provision of the said law, the labour director is obliged to implement workers' interests in the field of personnel and social matters. Nevertheless, his legal position, from the point of view of his responsibilities, is the same as for the other management board members.

610. In practice, few corporations have complied with this mandate and, hence few labour management board members have been appointed. Very few labour directors have been nominated so far in practice, mainly due to the controversial situation of the labour director in the existing legislation. There is an open discussion on how to amend the referring legislation to clarify the legal position.

§6. Liquidation of the Company

I. Ordinary Dissolution

A. *Reasons for Dissolution*

611. According to the LCC, a company is to be dissolved in the following situations (the articles may determine other reasons for the company to be dissolved):

- upon the expiry of the period for which it was formed;
- by resolution of a general meeting, which must be adopted by a majority of at least three-quarters of the subscribed capital represented (the Articles of Association may stipulate a larger majority and lay down other requirements);
- if the management is inactive for more than twelve months;
- if the court establishes that the company is null and void;
- if the company goes bankrupt;[139]
- on the basis of a court ruling;
- when the company is merged with another company;
- if the company's subscribed capital is reduced below the minimum amount provided in the LCC;
- if the company has no shareholders or if the company has only own shares (LCC-1I, 2015, Article 402).

612. Shareholders holding at least one-twentieth of the subscribed capital and any member of the management or supervisory body may lodge a suit requiring the court to decide on the dissolution of the company, if the company's goals cannot satisfactorily be achieved or other good reasons exist for the dissolution of the company, in particular defects in the provisions of the Articles of Association concerning:

- the amount of subscribed capital;
- the definition of shares; or
- the activities of the company not being in conformity with the LCC.

B. *Resolution on Dissolution (Liquidation)*

613. In the cases of an ordinary resolution mentioned above, the resolution for the dissolution of the company and commencement of liquidation (liquidation resolution) must be adopted by a general meeting.

614. A liquidation resolution must state the following details:

139. Bankruptcy procedure is regulated by the Law on company finance, insolvency and winding up procedures (LFIWP), Official Gazette of the RS, Nos 126/2007, 40/2009, 59/2009, 52/2010, 106/2010 (Slovene: ZFPPIPP).

- the registered name and registered office of the company;
- the body which adopted the resolution;
- the reason for the dissolution;
- the time limit for creditors and shareholders holding bearer shares to register their claims (the time limit may not be less than thirty days from the date of publication of the resolution); and
- the name, surname and address or the registered name and registered office of the liquidator.

615. A liquidation resolution may also contain other details connected with the dissolution and liquidation of the company.

C. Liquidation Procedure

616. After the entry of the commencement of liquidation in the register, the company must use the addition 'in liquidation' in its registered name.

617. Liquidation is carried out by one or more liquidators. The liquidators must be members of the management unless otherwise provided by the Articles of Association, the general meeting or the liquidation resolution. The liquidator may also be a legal person (liquidation undertaking).

618. On the motion of the supervisory board, the board of directors or shareholders accounting for one-twentieth of the subscribed capital, and where good reasons exist, a liquidator can be appointed by the court.

619. The provisions laid down in the LCC and in the Articles of Association on decision-making by the management apply *mutatis mutandis* to decision-making by the liquidators unless otherwise provided in the liquidation resolution.

D. Powers and Tasks of the Liquidator

620. A liquidator has the power to represent the company and to compile an opening liquidation balance sheet. In addition, the liquidator has the following powers:

- to conclude unfinished business;
- to pay the claims of creditors;
- to publish an invitation to creditors, calling on them to register their claims with him within a time limit which may not be less than thirty days from the day on which the invitation was published;
- to recover the claims of the company;
- to realize the liquidation estate to the extent necessary in order to pay off creditors;

- to prepare a proposal report on the progress of the liquidation procedure and the division of assets;
- to propose the deletion of the company from the register; and
- to carry out other tasks connected with the liquidation as laid down in law, the Articles of Association or the resolution for the liquidation of the company.

621. If, on the basis of registered claims, the liquidator establishes that the assets of the company are not sufficient to pay all the claims of creditors in full including statutory interest, the liquidation administrator must stop the liquidation procedure without delay and submit a motion for the commencement of a bankruptcy procedure.

622. After the company's debts have been paid off, the liquidator must prepare a report on the progress of the liquidation and a proposal for the division of the assets, unless otherwise provided in the liquidation resolution.

E. Division of Assets

623. After payment of all the company's liabilities, the remaining assets must be divided among the shareholders in proportion to their contributions. Contributions that have not yet been paid in must be paid in before the division in accordance with the Articles of Association.

624. When the division of assets has been completed, the liquidator must deliver to the registration body his report on the progress of the liquidation procedure adopted at the general meeting.

625. The general meeting resolution on the division of assets must declare that all the assets be divided in accordance with the resolution on the division of assets and propose the deletion of the company from the register.

II. Dissolution of a Company by a Simplified Procedure

626. A company may be dissolved by a simplified procedure without going into liquidation if all the shareholders apply to the registration body for the deletion of the company from the register without liquidation.

627. In this procedure, shareholders must attach with the application a resolution for the dissolution of the company by a simplified procedure and a declaration by all the shareholders, verified by a notary, to the effect that all the company's liabilities have been settled, that all relations with employees have been settled and that they assume liability to pay any potential outstanding liabilities of the company.

628. Creditors may pursue their claims against the shareholders who submitted the declaration within two years (LCC-1I, 2015, Article 425/2) of the announcement of the deletion of the company from the register. The shareholders are jointly and severally liable with all their assets for the company's liability to such creditors.

§7. Mergers and Takeovers

I. Mergers: General

A. Merger by Acquisition and by Formation of a New Company

629. LCC -1 lays down the following types of restructuring of the legal form of the company: merger, division, transfer of assets or change of legal form.

According to the LCC-1, two or more PLC may merge in one of the following ways:

- merger by acquisition, which is carried out by the transfer of all the assets of one or more PLC (the company being acquired) to another PLC (the acquiring company); or
- merger by formation of a new company which is carried out by the formation of a new PLC (the acquiring company) to which all the assets of the merging companies (the companies being acquired) are transferred.

The Act Amending the Companies Act[140] (LCC-1F, Slovene: ZGD-1 F), Article 579a lays down the issue of publishing of companies' information and communications. It stipulates, that information and communication, which the companies are obliged to publish in accordance with the provisions of VI. Part of LCC-1 (Mergers) must be published on a special website, managed by the Agency of the RS for Public Legal Records and Related Services (APLRRS, Slovene: AJPES[141]).

140. Official Gazette of the RS, No. 32/12 of 4 May 2012.

141. Agency of the Republic of Slovenia for Public Legal Records and Related Services (APLRS, Slovene: AJPES) is a primary source of official public and other information on business entities in Slovenia. Furthermore, as a member of European business register (EBR), AJPES provides direct online access to detailed and accurate European company information that is gathered from each of the member country's official register. AJPES also offers market services that are generally provided by credit rating agencies as the information on current and future business partners in one place. AJPES manages the Slovenian Business Register as a central public database on all business entities, their subsidiaries and other organization segments located in Slovenia which perform profitable or non-profitable activities. A constituent part of the business register is the court register, which includes legal entities (companies and their subsidiaries, subsidiaries of foreign companies, cooperatives, public and private institutes, public agencies and other legal entities).

B. Legal Consequences of a Merger

630. The companies being acquired (merged) are wound up when they merge without going into liquidation. Shareholders in the companies being acquired are provided shares in the acquiring company.

631. If each share in the company being acquired that is exchanged for shares in the acquiring company is not equal to one or more shares in the acquiring company, the shareholders receive a cash adjustment (not to exceed one-tenth of the value of the original shares).

632. When the merger is carried out, all the assets, rights and obligations of the company being acquired are transferred to the acquiring company. The acquiring company must enter into all legal relationships to which the company being acquired was a party as its universal successor in title.

C. Merger Procedure

633. The managements of the merging companies must conclude a merger by an acquisition contract (this must be in writing in the form of a notarial record).

634. The management of each of the companies participating in the merger by acquisition must draw up a detailed written report on the merger (they may draw up a joint report).

Following the Act Amending the Companies Act[142] (LCC-1 F, Slovene: ZGD-1 F,), Article 582/6, the management of each company participating in the merger must notify its general meeting of shareholders and the management of other companies involved in the acquisition, any significant changes in the company's assets that occurred since the merger contract was concluded, until the day of the general meeting, deciding on the approval of the merger.

635. A merger by acquisition contract must be audited by one or more auditors for each of the companies participating in the merger by acquisition (appointed by the supervisory board or by the management). The merger by acquisition auditors must draw up a written report on the audit of the merger by acquisition.

636. The supervisory boards of each of the companies participating in the merger by acquisition must review the intended merger on the basis of the report by the management and the report on the audit, and draw up a written report on such a review.

---

142. Official Gazette of the RS, No. 32/12 of 4 May 2012.

637. The consent of a general meeting of each of the companies participating in the merger by acquisition is required in order for the merger by acquisition contract to be valid (this requires a majority of at least three-quarters).

According to the Act Amending the Companies Act[143] (LCC-1 F, Slovene: ZGD-1 F), Article 582/6, shareholders are not entitled to have the opportunity to review the documents for the general meeting at the registered office of the company, if these documents are available free of charge on the website of the company, at least one month prior to the meeting.

In addition, the quoted act stipulates that the interim balance sheet need not to be drawn up if the company, following the publication of the last annual report, published half-yearly report in accordance with the law governing the financial instruments market, and the review of semi-annual reports to shareholders. The same amendment (ZGD-1 F) stipulate that the interim balance sheet need not to be drawn up if all the shareholders of each company participating in the merger make a declaration in the form of a notarial deed to their consent.

638. The management of each of the companies participating in the acquisition must submit an application for registration of the merger by acquisition with the registration body covering the area in which the registered office of the acquiring company is located. The application may also be submitted for a company being acquired by the management of the acquiring company.

639. Creditors of all the companies participating in the merger by acquisition have the right to demand protection of their non-matured, uncertain or conditional claims if they request such protection within six months following the notification of the entry of the merger in the register. Creditors who have the right to priority repayment in the event of a potential bankruptcy procedure do not have the right to demand protection.

D. *Simplified Merger by Acquisition*

640. For a merger by acquisition, the consent of a general meeting of the acquiring company is not required for the contract to be valid:

- when the acquiring company's participation in the capital of the company being acquired is at least nine-tenths; or
- when the shares which the acquiring company must provide to shareholders of the company being acquired do not exceed one-tenth of the subscribed capital of the acquiring company.

143. Official Gazette of the RS, No. 32/12 of 4 May 2012.

E. Merger by Formation of a New Company

641. The above-described provisions on a merger by acquisition apply *mutatis mutandis* to a merger by the formation of a new PLC. The newly formed company is considered the acquiring company. A decision may be taken to merge by the formation of a new company if each of the companies being merged has been entered in the register for at least two years.

642. The Articles of Association of the newly formed company and the appointment of the members of its supervisory board or board of directors must be confirmed by general meetings of the merging companies. The provisions laid down in the LCC on the formation of a PLC (described in the chapter on the formation of a company) apply *mutatis mutandis* to the formation of the new company. Upon the registration of the new company, the merged companies cease to exist. Upon registration, the shareholders in the merged companies become shareholders in the new company.

F. Cross-Border Mergers

643. The Act amending Law on Commercial Companies [Official Gazette of the RS], No. 10/08 of 30 January 2008 (LCC-1A) introduced cross-border mergers' directive to Slovene legal order.[144] LCC-1A regulates the cross-border merger of an LLC (public or private) and LP with share capital, with an LLC from another Member State if the national law of the relevant Member States permits mergers between such types of company.

644. LCC-1A provides for a single report on the common draft terms of the cross-border merger (cross-border plan) to be prepared on behalf of each of the companies that are merging. The common draft terms of the cross-border merger are to be approved by the general meeting of each of those companies and have to include at least the following:

- the form, name and registered office of the merging companies;
- the ratio applicable to the exchange of securities or shares (and additional cash payment, if any);
- the procedures related to transfer of shares and the terms for the allotment of securities or shares of the company resulting from the cross-border merger;
- the likely repercussions of the cross-border merger on employment;
- the date from which the holding of such securities or shares will entitle the holders to share in profits;

144. Directive 2005/56/EC of the European Parliament and of the Council of 26 Oct. 2005 on cross-border mergers of limited liability companies facilitates mergers of limited liability companies on a cross-border basis. The Directive covers all limited liability companies; there are special provisions for cooperative societies, last amended by the Directive (EU) 2017/1132 as regards cross-border conversions, mergers and divisions (COM(2018)0241 – C8-0167/2018–2018/0114(COD)).

- the date from which the transactions of the merging companies will be treated as being those of the company resulting from the cross-border merger;
- the rights conferred by the company resulting from the cross-border merger on members enjoying special rights;
- any special advantages granted to the experts or to members of the administrative, management, supervisory or controlling organs of the merging companies;
- the statutes of the company resulting from the cross-border merger;
- where appropriate, information on the procedures by which arrangements for the involvement of employees are determined;
- information on the evaluation of the assets and liabilities which are transferred to the company resulting from the cross-border merger;
- dates of the merging companies' accounts used to establish the conditions of the cross-border merger.

645. The management of each of the merging companies must draw up a report (might be single) intended for the members explaining and justifying the legal and economic aspects of the cross-border merger and explaining the implications of the cross-border merger for members, creditors and employees. An audit report (might be single) for members have to be drawn up for each merging company.

646. Under the cross-border directive, employee participation schemes should apply to cross-border mergers where at least one of the merging companies already operates under such a scheme. Employee participation in the newly created company will be subject to negotiations based on the model of the SE Statute.

According to the LCC-1 J (amended Article 622 k, paragraph 6 and 7), the registration authority with which the acquired company is registered, enters the deletion from the registry of that company ex officio, on the basis of a notification by the competent authority of acquiring company Member State; notification is received through a business registers integration system, established in accordance with the second paragraph of Article 4a of Directive 2009/101/EC. After the entry of a cross-border merger into a register, the register authority is obliged, ex officio to notify this entry through the business registers integration system to the competent register authority of all acquired companies in the Member States.

II. Takeovers

647. According to the TA (Takeover Act),[145] a takeover represents a situation in which the offeror, alone or together with persons acting in concert, achieves the takeover threshold, which is one-third of the voting rights in the target company.

145. The Takeover Act (TOL), Official Gazette of the RS, No. 79/2006, adopted on 14 Jul. 2006, transposes Directive 2004/25/EC of the European Parliament and of the Council of 21 Apr. 2004 on takeover bids (OJ L No. 142, 30 Apr. 2004, 12) into the law of the Republic of Slovenia (Slovene: ZPre-1).

648. Persons acting in concert are, according to the TOL, persons who act in concert on the basis of an explicit or implicit oral or written agreement and whose aim is to acquire or consolidate their control of the target company or to prevent the offeror from making a successful takeover bid. The TOL defines persons who are deemed to act in concert.

649. According to the TOL, a takeover bid must be made by an offeror achieving the takeover threshold. A renewed takeover bid must be made by the offeror after having acquired a 10% share of voting rights (an additional takeover threshold) after the completed successful takeover bid procedure; the obligation of making a renewed takeover bid ceases when the offeror that has already made a successful takeover bid acquires at least 75% of all the target company's voting shares (the final takeover threshold).

650. The Takeover Act applies if the target company is a public corporation and if its voting shares are traded on the regulated market. The TOL also applies if the target company is a company whose shares are not traded on the regulated market and has at least 250 shareholders.

III. Division

A. Complete Division

651. A PLC may carry out a complete division by the simultaneous transfer of all the assets of the transferring company, which is thereby wound up without going into liquidation, to:

- new companies formed as a result of the absolute division (a complete division by formation of new companies); or
- acquiring companies (a complete division by acquisition).

B. Partial Division

652. A partial division may be carried out by the transfer of individual parts of the assets of the company, which is not thereby wound up, to:

- new companies formed as a result of the partial division (a partial division by formation of new companies); or
- acquiring companies (a partial division by acquisition).

653. A division may also be carried out by simultaneous transfer of different parts of the assets of the transferring company to new companies and to acquiring companies.

C. The Legal Consequences of the Division

654. On the division of part of the assets of the transferring company to a new company or acquiring company, the new company or acquiring company must enter into all legal relationships in connection with the assets transferred to it, to which the transferring company was a party, as the universal legal successor of the transferring company.

655. The shareholders of the company being acquired must be provided with shares in the new company or acquiring company. If the ratio at which shares in the transferring company are exchanged for shares in the new or acquiring company is not equal, the shareholders of the company being acquired must receive a cash adjustment either from the acquiring company or from another person (not to exceed one-tenth of the value of the assets transferred).

IV. Inclusion

656. If 95% of all shares belong to another company (main company), a PLC can be according to LCC-1 included in the main company with the general meeting resolution only. The decision on the inclusion is valid subject to consent of the general meeting of the main company (at least three-quarters majority). The inclusion into the main company effects from the entry in the register. Main company can be LLC.

LCC-1, 2015, Article 555a stipulates that the publication of the inclusion as an item on the agenda of the general meeting should be the company name and registered office of the main company. There must be a statement of the main company with which the excluded shareholders are offered severance pay. This also applies to the agenda of the Assembly of the main company.

The inclusion must be examined by one or more auditors (the inclusion auditors) appointed by the court on the proposal of the supervisory or management board of the main company. The intended inclusion shall be proposed by the supervisory boards of both companies (report).

At least from the date of convening the general meeting of the main company, the shareholders of both companies involved shall be at the headquarters of these companies, provided an insight into: proposal for a decision on inclusion; annual reports of the companies for the last three financial years; written report by the management of the main company which in detail and explains the legal and economic reasons for the inclusion, and audit and supervisory board report (LCC-1, 2015, Article 555a).

§8. AFFILIATED COMPANIES, CONCERNS AND HOLDING COMPANIES

I. Affiliated Companies, a Majority-Owned Company, a Dependent and Dominant Company

A. *Affiliated Companies*

657. Affiliated companies are legally independent companies in a mutual relationship whereby:

- one company has a majority share in the other company (a majority-owned company and a company with a majority share);
- one company is dependent on the other (a dependent and a dominant company);
- the companies are part of a concern;
- the two companies have mutual capital participation; or
- the companies are affiliated by undertaking contracts.

658. If a majority of the shares in a legally independent company are held by another company or if a majority of the voting rights (the majority share) are held by another company, that company is considered a majority-owned company and the other company is the company with a majority share.

659. A dependent company is a legally independent company which is directly or indirectly controlled by the dominant company. It is presumed that a majority-owned company is controlled by the company which holds a majority share in it.

B. *Concerns of Companies*

660. The types of concern are the following:

- an actual concern: a dominant company and one or more dependent companies connected under the unified management of the dominant company;
- a contractual concern: companies connected by a controlling contract; and
- a concern with a relationship of equality: legally independent companies connected by unified management without the companies being mutually dependent.

In the case of a controlling contract (contractual concern), the parent company has the right to give instructions to its subsidiary to conduct business; it may also give instructions that are harmful to the company if they benefit the interests of the parent company or its groups of companies (if the contract provides otherwise). The management of the subsidiary must comply with the instructions of the parent company and may not refuse instructions, even if in its view, does not benefit the interests of the parent company or its groups of companies.

LCC-1I, 2015, Article 542/2,3 stipulates, that in the case of controlling contract (contractual concern) company may waive the damage claim for losses incurred, after the expiry of three years from the publication of the entry end of the contract in the register, provided that external shareholders with a special resolution agree (if minority shareholders whose holdings amount to a total of at least one-tenth is not opposing). Damage claims of the company may also be filed by each shareholder; however, they may require payment only for the company. Claims of the company may be also exercised by the creditors (or liquidator in the case of bankruptcy) of the company, if they are unable to repay. Waiver or compensation claim against creditors have no legal effect.

On the other hand, LCC-1I, 2015, Article 545/1 stipulates, that in the case there is no controlling contract (an actual concern) the parent company may not use its influence to draw up a subsidiary to do a detrimental legal transaction unless the damage or disadvantage is replaced. The management of the subsidiary must in the first three months of the financial year draw up a report on relations with affiliated companies. It shall give all legal transactions concluded by the parent company or affiliated company in the past financial year; that includes also the legal transactions on the initiative or in the interest of these companies, and any other actions committed by or suspended at the initiative or in the interest of these companies. When the refund is being curtailed, the report shall specify how the compensation during the year actually took place.

If the annual report is to be audited by an auditor, it is necessary to submit a report on relations with affiliated companies, together with annual report. LCC-1, 2015, new Article 546 has extensive instructions, how the auditor shall operate.

LCC-1, 2015, new Article 546a and 546b brings new duties of the management and supervisory board in relation to the report with affiliated companies. Management must immediately submit report on relations with affiliated companies to the supervisory board. This report should be read together with the auditor's report if the annual report is audited. The supervisory board shall verify the report on relations with affiliated companies and its findings inform the shareholders' meeting. On the proposal of any shareholder, the court appoints a special auditor to examine the company's business relationships with the parent company or affiliated company if the auditor had reservations or a negative statement on the report and if the supervisory or management board had comments on the report on relations with affiliated companies.

LCC-1, 2015 in the amended Article 547 brings a new regulation of responsibility of the parent company and its legal representatives. It is stipulated that if a parent company prepares its subsidiary to conduct themselves detrimental legal transaction without compensation until the end of the financial year, it has to repay to subsidiary company the resulting damage. The request for compensation for the damage also has shareholders regardless of the damage caused to the company. In addition to the parent company, its representatives are jointly and severally liable if they made subsidiary company to do the detrimental legal transaction.

C. Companies with Mutual Capital Participation

661. Companies with mutual capital participation are companies having their registered office in the Republic of Slovenia which are connected in such a way that each company holds more than one-quarter of the shares in the other company.

662. As soon as a company acquires more than one-quarter of the shares or stakes in another company having its registered office in the Republic of Slovenia, it must immediately notify this fact to the company in writing.

663. As soon as a company acquires a majority share in another company, it must immediately notify this fact to the company in writing. If a share is no longer of a size that would require the company to be informed, this fact must also be reported to the company immediately. The company which receives the notification must publish it without delay.

A company which has received notification may require proof of the existence of the relevant participation. A company, another company controlled by it or a third party acting for the account of the company or the other company controlled by it, may not exercise rights deriving from shares and capital shares in a company which it is obliged to notify as set out above, until the company has done so.

II. Corporate Contracts

664. LCC-1, 2015 (new Article 535.a, 535.b, 535.c in 535.č) introduces new regulation of corporate contracts concluded between companies for different purposes. Controlling contract (contract whereby a company subordinates its management to another company), contract on transfer of profit (total profits are transferred to another company) and contract of conduct of business of another company, are the most important corporate contracts under LCC. Besides, corporate contracts are contracts whereby the company (LCC-1, Article 534):

- its profit wholly or partially to merge with the profit of other companies, in order to share the total profit (profit community);
- part of its profit wholly or partially transfers to another company (contract on partial profit transfer), or
- a part of the company (e.g., a plant) lease or otherwise leave to someone else (contract for the lease of the plant).

Notwithstanding the contract, it cannot be transferred more than the amount of profit that was generated in the last financial year, less the amount of losses brought forward and the amount of legal reserves (LCC-1, 2015, Article 550).

LCC-1, 2015 (new Articles 535.a) stipulates, that the management of each company involved in the corporate contract, must prepare a detailed written report explaining the legal and economic explanation of the reasons for the conclusion and the content of the contract, especially the type and level of compensation. Management of the participating companies can produce a joint report on the contract.

LCC-1, 2015, new Article 535.b stipulates, that corporate agreement must be reviewed by one or more auditors (the contracted auditor). Contracted auditor is appointed by court, on the proposal of the supervisory board or by management. Audit is proposed and performed by the same contractual auditor (or auditors), for all participating companies if so agreed. The contracting auditors must produce a written report (could be common to all companies which enter into a contract).

LCC-1, 2015, new Article 535.c and 535.č stipulates, that the supervisory board of each company review the auditor's report and issue its written report and that the general meeting shall be convened. From the date of convening the General Meeting, which will decide on consent to the management contract, it is necessary to provide shareholders an insight into: corporate contract, annual reports of each of the contracting companies for the last three financial years and management report.

Each shareholder should be at its request free of charge given a copy of the mentioned documents.

III. The Holding Company

665. A holding company, in a broader sense, is every company which holds a majority of the shares of a legally independent company. In a more narrow sense, a holding company is a company with a majority share, which carries out principally the activities of:

- establishing new companies; or
- financing and managing dependent companies which it holds as a dominant company.

IV. Branches

666. A foreign company may pursue a gainful activity in the Republic of Slovenia through a branch. A branch shall act on behalf of and for the account of a foreign company, using the name of the parent company, its head office and its firm. For liabilities arising from the operation of branches, a foreign company with all its assets is liable. For each branch, one or more representatives representing a foreign company should be appointed (may be the same representatives to several branches)

The following provisions of LCC-1 apply *mutatis mutandis* to a branches: activities (Article 6, name (Articles 12–23); seat (paragraphs 29 and 30), procures (Articles 33–37), and business secrets (Article 39).

An application for registration of a branch in a register must be submitted by an agent of a foreign company and must include: the name and address of the branch; an indication of the activities and operations carried out by the branch, the name and surname of the person representing the branch and a foreign undertaking, identification information on the founder or partner, the nature and extent of the liability of the founder or partner, the date of entry and exit of the founder or partner, the amount of the founder or partner's contribution, and other information specified by law. The report shall be accompanied by an extract from the register showing the content and the date of registration of the parent company, the decision of the management to establish a branch, a copy of the rules or contract of partners, which must be notarized, and a certified business report of the last year of operations of a foreign company that establishes a branch in an abbreviated form.

According to the LCC-1 J (amended Article 683 a), the branch is deleted from the registry, on the basis of a notification from a representative of a branch or a foreign undertaking.

The branch may also be deleted from the registry ex officio, on the basis of a notification from the competent authority of the Member State, received through the system of integrated business registers that the winding-up proceedings against the foreign enterprise have completed, or insolvency proceedings, or any other procedure under which the foreign company has ceased to exist and has a legal successor.

§9. The LLC: General

I. Concept

667. An LLC is, according to the LCC, a company whose subscribed capital is made of subscribed contributions by members. The value of the contributions may differ. It is not possible to issue securities for the contributions; nevertheless, the company may issue a member a certificate as a proof of holding a stake.

668. Members may on the formation of the company contribute only one subscribed contribution and have only one business share. Members are not liable for the liabilities of an LLC. A company may be formed by one or more natural or legal persons who will become the members upon the formation of the company.

A company may have a maximum of fifty members. A company may have more than fifty members only with the permission of the minister with responsibility for the economy.

669. A company is formed by a contract of members, which can be concluded in the form of a notarial record or on a special form, on paper or in an electronic version.

II. The Members' Contract

670. The members' contract must state:

- the name, surname and address or the registered name and registered office of each of the members;
- the registered name, registered office and activity of the company;
- the amount of the share capital and of each subscribed contribution separately, and the members who invested each subscribed contribution and their stake;
- the duration of the company if it is formed for a fixed period; and
- any obligations which the members have towards the company other than payment of the subscribed contribution and any obligations which the company has towards the members.

671. The members' contract may also contain other elements in addition to the elements listed above.

672. If the subscribed capital or any part of the subscribed capital is given in the form of a non-cash contribution, the members' contract must state the subject of each non-cash contribution separately, the value of the basic contribution for which the non-cash contribution is given, and the member who invested the non-cash contribution.

III. The Subscribed Capital, Cash and Non-cash Contributions

673. The subscribed capital must amount to at least EUR 7,500, and each subscribed contribution must amount to at least EUR 50.

674. Before the application for entry in the register, each member must pay in at least one-quarter of the amount of his subscribed contribution, and the value of all contributions must amount to at least EUR 7,500.

675. A subscribed contribution must be provided in money or in the form of a non-cash contribution or non-cash acquisition.

676. A non-cash contribution may be provided in the form of movable or immovable property, rights, an enterprise or part of an enterprise. Non-cash contributions must also include payment for items of property acquired by the company and which it treats as a member's contribution.

677. Non-cash contributions must be delivered in full prior to the application for entry in the register. If the total value for which non-cash contributions are given amounts to more than EUR 100,000, the parties who invested the non-cash contributions must ensure, at their own cost, that the non-cash contributions are assessed by an auditor.

IV. Entering the Company in the Register

678. The manager must apply to enter the company in the register. The application must be accompanied by:

- the original members' contract or a verified copy;
- a list of members and the subscribed contributions which they have acquired in the company;
- the report on non-cash contributions; and
- confirmation from a bank of the deposit of monetary contributions with a statement from the bank that the company can freely dispose of the assets.

§10. THE RELATIONSHIP BETWEEN THE COMPANY AND THE MEMBERS

I. Transfer of a Business Share

679. Business shares may be disposed of and inherited. The disposal of a business share requires a contract drawn up in the form of a notarial record.

680. Unless otherwise provided in the members' contract, the members have priority under equal conditions to the purchase of a (further) business share ahead of other persons (members' priority right). A member who intends to sell his business share must notify the other members in writing of his intention to sell and of the conditions of the sale, and invite potential buyers to notify him of their willingness to buy the business share within one month of receipt of the notification. If more than one member is prepared to buy the business share, they become holders of the business share together.

681. The members' contract may determine that the disposal of a business share to persons who are not members requires the consent of a majority or all of the members, and determines the conditions for the giving of such consent.

682. If none of the members are prepared to buy the business share and the members have not given their consent to the sale of the business share to a person who is not a member, the member may withdraw from the company.

II. Distribution of Profit, Preservation of Subscribed Capital

683. The members have the right to a share in the profits for appropriation as established in the annual balance sheet, unless otherwise provided in the member's contract. The profits must be distributed in proportion to the amount of the business share, unless otherwise provided in the member's contract.

684. Assets which are required in order to preserve the subscribed capital may not be paid out to the members.

685. Under no circumstances are members liable to repay sums which they received in good faith as a share in the profits, except in the case of illegal payments.

According to amended Article 482/1, of the LCC-1I, 2015, the property, which is required to maintain a minimum share capital (EUR 7,500), shall not be considered a loan of the company to shareholder or manager or his family, or legal person, where a shareholder or manager or member of his family or all together hold at least one-tenth of management rights. Such a transaction is void.

III. When Loans Were Given to the Company Instead of Its Own Capital

686. There is a special regulation for cases where loans were given to the company instead of its own capital. A member who, acting as a good manager, should have provided his own capital but gave a loan to the company instead, may not pursue a claim against the company for repayment of the loan in a bankruptcy procedure or a compulsory settlement. Such a loan is considered to be a part of the assets of the company.

687. Another special regulation aimed at preserving the subscribed capital refers to repayment of a loan, made in the circumstances described above, which was repaid prior to the commencement of a bankruptcy or compulsory settlement. If the company repaid a loan in the year prior to the commencement of bankruptcy or compulsory settlement, a member who granted the loan, provided insurance or who stood as a guarantor must compensate the company for the sum of the repaid loan.

688. The assets necessary for the maintenance of fixed capital and related reserves are not to be paid to shareholders. A company loan to a member (or a manager, or a member of his family, or to a legal person in to which the member or manager or his family member who has a share, at least one-tenth) and any other legal transaction to achieve the same effect is void (LCC-1 J, Article 495).

IV. A Company May Acquire Its Own Business Shares

689. There is a provision in the LCC to the effect that a company may acquire its own business shares for a consideration which it has paid in full. However, the company may not make payments to acquire its own business shares until it has created the reserves for its own business shares.

690. There is no provision to limit the extent to which a company may acquire its own shares, except a rule that a company may not acquire all the business shares.

V. Exclusion and Withdrawal of a Member

691. The member's contract may determine that a member may withdraw from the company or be excluded from the company and set out the conditions, the procedure and the consequences of a withdrawal or exclusion.

692. If nothing is determined in the member's contract, a member may request to withdraw from the company in a lawsuit if good reasons exist for doing so. For example: if the other members or a manager are causing damage to the member, if the company or members are obstructing or preventing the exercise of the member's right to withdraw, if he is obstructed in the exercise of the rights he enjoys under the law or under the members' contract, or if the general meeting or the managers impose disproportionate duties upon him.

693. Any member may require in a suit that another member be excluded from the company if good reasons exist for doing so, such as the following: the other member is causing damage to the company or the members, he is violating general meeting resolutions, he is failing to cooperate in the management and thereby hindering the regular functioning of the company or the exercise of other members' rights or he is otherwise committing a serious violation of the contract of the members.

694. A member who has withdrawn or is excluded from the company has the right to repayment of the estimated value of his business shares at the time of withdrawal. The company must pay this value to him within three years (where a member has been excluded within six years of becoming a member) of the day of withdrawal at the latest, including interest at the rate at which interest is paid on bank demand deposits.

VI. Lawsuit by a Member

695. A member can file a lawsuit on his own behalf or on behalf of the company against another member who failed to meet the member's obligations in the formation or management of the company.

696. A member is only to be entitled to file the lawsuit, provided that he ineffectually requested another member to meet his obligations or informed the company of the non-compliance, and if:

- he proposed to a general meeting the adoption of a resolution for the filing of such lawsuit but the general meeting rejected it;
- the general meeting adopted such a resolution but failed to appoint a special representative for the filing of a lawsuit, if necessary; or
- the general meeting adopted a resolution but the manager or the special representative failed to file a lawsuit.

697. A member is also entitled to lodge a lawsuit against a manager who failed to meet his obligations in respect of the management of the company.

698. The costs of the special representative and the legal costs are covered by the company.

§11. MANAGING OF A COMPANY

I. Members' Decision-Making

699. If the members' contract does not contain provisions for the management of a company, the LCC rules regarding decision-making by the members, members' voting rights, the general meeting of members, rights of minority members, members' right to information and inspection and managers, apply.

700. According to the LCC, the members must decide on:

- the adoption of the annual balance sheet and profit and loss account as well as distribution of the profits for appropriation;
- a demand for payment of subscribed contributions;
- the repayment of subsequent payments;
- the division and termination of business shares;
- the appointment and recall of managers;
- measures to review and supervise the work of the managers;
- the appointment of a procurator and a proxy;
- the pursuit of the company's claims against the managers or members for recovery of damage caused in the formation or managing of the company;
- the representation of the company in judicial processes against the managers; and
- other matters where so determined by the LCC or by the members' contract.

701. Each complete EUR 50 of a subscribed contribution secures the member one vote. The members' contracts may determine that certain members have a higher number of votes for each complete EUR 50 of a subscribed contribution, or that the voting rights of certain members are restricted.

II. General Members' Meeting

702. The general meeting must be convened by the manager (by registered letter to all members, who are on the date of convening the assembly entered in the register (LCC-1I, 2015, Article 509/1). Invitation letter must state the agenda of the general meeting, at least twenty-five days prior to the date on which the general meeting is to be held):

- if the members are required to decide on matters (*see* above);
- if it is necessary in the interests of the company;
- if it is established in the annual balance sheet or an interim balance sheet that half of the subscribed capital has been lost; or
- in other cases determined by law or the members' contract.

III. Rights of Minority Members

703. Members whose business shares account for at least one-tenth of the subscribed capital may require a general meeting to be convened, stating the matters which the general meeting should decide and the reasons for the convening of the general meeting.

704. In addition, members who fulfil the above conditions may require a vote on a particular matter to be included on the agenda of a general meeting that has already been convened.

705. Furthermore, members whose business shares account for at least one-tenth may convene a general meeting or include a matter on the agenda themselves if their request was not approved or if persons to whom a request should have been addressed were absent. A general meeting so convened decides whether the company is to bear the costs of convening the general meeting or expanding the agenda.

IV. Members' Rights to Information and Inspection and Court Orders on This Right

706. The manager must inform a member immediately upon request about the company's affairs, and enable a member to inspect the books and documents.

707. The manager may refuse a request for information or inspection if it is probable that the member will use the information obtained for a purpose that would be in conflict with the interests of the company, thereby causing significant damage to the company or an affiliated company. A final decision on such a refusal must be taken by the members.

708. A member who was not given information or who was not allowed to inspect the company's books or documents or whose request was refused by the manager may request the court to issue an order permitting him to receive the information or inspect the books and documents.

V. Manager of a Private Limited Company

709. Members of a private limited company, like shareholders of a public company, are free to choose between the one or two-tier system of corporate governance.

710. If members' contracts provide that the company has a supervisory board, the provisions regarding the supervisory board of a PLC apply *mutatis mutandis* to it, unless otherwise provided by the contract. If the company has a supervisory board, the manager must be appointed and recalled by that board.

711. A company may have one or more managers. If there are more, the members' contracts must determine whether they work jointly or as individual managers. The duty of a manager is to manage the operations of the company on his own responsibility and to represent the company.

712. The members' contracts may provide that a manager be appointed for a fixed period which may not be shorter than two years. The same person may be reappointed as a manager.

713. A general meeting of members may recall a manager at any time irrespective of whether he was appointed for a fixed period or indefinitely. The members' contract may determine that a manager can only be recalled for reasons laid down therein.

§12. Dissolving a Company

I. Reasons for Dissolving a Company

714. Normally, a company is dissolved upon the expiry of the period for which it was formed. A company can also be dissolved if so decided by the members by a majority of at least three-quarters of the votes of all the members; the contract of the members may determine a larger majority.

715. There are other reasons for a company to be dissolved, such as:

- the court establishes that the corporation is null and void;
- the company goes bankrupt;
- the court makes a ruling in accordance with the LCC;
- the company is merged with another company; or
- the company's subscribed capital is reduced below the statutory amount;
- the company does not have shareholders or if the company has only its own shares;
- the company's management does not work for more than six months (LCC-1I, 2015, Article 521/1).

716. Any member whose business share amounts to at least one-tenth of the subscribed capital may, in a suit, request that the court dissolve the company if he believes that it is not possible to achieve to a satisfactory degree the plans of the company or that some other good reasons exist for the dissolution of the company.

II. Application of the Rules Laid Down for a PLC

717. The provisions laid down in the LCC on PLC apply *mutatis mutandis* to the liquidation procedure, dissolution by abridged procedure, and establishing the nullity and contestability of resolutions of general meetings.

Part II. Partnerships

Chapter 1. Concept of a Partnership

718. Commercial companies under the LCC are organized either as 'personal companies' (a UC, an LP and a dormant partnership), or as 'companies with share capital' (an LLC, a PLC an LP with share capital and a European PLC).

719. The term 'personal companies' corresponds to partnerships, whether it be a general partnership (a company with unlimited liability, according to the LCC), a UC (in German: Oefentliche Handels Gesellshaft) or an LP (in German: Komandit Gesellshaft).

720. Each commercial company, including all personal companies, is a legal person within the meaning of the LCC, which independently pursues an activity with a view to deriving a profit in the market, as its exclusive activity (any activity pursued in the market for the purposes of obtaining a profit).

Chapter 2. Unlimited Companies (General Partnerships)

§1. Concept of a UC

721. A UC is a legal person, and is liable for the obligations of the company with all its assets. It can be formed by two or more persons who are liable for the obligations of the company with all their assets.

722. It is formed by means of a contract concluded by the members, and the legal relationship between the members is regulated by such a contract of the members. Unless otherwise provided in the LCC, the rules governing a contract of the members in civil law (the Obligation's Law) apply *mutatis mutandis* to a UC.

§2. Contributions to a Company

723. Unless agreed otherwise, the members pay in equal contributions. A member may contribute money, things, rights or services to a company. The members must estimate the monetary value of a non-cash contribution by agreement.

724. A member is liable for damage which he causes to a company either wilfully or through gross negligence.

725. A member can file a lawsuit on his own behalf or on behalf of the company against another member who fails to meet the members' obligations in the formation or management of the company.

§3. Business Conduct

726. Members conduct the business in a UC. The conduct of business may be transferred by the members' contract to one or more members. In that case, the other members may not conduct the business.

727. If all the members or more than one of the members is entitled to conduct the business, each of them is entitled to conduct the business alone. If another member who is entitled to conduct the business opposes a particular operation, that operation may not be carried out.

728. If the members' contract provides that the members who are entitled to conduct the business may only conduct business jointly, the consent of all of the members is required for each operation.

729. The members' contract may provide that the members who conduct the business are obliged to take account of the instructions of the other members. If a member believes that in view of the circumstances, the instructions are not sensible, he must inform the other members of this and wait for their decision.

730. A member who conducts the business is obliged to provide the company with the necessary reports, to inform the company on request as to the state of operations and to submit accounts statements to it.

731. All members, including those not entitled to conduct the business, may examine the company's affairs and have the right to inspect the company's books and documents.

732. Members who are entitled to conduct the business take decisions unanimously unless the contract of the members determines that a majority is required.

§4. Annual Financial Statement, Division of Profit and Loss

733. At the end of each financial year, the profit or loss must be established on the basis of the annual financial statements and the share of each member in the profit or loss must be calculated.

734. The profit accruing to a member must be added to his capital share; the calculated share of a member in any loss and money which he has withdrawn during the course of the financial year must be deducted from his capital share.

735. Each member may initially be allocated a share of the profit in the amount of 5% of his capital share. If the profit does not allow for this, the allocation must be reduced accordingly.

According to LCC-1I, 2015, Article 95, new par 4, members may decide, if the partnership agreement so provides, that the profits is distributed otherwise.

736. Each member may withdraw money from the company to his own debit, up to an amount of 5% of his capital share established in the previous financial year, and may also require, unless it would clearly damage the company, the payment of his share of profits for the previous financial year which exceeds the aforementioned amount. A member may not reduce his capital share without the consent of the other members.

§5. Representatives

737. Each of the members is entitled to represent the company unless he is barred from doing so by the contract of the members. The contract of the members may provide that all or some of the members are only entitled to represent the company jointly.

738. Members who are entitled to represent the company jointly may choose an individual from among their number and authorize that individual in writing to carry out certain operations or certain types of operations. For an expression of will to be given to the company, it is sufficient for it to be expressed to one of the individuals entitled to represent the company jointly.

739. On the motion of the other members, the court may withdraw the right of representation from a member if good reason exists, especially in the case of a serious breach of obligations or inability to represent the company properly.

§6. Members' Personal Liability

740. All the members are personally liable to creditors for the liabilities of the company to the full extent of all their assets. Their liability is subsidiary to that of the company – if the company fails to fulfil a liability to a creditor on his written request, all the members are jointly and severally liable. Any agreement to the contrary by the members in respect of their liability to third persons is without legal effect.

741. If a member ceases to be a member of the company, that member is responsible for the liabilities of the company that were incurred up to the time of the announcement of the entry in the register of the termination of his membership.

742. If a claim is lodged against a member arising from the liabilities of the company, the member may make personal objections or objections which the company could make.

743. Anyone who joins an existing company is liable in the same way as the other members for the liabilities of the company which arose before he joined irrespective of whether or not the registered name was changed.

§7. Dissolution of a UC

744. A UC is dissolved upon the expiry of the period for which it was formed or by resolution of the members. A UC can also be dissolved if the company goes bankrupt. There are other reasons for dissolution, such as the following:

- the death or dissolution of a member, unless otherwise provided for in the member's contract;
- notice being given;
- a court ruling;
- the number of members falling below two; and
- other cases laid down in law.

745. If a company is founded for an indefinite period, a member may give notice to cancel the contract of the members at the end of the financial year, provided such notice is given in writing to the other members at least six months prior to this date.

746. If a good reason exists, a member may take legal action for the dissolution of a company before the expiry of the time determined for its duration, or without a notice period if the company was formed for an indefinite period.

747. A good reason is deemed to exist if another member wilfully or through gross negligence violates any substantial obligation under the contract of the members or if the fulfilment of such an obligation becomes impossible.

748. If for any reason a company is left with only one member, that member is obliged within one year to take all action necessary to bring the company into compliance with the conditions laid down in the LCC or continue the activity as an entrepreneur.

§8. Liquidation of a UC

749. Liquidation must be carried out in all cases of dissolution of the company except if the company goes bankrupt.

750. Liquidation is carried out by all the members as liquidators unless it is entrusted to particular members or third persons by resolution of the members or in terms of the contract of the members.

751. Liquidators must conclude current operations, recover claims, realize the remaining assets and pay off creditors, and new operations may be undertaken in order to conclude unfinished operations.

752. Liquidators must add the words 'in liquidation' to their signature and the registered name. After payment of the debts, the liquidators are to divide the remaining assets of the company among the members in proportion to their respective interests in the capital established on the basis of the closing liquidation account.

Chapter 3. Limited Partnerships

§1. Concept

753. An LP is a company formed by two or more persons in which at least one of the partners is personally liable for the liabilities of the company with all his assets (a general partner) and at least one partner is not personally liable for the liabilities of the company (a limited partner).

754. Unless otherwise provided in the LCC, the provisions of LCC applicable to a UC apply *mutatis mutandis* to LP. An application for entry in the register must, in addition to the data required for a UC, also contain details of the limited partners and the amount of their contributions. The legal relations between the partners are regulated in the partnership agreement (contractual freedom).

§2. Managing the LP

755. Limited partners are not entitled to conduct the business of the partnership. A limited partner may not oppose the operations of a general partner, provided they do not exceed the normal scope of activity of the company. A limited partner becomes liable in the same manner as a general partner if he involves himself in the conduct of the business of the partnership. A limited partner has the right to demand a copy of the annual report and to inspect the business books and accounting documents in order to check their accuracy.

756. Where good reasons exist, the court may at any time, on the motion of a limited partner, order that a copy of the annual report be delivered to the limited partner, or that other explanations be given or that the books of account and accounting documents be submitted to the limited partner.

757. A limited partner is not entitled to represent the company but may be granted procuration or proxy.

§3. Profit and Loss

758. The profit of a limited partner only accrues to his share in the capital until it reaches the amount of his set contribution. A limited partner only shares in a loss up to the amount of his share in the capital and the unpaid part of his contribution. A limited partner may not demand payment of profits until his share in the capital has been reduced as a result of loss to below the amount paid for his set contribution or would be reduced below this amount if the payment were made.

§4. Limited Partners' Liability to Creditors

759. A limited partner is personally liable to creditors for the liabilities of the company up to the amount of the unpaid contribution which he would have to pay in under the partnership agreement.

760. Creditors may not appeal for an increase in the contribution by a limited partner which is not entered in the register unless the company has informed them of such an increase in another manner.

761. Anyone who joins an existing company as a limited partner is liable for the liabilities assumed by the company before he joined.

Chapter 4. Dual Companies

762. An LP in which the sole general partner is a company, in which there are no personally liable partners, or where all general partners are such companies, is a DP.

763. The following rules apply to a dual partnership:

- A company may be formed for the sole purpose of incorporating it as a general partner into a DP.
- PLC, LLC and LPs with share capital may not be restructured as DP.
- A DP may not be a general partner in an LP.
- All business documents must, in addition to the registered name of the DP, state the names and surnames of the members of the management board of the general partner in the DP.
- In matters relating to the business conduct of a DP, the registered name of the general partner must be added when a natural person signs for the company.

764. The above-explained rules apply *mutatis mutandis* to a UC in which all the partners are companies that do not have personally liable partners.

Court Procedure

765. 900 On several corporate issues (listed below), the law provides that the court shall decide on the matter in the civil non-contentious procedure. The procedure is fast; the court must decide within five days of receipt of the proposal. The deadline for an appeal against the decision by which the court decides in these cases is three days of notification of the decision. An appeal does not prevent the execution. Where a proposal is well founded, the applicant costs are borne by the company, if this law provides otherwise.

Court in non-contentious procedure to decide on the following matters:

- withdrawal of entitlement to conduct business or representation to the shareholder (90 and Article 99);
- permit the shareholder to take over the company without liquidation (the first paragraph of Article 116);
- the appointment or dismissal of liquidators (Article 119 and Article 120 and Article 408);
- establishing a shareholder or a third person to keep the books after the liquidation of the company (the second paragraph of Article 132);
- delivery of a copy of the annual report to general partner (the second paragraph of Article 140);
- the appointment of the founding auditor, a special auditor, extraordinary auditor, merger and division auditor, contractual auditors, special auditors for the relationship with the parent company, assimilation auditor. (Article 194, second paragraph of Article 318, the first paragraph of Article 322, second paragraph, 360, 386, 583, 535.b, 546.b, second paragraph 555 and 627. Article) (LCC-1I 2015);

- disagreements between the founders and the founding auditors (second paragraph of Article 196);
- extending the deadline for implementation of the Founding Assembly (third paragraph of Article 214);
- publish the announcement to subscribers of shares to raise contributions (third paragraph of Article 215);
- the market value of shares traded on a regulated market (sixth paragraph of Article 237);
- the authorization for the annulment of shares (second paragraph of Article 244);
- the appointment or dismissal of members of management or supervisory bodies (Article 256 and the second paragraph of Article 276);
- the mandate for convening the General Meeting or the publication of the item on which it decides (fourth paragraph of Article 295);
- the right of a shareholder or interested person to information (306 and Article 513 and the second paragraph of Article 637);
- appropriate severance to minority or withdrawing shareholders (the second paragraph of Article 388 and the third paragraph of Article 556);
- the amount of payment to the liquidator (first paragraph of Article 423);
- compensation and cash payments to external shareholders (fourth paragraph of Article 552 and the fifth paragraph of Article 553);
- appointment of a special or common representative (second paragraph of Article 595 and the first paragraph of Article 608);
- the proposal for a court test of the exchange ratio (the first paragraph of Article 605);
- matters relating to the SE established in 8, 25, 26, 55 and Article 64 of Regulation 2157/2001/EC;
- matters relating to cross-border mergers of LLC (Second section 4 of Chapter VI. Part of this Act) and
- other matters for which the law provides that the court shall decide on the civil procedure.

If an unlimited partnership, LP or LLC does not have a manager because of his death, permanent or long-term incapacity for work, or in other emergency situations, the court appoints the manager on a proposal in a non-contentious procedure.

The proposal may be lodged by anyone who has a legal interest. The function of court-appointed manager expires no later than the expiry of the period for which he was appointed by the court, or by appointing a new manager in accordance with the Articles of Incorporation.

Court-appointed manager has the right to remuneration and settlement costs. If the court-appointed manager and the company do not agree on the amount of the expenses and the payment, the decision on costs and payment is taken by the court.

Selected Bibliography

Books and Articles

Bohinc, Rado. *Comparative Company Law* (An Overview on US and some EU Countries' Corporate Governance Legislation, VDM Verlag, Dr Miler, 2011).

Bohinc Rado Korporacije, pregled pravnih pravil in sodne prakse. Ljubljana: NEBRA, 2008.

Bohinc, Rado, Borut Bratina & Hilda Marija Pivka. Pravo gospodarskih druĭb. Ljubljana: FDV, 1998.

Bohinc, Rado & M. Schauer. Stellung der Organe der Aktiengesellschaft, Nach slowenischem Recht und im Rechtsvergleich, Pravni poloĭaj uprave delniške druĭbe, po slovenskem pravu in primerjalno. Wirtshaft Universitet Wien: FOWI, 2000.

Bratina Borut,Grah Petra, Application of the Partial Offer Concept, as Stipulated in the Takeover Act, Podjetje in delo, 2018.

Bruckmüller, M. Ustanovitev gospodarskih družb v luči novejše sodne prakse Evropskega sodišča, Podjetje in delo, letnik 2003, številka 6, stran 1122, eGV d.o.o., 1. 10. 2003.

Gregor Drnovšek, Safeguarding Creditors in the Course of Simplified Reduction of Subscribed Capital, 2015, de Gruyter, Naše gospodarstvo, https://www.degruyter.com/downloadpdf/j/ngoe.2015.61.issue-3/ngoe-2015-0011/ngoe-2015-0011.pdf.

Ivanjko, iime. Podjetje in družba, Podjetje in delo. dt. 2, Gospodarski vestnik, 1994.

Ivanjko, Šime. Organi upravljanja d.d. – sporni pojem, Odločanje o pravicah, Pravna praksa, no. 10. Ljubljana, 1996.

Ivanjko, Š. & M. Kocbek. Korporacijsko pravo, GV Založba, in Pravna fakulteta Maribor 2003.

Juhart, Miha. Financial collateral in Slovenian law. V: Campbell, Dennis (ur.). Comparative Law Yearbook International Business: Volume 33, 2011. Alphen aan den Rijn: Kluwer Law International, cop. 2012, str. [435]-453. [COBISS.SI-ID 12308561].Keresteš, T. Družba XY Ltd – nujnost poznavanja statusnih oblik v drugih državah članicah EU Podjetje in delo, letnik 2004, številka 7, stran 1005.

Knez, R. Intenzivna šola evropskega prava, Narava prava Skupnosti – Evropsko pravoznanstvo, Nebra, Ljubljana, 2004.

Kocbek, M., Prelič, S. Zakon o gospodarskih družbah z uvodnimi pojasnili z novelo ZGD-1J, 2018, Litteralis d.o.o.

Kocbek, M., Prelič, S. Zakon o gospodarskih družbah z uvodnimi pojasnili (ZGD-1D do ZGD-1G), GV Založba 2012.

Selected Bibliography

Kocbek, M., et al. Veliki Komentar Zgd-1, GV Založba, Ljubljana 2014, 1., 2. in 3. del.

Kocbek, M. The Majority Owner and Decisions on the Conduct of Business in a Public Company – Differences Between the One-Tier and Two-Tier Management Systems, Podjetje in delo 2018.

IVANJKO, Šime, KOCBEK, Marijan, PRELIČ, Saša (2009). Korporacijsko pravo (2., predelana in dopolnjena izdaja). GV Založba, Ljubljana.

Kocbek, M. Evropska delniška družba in njena vključitev v slovensko pravo družb, Podjetje in delo, letnik 2004, številka 3, stran 455, 14. 6. 2004 (Kocbek, 2004).

Kocbek, M. Novela ZGD-F, Uskladitev z EU in dograditev, Podjetje in delo, št. 3–4/ 2001.

Kocbek, Marijan. Varstvo manjšinskih delničarjev v zvezi z oddkodninskimi zahtevki in zahtevami za izredne revizije, Podjetje in delo, nos 5–6 (1996).

Prelič, S. et al., Družba z omejeno odgovornostjo, GV Založba, Ljubljana 2009.

Prelič, S. Materialno statusno preoblikovanje, GV Založba, Ljubljana 2005. M. Seibert, U. Aktienrechtsreform in Permanenz, Die Aktiengesellschaft, št. 8/2002.

Podgorelec, P. et al., Koncerni, GV Založba, Ljubljana 2014.

Rozman, T., Vpliv obvladujoče družbe v dejanskem koncernu, Pravna praksa, GV Založba, Ljubljana 2012.

Research

Report of the High Level Group of Company Law Experts on a Modern Regulatory Framework for Company Law in Europe Brussels, 4 November 2002, Jaap Winter.

Action Plan and the Communication from the Commission to the Council and the European Parliament of 21 May 2003 entitled 'Modernising Company Law and Enhancing Corporate Governance in the European Union – A Plan to Move Forward'.

Directors' Remuneration in Listed Companies: Consolidated Answers for the fifteen EU Member States.

The Real Difference in Corporate Law between the United States and Continental Europe: Distribution of Powers, Sofie Cools, Discussion Paper No. 490, 09/2004, Harvard Law School, Cambridge, MA 02138.

The OECD Principles of Corporate Governance, OECD Observer, 2004.

Beyond Sarbanes-Oxley, The Benefits of BPM for Compliance, David Kelly and Heather Ashton, Upside Research, Inc.

Entwurf eines Gesetzes zur Einführung der Europäischen Aktiengesellchaft, Stand: 5 April 2004, www.bmj.de/media/archive/666.pdf. Draft, European Public Limited Liability Regulation 2004, www.dti.gov.uk/er/archive.htm.

The current system of employee representation in Slovenia; Country and practitioner reports Slovenia (by Janja Hojnik and Branko Sparavec) in: Worker Board level Representation in the New EU Member States – Country Reports on the National Systems and Practices (edited by Social Development Agency asbl and ETUI-REHS, 2005).

Cost Benefit Analysis of Transparency Requirements in the Company/Corporate Field and Banking Sector Relevant for the Fight Against Money Laundering and Other Financial Crime, A study Financed by the European Commission – DG JLS, Final Report 27 February 2007.

Legislation

See the list of abbreviations.

Codes

The Corporate Governance Code for Joint Stock Companies, adopted by the Ljubljana Stock Exchange, Inc., Ljubljana, the Association of Supervisory Board Members of Slovenia, and the Managers' Association of Slovenia on 18 March 2004, agreeing on adopting its amendments on 14 December 2005, 5 February 2007 and 8 December 2009. The current wording entered into use on 1 of January 2010.

German Corporate Governance Code, as amended on 21 May 2003, Government Commission.

Main EU Sources of Company Law

Directives in the Field of Company Law

For details see the list in the chapter Legal sources

First Council Directive 68/151/EEC of 9 March 1968 on coordination of safeguards which, for the protection of the interests of members and others, are required by Member States of companies within the meaning of the second paragraph of Article 58 of the Treaty, with a view to making such safeguards equivalent throughout the Community (OJ L No. 65, 14. 3. 1968, p. 8) with amendments (hereinafter: 'Directive 68/151/EEC').

Second Council Directive 77/91/EEC of December 1976 on coordination of safeguards which, for the protection of the interests of members and others, are required by Member States of companies within the meaning of the second paragraph of Article 58 of the Treaty, in respect of the formation of public limited liability companies and the maintenance and alteration of their capital, with a view to making such safeguards equivalent (OJ L No. 26, 31. 1. 1977, p. 1) with amendments (hereinafter: 'Directive 77/91/EEC').

Third Council Directive 78/855/EEC of 9 October 1978 based on Article 54(3)(g) of the Treaty concerning mergers of public limited liability companies (OJ L No. 295, 20.10. 1978, p. 36) with amendments (hereinafter: 'Directive 78/855/EEC').

Fourth Council Directive 78/660/EEC of 25 July 1978 based on Article 54(3)(g) of the Treaty on the annual accounts of certain types of companies (OJ L No. 222, 14. 8. 1978, p. 11) with amendments (hereinafter: 'Directive 78/660/EEC').

Sixth Council Directive 82/891/EEC of 17 December 1982 based on Article 54(3)(g) of the Treaty concerning division of public limited liability companies (OJ L No. 378, 31. 12. 1982, p. 47) with amendments (hereinafter: 'Directive 82/891/EEC').

Seventh Council Directive 83/349/EEC of 13 June 1983 based on Article 54(3)(g) of the Treaty on consolidated accounts (OJ L No. 193, 18. 7. 1983, p. 1) with amendments (hereinafter: 'Directive 83/349/EEC').

Eighth Council Directive 84/253/EEC of 10 April 1984 based on Article 54(3)(g) of the Treaty on the approval of persons responsible for carrying out the statutory audits of accounting documents (OJ L No. 126, 12. 5. 1984, p. 20) with amendments (hereinafter: 'Directive 84/253/EEC').

Eleventh Council Directive 89/666/EEC of 21 December 1989 concerning disclosure requirements in respect of branches opened in a Member State by certain types of company governed by the law of another State (OJ L No. 395, 30. 12. 1989, p. 36) with amendments (hereinafter: 'Directive 89/666/EEC').

Twelfth Council Company Law Directive 89/667/EEC of 21 December 1989 on single member private limited liability companies (OJ L No. 395, 30. 12. 1989, p. 40) with amendments (hereinafter: 'Directive 89/667/EEC').

Council Directive 2001/86/EC of 8 October 2001 supplementing the Statute for a European Company with regard to the involvement of employees.

European Community Regulations in the Field of Company Law

For details see the list in the chapter Legal sources

Council Regulation (EEC) No. 2137/85 of 25 July 1985 on the European Economic Interest Grouping (EEIG) (OJ L No. 199, 31. 7. 1985, p. 1) (hereinafter: 'Regulation 2137/85/EEC').

Regulation (EC) No. 1606/2002 of the European Parliament and of the Council of 19 July 2002 on the application of international accounting standards (OJ L No. 243, 11. 9. 2002, p. 1) (hereinafter: 'Regulation 1606/2002/EC').

Commission Regulation (EC) No. 1725/2003 of 29 September 2003 adopting certain international accounting standards in accordance with Regulation (EC) No. 1606/2002 of the European Parliament and of the Council (OJ L No. 261, 13. 10. 2003, p. 1) with amendments (hereinafter: 'Regulation 1725/2003/EC').

Council Regulation (EC) No. 2157/2001 of 8 October 2001 on the Articles of Association of a European Company (OJ L No. 294, 10. 11. 2001, pp. 1–21) (hereinafter: 'Regulation 2157/2001/EC').

Council Regulation EC 2157/2001 on the Statute for a European company (SE), OJ L No. 294, 10. 11. 2001.

Main Directives in the Field of the Securities Market

Council Directive 93/22/EEC of 10 May 1993 on investment services in the securities field (OJ L No. 141, 11. 6. 1993).

Directive 2001/34/EC of the European Parliament and of the Council of 28 May 2001 on the admission of securities to official stock exchange listing and on information to be published on those securities (OJ L No. 184, 6. 7. 2001).

Directive 2003/6/EC of the European Parliament and of the Council of 28 January 2003 on insider dealing and market manipulation (market abuse) (UL L 096, 12 April 2003).

Commission Directive 2003/124/EC of 22 December 2003 implementing Directive 2003/6/EC of the European Parliament and of the Council of 28 January 2003 on insider dealing and market manipulation (UL L 339, 24 December 2003).

Commission Directive 2003/125/EC of 22 December 2003 implementing Directive 2003/6/EC of the European Parliament and of the Council as regards the fair presentation of investment recommendations and the disclosure of conflicts of interest (UL L 339, 24 December 2003).

Commission Directive 2004/72/ES of 29 April 2004 implementing Directive 2003/6/EC of the European Parliament and of the Council as regards accepted market practices, the definition of inside information in relation to derivatives on commodities, the drawing up of lists of insiders, the notification of managers' transactions and the notification of suspicious transactions (UL L 162, 30 April 2004).

Selected Bibliography

Index

The numbers here refer to paragraph numbers

Index

Index

www.ingramcontent.com/pod-product-compliance
Lightning Source LLC
Chambersburg PA
CBHW071437230926
51846CB00001B/263
9789403530130